WRITING A
UNIX™
DEVICE DRIVER

Janet I. Egan and Thomas J. Teixeira

John Wiley & Sons, Inc.

New York • Chichester • Brisbane • Toronto • Singapore

Publisher: Stephen Kippur
Editor: Therese A. Zak
Managing Editor: Andrew B. Hoffer
Production Service: Pipeline Associates, Inc.

This publication is designed to provide accurate and authoratative information in regard to the subject matter covered. It is sold with the understanding that the publisher is not engaged in rendering legal, accounting, or other professional service. If legal advice or other expert assistance is required, the services of a competent professional person should be sought. FROM A DECLARATION OF PRINCIPLES JOINTLY ADOPTED BY A COMMITTEE OF THE AMERICAN BAR ASSOCIATION AND A COMMITTEE OF PUBLISHERS.

Related Titles of Interest from John Wiley & Sons

C Programming Language: An Applied Perspective, **Miller and Quilici**

C Wizard Programming Reference, **Schwaderer**

The 80386/387 Architecture, **Morse, Isaacson, and Albert**

Assembly Language Programming for the 68000 Family, **Skinner**

Library of Congress Cataloging-in-Publication Data

Egan, Janet I., 1951-
        Writing a UNIX Device Driver

        Bibliography: p. 351
        1. UNIX (Computer operating system) 2. Computer
input-output equipment. 3. Electronic digital computers—
Programming. I. Teixeira, Thomas J., 1954- . II. Title.
QA76.76.063E35 1988   005.4'2   87-31638
ISBN 0-471-62811-5
ISBN 0-471-62859-X (pbk.)

Printed in the United States of America

88 89 10 9 8 7 6 5 4 3 2

ACKNOWLEDGEMENTS

This book is based on a MASSCOMP manual, *Guide to Writing a UNIX Device Driver*. The first version that MASSCOMP published as part of the documentation set for the MC-500 was based in part on preliminary drafts prepared for MASSCOMP by Cliff Cary and Tom Alborough of Creare R&D. Those drafts, plus additional original material, were turned into a manual by Janet Egan and Tom Teixeira and reviewed by Miche Baker-Harvey and Eric Finger. That manual was also used as course material for a course on writing device drivers given by MASSCOMP's customer training department.

MASSCOMP gave us permission to use the material in the manual as the basis for the book. Henk Schalke, Vice President of Engineering, was most helpful in securing all the necessary permissions.

Joan Stigliani provided some of the information on VME in Chapters 3 and 4. Don Barstow reviewed the chapter on debugging and provided answers to our questions. Rod MacDonald also answered questions on the debugging chapter. Alan Atlas provided formatting help with Appendix F.

PREFACE

This book describes how to write a device driver and connect it to a UNIX system. It is intended for C programmers who are already experienced at using the UNIX operating system. However, enough background information on UNIX concepts is provided in the first two chapters to enable a reader who has written device drivers for other operating systems to relate that experience to the UNIX operating system.

Throughout this book we have used MASSCOMP's implementation of UNIX, RTU, as the basis for the discussion and as the source of specific examples. Information that is specific to RTU is identified as such in the text. Where RTU differs from System V, the differences are described in the main text. Separate appendices deal with the differences from the Berkeley 4.2 implementation and from the XENIX implementation.

Likewise, in discussing the hardware context for device drivers, we have used MASSCOMP's hardware as the basis of discussion and have pointed out how other types of hardware affect how you implement a device driver.

This book is meant to be used in conjunction with the documentation for your particular system. There are cross references that indicate when to look for information in the hardware documentation for your system and when to look at the system management documentation. UNIX command names are followed by a number in parentheses that refers to the section of the *UNIX Programmer's Manual* in which they can be found.

C O N T E N T S

C H A P T E R

1

UNIX AND ITS
I/O SUBSYSTEM

This chapter gives an overview of the UNIX™ operating system and the methods it uses to perform input/output (I/O) operations. Some of the topics discussed are only of passing interest—you will not need a knowledge of their details in order to write a device driver. Other topics are central to the subject but are not treated in full detail in the initial discussion. Wherever inexact or intuitive descriptions are used, the subject under discussion is either not central to device drivers or is described more precisely in a later chapter.

Since its original development in the early 1970s, the UNIX operating system has undergone much development both within Bell Laboratories (and later AT&T Information Systems) where it was developed and at the many universities and companies that have adopted UNIX as the basis for their software systems. As a result, any two systems that have been derived from UNIX systems may differ widely in their internal implementation. A complete treatment of the internal operation of even one UNIX system is beyond the scope of this book, although the interface to device drivers is conceptually similar in most versions of UNIX.

Throughout this book we will use MASSCOMP's implementation of UNIX, RTU, to provide specific examples of internal operation as they affect someone writing a device driver. Examples will also be drawn from other common versions of UNIX as required.

Readers interested in discovering more about how to use the UNIX system should refer to any of the many books about UNIX listed in the bibliography.

More information about the implementation of the UNIX system can be found in the following articles, which appear in Volume 2 of the *UNIX Programmer's Manual*:

- *The UNIX Time Sharing System* by D. M. Ritchie and K. Thompson

- *UNIX Implementation* by K. Thompson

- *The UNIX I/O System* by D. M. Ritchie

Note that these articles were written several years ago and do not give accurate descriptions of any modern UNIX system in every detail. However, they do provide an overview of UNIX as seen by its original developers.

• The UNIX Operating System •

Using the most general terms, the software system known as UNIX is made up of three components:

1. The UNIX kernel
2. A varying number of user processes
3. A system of data files stored on secondary memory

The kernel is the heart of the system since it is the only program that has direct access to and control of the system hardware, including the processor, primary memory, and the I/O devices. User processes respond to commands entered at terminals and perform tasks for users. The function of the kernel is to provide these processes with access to the system resources, including the file system. It acts as a coordinator to allow the complete hardware and software system to act as a multiuser, multiprocessing, time-sharing system.

To a user who examines an active UNIX system from an interactive terminal the kernel is essentially invisible. All the programs that can be run, including compilers, I/O utilities, and the terminal command interpreter, are user processes. To a programmer writing an application the kernel is visible in the form of system calls. These look like ordinary functions or subroutines, but they perform actions that must be controlled and coordinated on a systemwide basis.

The user processes have specific jobs to perform that require the use of shared system resources. Normally there are many active user processes that are competing for resources. The kernel maintains a global view of the needs and priorities of all user processes and determines the order in which they will be served.

The Kernel

The UNIX kernel consists of a single large executable binary image. Most of its modules are written in the C language, but a small part of it is written in assembly language. Its modules are compiled and assembled using the standard UNIX program development utilities, and then linked into a binary image. It is loaded into primary memory and its execution is started by a bootstrap procedure whose details do not concern us here.

The kernel has three basic jobs to perform:

- Create user processes and schedule their execution
- Provide them with system services
- Service hardware interrupts and exceptions

An overview of the logic of the kernel can be given as follows:

- It maintains a list of existing user processes and associates a scheduling priority with each of them.

- It reviews this process list and separates those that are ready to run from those that are not. A process may not be ready to run for many reasons. The most common are processes waiting for I/O operations to complete and waiting for other processes to finish executing. Processes can also wait for resources such as main memory to become available.

- Of those that are ready, the one with the highest scheduling priority is selected for execution. It gains control of the central processor (CPU), and execution of the kernel is temporarily suspended.

- The selected process runs until it makes a system call; when that happens the user process is suspended and the kernel is reactivated. The kernel processes the system call and then makes a fresh determination of which user process to run.

Figure 1-1 shows a simplified process table. Processes 1, 40, and 41 are runnable (R). Processes 20 and 24 are sleeping (S) and waiting for a specific event. Process 24 is waiting to read from a device. Process 20 is waiting for a child process to exit.

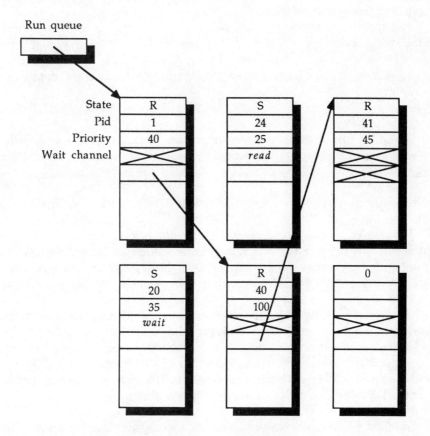

Fig. 1-1. Process table entries

Some system call requests can be fully satisfied by executing code in the kernel. For example, a call to lseek that sets a file seek pointer falls in this class. Requests to perform I/O to a peripheral device, however, usually require some action on the part of the device. In these cases the kernel initiates the device action asynchronously but does not wait for it to complete. The process that requested the service is marked as not ready and remains that way until a device interrupt indicates that the I/O operation is complete.

User Processes

The source code for an application program that is to be run on a UNIX system is compiled and linked into a binary file known as an executable image. See a.out(5) in the *UNIX Programmer's Manual* for a description of the format of this file. A *user process* is an execution of an image by the UNIX kernel.

When an image is to be executed by a user process, the sharable instructions (the text segment) are loaded into a read-only area of memory. (The kernel makes the area read-only, not the hardware.) Two additional sections of memory are allocated to serve as read/write data areas for the process, the first for its named variables and the second for its stack. The kernel makes some other preparations and then starts the process by loading the proper value into the hardware program counter.

A complete description of the state of a process at a given moment includes the following items:

1. The contents of its memory space, including the code and data areas.

2. The contents of the CPU general purpose registers and program counter (the *hardware context*).

3. Other information, such as open files, the current working directory, and the status of any outstanding system call request (the *software context*).

The software context information is stored in data structures maintained by the kernel.

While a process is being executed its code and data areas are in primary memory and its register and program counter values are loaded in the real CPU registers. If the process must be suspended the register and program counter values are copied to a data structure in memory so that another process can use the CPU.

As long as a suspended process remains in primary memory it can be restarted by loading these values back into the CPU. However, the kernel may choose to swap the process images out to secondary memory (disk) in order to free up primary memory for other users. When this happens only a very small amount of information about the process remains in memory—just enough to allow the kernel to determine when the process should be restarted and how to find it on the disk.

In effect a user process runs on a pseudocomputer that is implemented by the UNIX kernel and is not identical to the real system hardware. The pseudo-computer executes some additional commands (system calls), but does not allow access to all parts of the machine, for example, device interrupts and privileged instructions. If a process is suspended, swapped to secondary memory, and subsequently restarted, these events are completely invisible to the process. Code and data areas in memory that belong to the kernel and to other user processes are also totally invisible to a user process.

System and User Address Spaces

RTU is a demand paged virtual memory system. Each user process has its own address space, which begins at location zero and can be large (16 megabytes or more), subject to limitations based on the processor type and the amount of secondary memory available on the system. The UNIX kernel has its own logically distinct address space. These address spaces are referred to as user and system virtual address spaces, respectively. On MC68000 systems, the system virtual address space is completely separate from user virtual address space while on MC68020 systems, user virtual address space is a subset of system virtual address space.

The MASSCOMP hardware and operating system map user and system virtual address spaces onto physical memory in 4096-byte pages. The contiguous, zero-based virtual address space of a user process is mapped onto scattered noncontiguous pages of physical memory. Furthermore, individual pages in the address space of a user process may be moved to secondary memory by the kernel in order to free up primary memory for another process. See Figure 1-2.

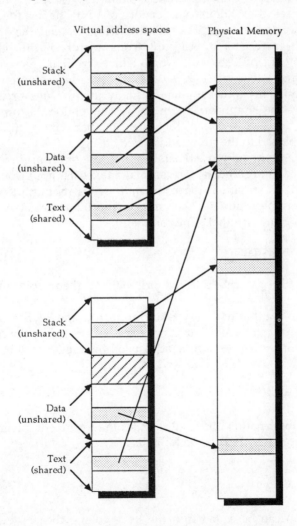

Fig. 1-2. Virtual to physical address space mapping

Programmers of ordinary user processes usually do not need to be aware of virtual-to-physical address mapping since the kernel and hardware handle it transparently. Writers of device drivers, however, must be aware of these addressing issues. Drivers deal simultaneously with user process addresses, system (kernel) addresses, and a third distinct type of address, the I/O bus address. This book specifies in detail the address types that appear in each situation faced by device drivers. It also describes the kernel functions that are called by drivers to copy data from one address space to another and to make data appear in another address space without copying it (this is done by manipulating various address mapping tables).

▪ A User's View of UNIX ▪

The UNIX system was originally designed and built as a time-sharing system. Consequently, most users interact with UNIX through a terminal, which has a typewriter-like keyboard for input and a small television screen or monitor for displaying characters. While recent versions of UNIX have added many powerful user interface features such as multiple windows and the ability to invoke operations using menus or by selecting icons (pictures) with pointing devices, the vast majority of UNIX software works with a terminal.

A user issues a sequence of *commands* that may have an arbitrary number of *arguments*. Arguments to a command usually identify one or more *files* to be manipulated by the command although by convention, arguments beginning with a hyphen are *flags* or *options* that affect the behavior of the command. The arguments are passed to the command as text strings.

Most UNIX commands are flexible in their use of file arguments: if no input files are specified as arguments, the command takes its input from the keyboard; if no output file is specified, the command writes its output on the terminal screen. For example, the `cat` command (short for concatenate) copies any number of files to the terminal. The command:

```
cat preamble data
```

first copies the file `preamble` to the terminal and then copies the file `data` to the terminal.

Any command that normally takes input from the keyboard or writes output to the terminal can have its input or output redirected by the command interpreter. For example, the `ls` command lists all the files in a directory. The command:

```
ls -l
```

will print long information about all the files in the current directory on the terminal. This output may look something like:

```
-rw-rw-rw-  1 fred    user     101     Jun  4 14:55 preamble
-rw-rw-rw-  1 fred    user     5428    Jun  4 15:13 data
```

This information can be saved in a file by invoking the `ls` command again, directing the output into a file named `dir`:

```
ls -l >dir
```

Similarly, wc is a command that counts the number of words, lines, and characters in a file. While one would usually specify file arguments to wc, wc also
counts the number of words, lines, and characters typed into it as input. This
input can be redirected from the file data by the command:

```
wc <data
```

Finally, the output of one command can be used as the input to another command using a *pipe*, a special mechanism for sending data between programs. A
pipe looks like a file to each program. The command line:

```
cat preamble data | wc
```

can be used to count the total number of words, lines, and characters in the files
preamble and data without having to create a temporary file. Command lines
in UNIX systems are often called pipelines since they typically contain several
commands connected by pipes. The commands in these pipelines (particularly
the commands in the middle) are called *filters* since they process the data that is
flowing through the pipeline. See Figure 1-3.

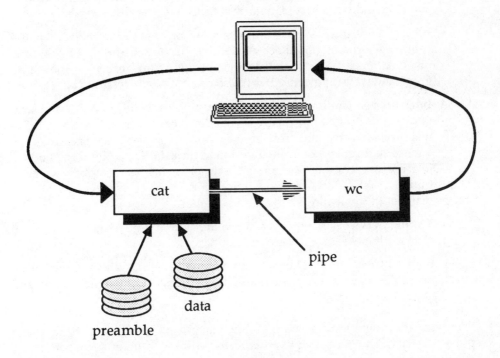

Fig. 1-3. Pipeline execution

· A Programmer's View of UNIX ·

A program on the UNIX system begins execution with the arguments for that command in the area of memory reserved for a subroutine call stack. In higher level languages, the command arguments are often made available as parameters to the "main" routine of the program. If this is not possible, special library functions are provided to access the command arguments. The arguments are simply text strings, although each "word" of the command line is passed as a separate argument. For the most part, command arguments are not changed by the shell, although the shell expands file-name "wild cards" to as many arguments as are required. The shell also has special syntax for variable substitution as well as quoting characters to prevent any alteration of the argument. I/O redirection is also handled by the shell itself and is described in more detail below. Consequently, even the simplest program in UNIX is able to "implement" these features with no effort by the programmer.

UNIX implements a wide variety of system calls. These are documented in Section 2 of the *UNIX Programmer's Manual* provided with each UNIX system. The system calls provide a variety of categories of service:

- **I/O Operations.** These services provide access to shared I/O devices and to the global data structures that describe their status. They open and close files and devices, read and write data, set the state of a device, and read and write system data structures.

- **Process Control.** System calls that allow a process to control its own execution. A process can allocate memory, set its scheduling priority and other parameters, lock itself in memory, load and execute a new program, and wait for events. It can also cause new processes to be created.

- **Inter-process Communication.** System calls that allow a process to send information to another process. There are many ways of sending information between processes: signals, pipes, shared memory, message queues, and semaphores. In addition to these fairly standard methods of interprocess communication, RTU implements asynchronous system traps (ASTs), which are similar in many ways to signals but remove many of the awkward restrictions of signals.

- **Timing Services.** A process can use the system time of day and interval clocks to synchronize its activities.

- **Status Information.** There are numerous calls that return information about the status of the process and its children, about the file system, and about I/O devices.

When you are programming in a high-level language, system calls behave like special library calls. Since many system calls return a value of some sort, these calls customarily reserve a set of illegal values to indicate that an error has occurred. A special variable is used to store an error code that identifies the particular error that occurred.

I/O System Calls

In general, a file must be opened before any other operation can be performed on the file. This allows the operating system to initialize various internal data structures to allow subsequent I/O operations to be performed more efficiently. When a file is opened, the operating system returns a *file descriptor*, which is a small integer identifying the open file. Other I/O operations take a file descriptor as an argument instead of a path name so the name of the file only has to be checked once.

There are two system calls that open files. They are:

```
fd = open(file, mode)
```

Here, file is a character string specifying the path name of the file to be opened and mode contains various flag bits indicating what operations should be allowed on the file after it has been opened. The most common values of mode will open an existing file for reading only; open an existing file for writing only; or open an existing file for both reading and writing.

The other system call that opens a file creates a new file or overwrites an existing file (replacing all information that was previously in the file):

```
fd = creat(file, protection)
```

Again, file is a character string specifying the path name of the file to be created. protection is a number that specifies which other users will be able to open the file for various types of access. Note that most recent versions of UNIX allow a file to be created with the open system call specifying the correct mode bits and providing the protection as an additional argument. However, creat is provided for compatibility with existing programs.

Once a file is open, the major operations that can be performed on the file read or write data to or from that file. The system call

```
actual = read(fd, address, count)
```

reads up to count bytes of data from the previously opened file specified by fd into memory at address. read returns the number of bytes that were actually transferred. If this value is less than zero, an error occurred while reading from the file. A return value of zero indicates that the end of the file has been reached but is not an error. Otherwise, the actual number of bytes read is usually equal to the number of bytes requested, although actual may be less than count if the end of the file is reached. This can also occur when the file specified by fd refers to a special file (either a device or a pipe). For example, device drivers for terminals will generally not read more than one line of data, regardless of how many bytes of data are requested.

The system call:

```
actual = write(fd, address, count)
```

behaves like read except it writes data to the file. Although a device driver has the option of writing fewer bytes than were requested, nearly all programs will interpret this as an error.

I/O operations are normally sequential so the next `read` or `write` call will access the next block of data in the file. Data can be accessed in any order by preceding `read` or `write` calls with:

```
new_location = lseek(fd, offset, whence)
```

Here, `whence` specifies whether `offset` should be interpreted as a number of bytes from the beginning of the file, a number of bytes from the end of the file, or an offset from the last byte previously read or written to that file. The `lseek` system call returns the new location of the "seek point" for that file as the number of bytes from the beginning of the file.

When an open file is no longer needed, it can be closed with the call:

```
result = close(fd)
```

`result` will be equal to zero if the close was successful. In general, `close` will succeed unless the file descriptor specified by `fd` was not open in the first place.

After a file descriptor is closed, an attempt to read or write using that file descriptor will fail. However, that file descriptor can be reused, so some subsequent call to `open` or `creat` may return the same value as some previous call to `open` or `creat`. This is in fact useful and is used to implement I/O redirection. Each program begins execution with several file descriptors already open. For programs executed by the command interpreter, these file descriptors are:

- **0**. The *standard input* file. This is normally the terminal but can be changed by I/O redirection such as `<file`.

- **1**. The *standard output* file. Again, this is normally the terminal but can be changed by I/O redirection such as `>file`.

- **2**. The *standard error* file. Again, this is normally the terminal but can be changed by I/O redirection. The syntax required for the I/O redirection varies with different shells, but `2>file` will redirect the standard error file in the standard UNIX shell.

Basically, the command interpreter implements I/O redirection by first closing one of these standard file descriptors and then opening the specified file for reading or writing. The actual details must be a little more complicated since otherwise the command interpreter would not be able to read any more commands once it closes its own standard input file. To avoid this problem the command interpreter first creates a new process with the `fork` system call:

```
pid = fork()
```

This creates a new process and returns different values in the old and new processes. The newly created process is called the *child* process and the original process is the *parent* process. See Figure 1-4. The parent process is able to exercise some privileged control over the child process. In particular, the parent process can wait for the child process to finish executing with the system call:

```
pid = wait(status)
```

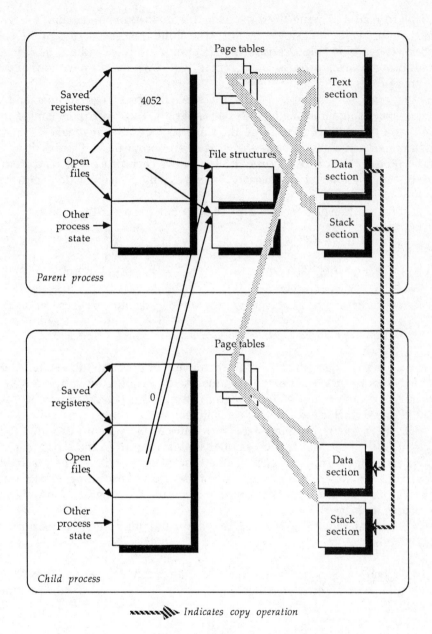

Fig. 1-4. Operation of fork

Here pid identifies which of several child processes finished executing. The reason the child process finished executing is returned in the status parameter. A process may exit voluntarily and specify a completion code that appears in status. A process may also finish executing as a result of an error or receiving a signal from the terminal or another process.

Returning to the fork system call, the child process is a nearly perfect copy of the parent process, but pid will be zero in the child process while pid is the process ID of the newly created child process in the parent. Both processes are able to read and write from the same file descriptors and initially have the same memory contents. However, since the child process is a *copy* of the parent process, it can close file descriptors and open new files without affecting the parent process. Each process can also modify its own memory without affecting the other process.

The open file descriptors are not complete copies of each other and continue to share some information. In particular, the file descriptors copied in the parent and the child process share the same seek point. This makes it easy for both a parent and a child process to write to an output file without writing over data written by the other process. It also allows each process to read from the same file while guaranteeing that data is read exactly once (provided neither process calls lseek).

A program can also make a copy of any open file descriptor using:

```
new_fd = dup(old_fd)
```

This will copy the file descriptor specified by old_fd to the lowest numbered file descriptor not currently in use.

Any process may execute a new program by executing the system call:

```
result = exec(program, argument0, argument1, argument2, ...)
```

Here program is the path name of the command or program to execute; argument0, argument1, ... are the arguments to the program. By convention, argument0 is the name of the program itself. The list of arguments is terminated by zero, which can never be a valid character string.

The new program replaces the program currently being executed by the process. If the exec call is successful, it will not return in the sense that statements following the call to exec in the first program will not be executed by that process. However, it is possible to get the effect of executing a program in a subroutine call by creating a new process to execute the program and waiting for that process to exit.

The actual sequence used by the command interpreter to perform I/O redirection is:

1. Open the file specified in the I/O redirection. If the open is unsuccessful, print an error message and go back and wait for another command line.

2. Call fork to create a new process.

3. The parent process should close the file descriptor opened for the I/O redirection and then call wait.

4. The child process will call close with an argument of 0, 1, or 2 depending on whether the I/O redirection affects the standard input, standard output, or standard error.

5. The child process uses dup to set up the standard input, standard output, or standard error to reference the file descriptor that was opened for redirection. This file descriptor can be closed after calling dup.

6. Finally, the child process executes the program specified on the command line.

There are other file system related system calls, most of which will not concern us. For example, the calls `link` and `unlink` create new names for files or remove names for files, but these calls do not need to call any device drivers. Similarly, the calls `stat` and `fstat` return information about a file specified by either a path name or an open file descriptor, but again, these calls do not call any device drivers (this information is essentially the same as that printed by the long form of `ls`).

However, a very important system call for device driver implementors is `ioctl` (for I/O control). This is a catchall for any function other than reading or writing data. The form of the call is deceptively simple:

```
result = ioctl(fd, command, arg)
```

where `fd` identifies an open file descriptor, as usual; `command` specifies the operation to be performed; and `arg` provides any other information that may be required. `arg` is often the address of a control block in memory so it is possible to provide arbitrary amounts of data as parameters to an `ioctl` operation.

The interpretation of `command` is left entirely up to the device driver, although by convention, different device drivers will not implement the same command unless they are drivers for different instances for the same type of device. For example, terminal device drivers implement a common set of commands that allow programs to change the data rate of the communication lines or to change how characters are echoed. Device drivers for magnetic tape devices implement a different set of commands to rewind the tape or to skip to the next file on the tape. However, terminal device drivers will generate an error if a program asks them to rewind, and magnetic tape drivers will generate an error if a program requests them to stop echoing.

▪ Process Control and Scheduling ▪

This section discusses how a user process comes into existence, how its state is represented, and how its execution is scheduled.

Process Creation and Deletion

Two fundamental processes are created during the initial system bootstrap procedure:

- Process 0. The swapper process
- Process 1. The init process

These processes remain in existence as long as the UNIX system is active. The swapper supports memory management operations. The init process is responsible (directly or indirectly) for starting all other user processes. Other processes may be created by the system to service activities such as paging.

After these processes are created, user processes are created by calling fork. When a user process calls fork the kernel creates a new process that is almost an exact copy of the calling process. The only difference is that the new process has a new, unique process identification number (PID) and a new parent process identifier (PPID). The original process is referred to as the parent and the newly created one is called the child.

A user process can call exec to replace the code image that it is executing with a new one. Thus to create a new process running a new program, an existing process must call fork and then exec. At system startup time the init process forks several additional processes based on a script in the file /etc/inittab. See init(8) in the *UNIX Programmer's Manual* for a complete discussion. init typically creates several background processes (daemons) and other processes, gettys, that monitor each interactive terminal for user logins.

When a user logs into the system, the process monitoring a terminal typically calls exec several times to run different programs that are part of the login sequence. Finally a shell or command interpreter program is loaded to read user commands from the terminal. The shell can carry out some commands on its own, but frequently it must run another program (i.e., execute a known image). To do so, it uses fork to create a new process that then uses exec to load and execute the required image. The parent shell process either waits while the new process is running or continues to read and execute other commands. When a command process started by the shell completes its work, it calls exit and then ceases to exist. When the shell receives the logout command it also calls exit. init, which has been waiting for the shell to exit, then forks a new process, getty, to monitor the terminal for the next login.

The preceding discussion shows that the number of user processes in existence at any time is variable. There is at least one process for each interactive terminal, and the terminal shell processes frequently create additional processes in response to commands. Those processes may in turn fork additional processes.

Process Definition Structures — user and proc

The kernel maintains two descriptive data structures for each process:

- user. Contains all the information about the process that is needed only while the process is active. The user data structure for the current active process is named u. Drivers make frequent use of many fields in the user structure.

- proc. Contains information about the process that is needed while it is inactive and perhaps swapped out of memory. Device drivers do not explicitly access fields in the proc structure, but they often pass a pointer to that structure as an argument when calling kernel routines.

These data structures are defined in usr/include/sys/user.h and /usr/include/sys/proc.h, respectively.

When a process is swapped out to disk, its user structure is written out with it. The proc structures for all processes are kept in an array known as the process table, which remains in primary memory at all times. The state of a user process is completely defined by the data in these two structures.

Process Scheduling, Paging, and Swapping

Typically there are many user processes contending for use of the CPU, memory, and other hardware. The RTU kernel includes code to settle this contention through execution scheduling, memory paging, and image swapping. At any given time there may be many user processes that are ready to run. A scheduling routine within the kernel scans the process table and selects the process that is ready and has the highest priority. That process gains control of the CPU. The scheduler performs this selection at frequent intervals, and eventually every user process obtains a share of execution time.

Because RTU is a demand-paged virtual memory system, it is possible for the total virtual address space occupied by the kernel and active user processes to exceed the amount of physical memory attached to the system. When this situation occurs, the kernel removes individual 4096-byte pages belonging to user processes from physical memory; these pages are copied to secondary storage from which they can be retrieved when needed. This shuffling of individual pages to and from secondary memory is referred to as *paging*, and is performed by the kernel. Paging is driven by individual memory references. A reference to a virtual page that is not in primary memory causes a hardware trap that initiates execution of code to load the needed page. If there is no unused page of physical memory available, a resident page of virtual memory is written out to the paging file in order to free up the needed space.

Process 0, the swapper, moves complete process images to and from a file in secondary memory. Excessive paging and other conditions also cause the swapper to select one or more processes to be swapped out.

NOTE: Part or all of a user process may not be memory resident at certain times. Before a driver initiates a direct memory access (DMA) data transfer by an I/O device, it must take steps to guarantee that the target area in user process virtual address space is locked into physical memory. The RTU kernel provides support routines that drivers can call to accomplish this and other related tasks.

Context Switches—The Current Process

The user process that has been selected for execution and given control of the CPU is known as the current process. Selecting a new current process and starting it executing is called context switching. When a context switch takes place, the contents of u are replaced by remapping one or more pages of system virtual address space.

• System Calls •

User Calls to System Calls

To the application programmer a system call is in fact a subroutine or function call—it causes a jump to a routine linked into the user process image. However, during execution of the called routine a more profound change of state takes place. The process enters the kernel mode and begins to execute code linked into the kernel.

The difference between execution in user mode and kernel mode is a fundamental one. The switchover from the former to the latter is accomplished through a hardware trap or exception. The hardware processor is placed in a different state; it executes in a different virtual address space and is able to execute privileged instructions. One way of looking at this event is to say that the user process continues to execute but is now in the kernel mode. It has, in effect, called a kernel routine. Another way of looking at the situation is to say that the user process has been suspended and that the kernel has been activated in order to perform a service for the user process.

When a user process issues a system call and activates the kernel, it is still the current process; its `user` structure occupies the kernel `u` structure. It is in this context that device driver routines such as `read` and `write` are called.

I/O Services

The type of system call of greatest interest to programmers writing device drivers is the I/O operation. I/O services provided by the UNIX kernel allow user processes to move data to and from hardware devices such as terminals and disks. Devices are usually not owned or controlled directly by a user process—their memory-mapped registers do not appear in the process address space.

For every I/O device, there is within the kernel a group of routines and tables known collectively as a device driver. One driver may control several similar devices, but every device must have a driver. The device driver is the only code anywhere in the UNIX system that directly interacts with the device. On MASSCOMP systems this interaction consists of reading and writing memory-mapped device registers (i.e., hardware registers that appear to the software to be memory locations) and fielding device interrupts. Other processors may use special I/O instructions to access devices.

The UNIX kernel includes a large amount of code devoted to I/O that is not a part of any device driver. This code implements a device-independent I/O and file system that serves all devices. The purpose of a device driver is to provide this device-independent I/O system with a standard, uniform interface to the device. To the greatest extent possible the driver hides the unique characteristics of the device from the kernel and from user programs.

In addition to services that perform real I/O actions (read or write data or set the device state), there are many auxiliary control services that update global data structures or return status information. Some of the auxiliary services can be completed entirely by the device-independent I/O system. Requests that require device activity always produce calls to one or more device driver routines, either immediately as a direct response to the request, or indirectly and perhaps asynchronously.

2

THE UNIX I/O SYSTEM

This chapter gives an overview of the implementation of the UNIX I/O system within the kernel. This implementation is organized around several fundamental ideas:

- The file system, a single logical entity that controls access both to ordinary data files and to all I/O devices
- An `inode` structure for each open file in the system
- A `file` structure for each file descriptor in the system
- The block buffering system
- Device drivers, which present an interface to each I/O device

The UNIX operating system takes a unique and unusual approach to I/O services. In many operating systems (e.g., VAX/VMS™) user processes perform I/O on devices, some of which may contain file systems. In such systems, file-structured devices depend on special software modules outside the kernel to define and maintain their file systems. Under UNIX this order of priorities is reversed—all I/O is performed on files, some of which are actually devices. A single systemwide file system is maintained by the kernel itself, and all user I/O requests refer to "files" within this system.

This approach to I/O is designed to minimize the difference in user code between I/O to a named file on a file-structured device and I/O to a device such as a terminal or printer. Within the kernel, however, there is a major difference between the way I/O is handled for structured and nonstructured devices. This section describes how the UNIX file and I/O systems are implemented within the kernel.

• The File System •

We will begin by describing the file system, since every I/O service request initially refers to a named file within this system. By tracing the way that the kernel handles the request we will see how each type of request eventually reaches a device driver.

Overview of the UNIX File System

An important service provided by any operating system is the capability to efficiently organize data that must be permanently stored on the computer system. This data is usually stored on magnetic disks. A disk system contains one or more disks that have been coated with magnetic oxide, which record the actual data. Each disk surface has one or more heads that read and write the data. The heads are held stationary while the disk itself rotates past the heads. The disk surface is divided into concentric *tracks*. The disk heads can be moved to be positioned over any track on the disk. Each track is divided into a number of *sectors* each of which can store a fixed amount of information (typically 512 characters). See Figure 2-1.

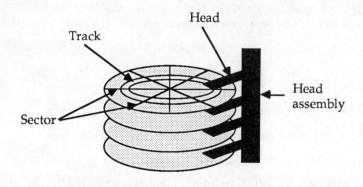

Fig. 2-1. Physical disk addressing

It would clearly be extremely awkward to require users to specify the physical disk address (head, track, and sector) of any information they want to access. Instead, the operating system implements a file system that allows users to specify names for collections of data called files. The operating system is then responsible for finding unused portions of the disk to be used for storing data in a file and for accessing the data on the disk using the full physical address of disk number, head number, track, and sector.

The UNIX file system contains three types of files:

• Regular files

• Directories

• Special files

A *regular file* is an array of bytes stored on the disk. Any additional interpretation of the data must be done by the user or the program. For example, a file containing a data base may be thought of as storing some number of records. However, the UNIX file system is not aware of this organization and accesses this file the same way as it accesses a file that contains ordinary text, or indeed any regular file.

A *directory* is a file that contains names of other files. The UNIX file system is *hierarchical*, since any directory can contain other directories. This makes it easy for many users to keep their files separate since all users can have their own directory. It is also possible for each user to keep a very large number of files organized efficiently by making use of subdirectories within one's own directory.

Hierarchical directory structures are often illustrated as an upside down tree with the "root" of the tree at the top. Each file in the tree is named by the path that must be taken along the branches of the tree to reach the file. UNIX systems use a slash character (/) to separate the names along each branch. For example, to find the file specified by the path name /usr/tjt/book/ch01.s, start at the root and look for a file named usr. This file should be a directory. Next, look in this directory for a file named tjt, which should also be a directory. Look in the directory tjt for another directory named book. Finally, look in this last directory for a file named ch01.s. See Figure 2-2.

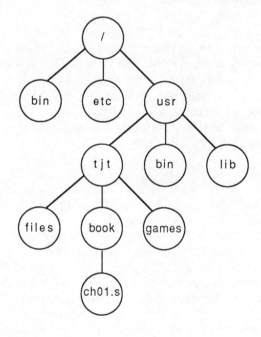

Fig. 2-2. A portion of a hierarchical file system

Special files behave differently from regular files and generally cannot be used to store information for later use. There are, in fact, several types of special files. Pipes and named pipes or FIFO (First-In, First-Out) files are special files.

The type of special file we will be most concerned with are I/O device files, which are used to access other devices on the system such as printers, tape drives, terminals, and even the disk drives that are used to store a file system. Device files are divided into two classes: block devices and character devices.

A block device is able to store data in fixed size blocks at numbered locations and retrieve them at a later time. A block device must be randomly addressable in BSIZE-byte units. BSIZE is defined in the file /usr/include/sys/param.h and is usually 512. Block devices are usually disks or magnetic tape systems. Although the the operating system accesses a block device in fixed size blocks, a data buffering and caching system (block I/O) implemented within the operating system allows programs to read and write data to a block device in arbitrary units. A block device can be "mounted" so that it holds a portion of the UNIX file system.

Devices that do not meet the requirements of a block device are interfaced as character devices. Many character devices do not store data (e.g., line printers, plotters, and terminals). Other character devices may store data but must be able to read or write data in block sizes different from BSIZE (e.g., reel-to-reel magnetic tape may contain variable size blocks). Finally, the internal interface to character devices is not forced through any internal data buffers (although some character devices may use their own data buffering system). For this reason, character devices are sometimes referred to as *raw* devices.

To most users of a UNIX system, there is no substantial difference between block and character special files. Although the documentation for many programs may specifically recommend using a raw device, using a block device instead will work but may be slightly less efficient. In fact, for most devices there is no choice to be made, and only one type of special file can access the device. The main exceptions are disk and tape devices, which typically have both a block device and a raw or character device. The names of the raw device usually have an "r" at the start of the last name in the path name. For example, /dev/mt0 is usually a block device accessing magnetic tape drive 0 while /dev/rmt0 would be a raw device for magnetic tape drive 0. However, you cannot rely on the name of a file to tell you anything about the file itself. The long format of the ls command will provide this information:

```
ls -l /dev/mt0 /dev/rmt0
brw-rw-rw-  1 root  sys   5,  0  Jun  5 11:44 /dev/mt0
crw-rw-rw-  1 root  sys   8,  0  Jun  3 15:32 /dev/rmt0
```

Here, the first character of the directory listing contains the character "b" to indicate /dev/mt0 is a block device while the character "c" indicates /dev/rmt0 is a character device.

The long information for a special file prints two numbers separated by a comma for special files instead of printing the length of the file. These two numbers are called the *major* and *minor* device numbers. The major device number identifies what device driver is used to communicate with the device. The minor device number can be used for several things, but generally identifies one of several devices or controllers attached to the same device driver. The minor device number can also be used to specify operating modes of a device. For example, /dev/nrmt0 might have minor device number 128 and would also access magnetic tape drive 0, except the tape is not rewound when the device is closed.

The major device numbers for the block and character device for magnetic tape are different. This does not mean they do not share the same device driver. Major device numbers are assigned independently for block devices and character devices.

While many devices use special data formats and need special programs to drive them, it is possible to use device files the same as regular files, including using device files for I/O redirection. For example, on most UNIX systems, the file /dev/lp refers to the line printer. You could get a listing of your directory printed on the line printer with the command:

```
ls -l >/dev/lp
```

While this may work, it does not take into account the fact that other users of the system may also try to use the line printer at the same time. For this reason, printers are usually accessed through a special "spooling" program that saves your output in a file and automatically waits for the printer to become available. However, the principle of accessing the device itself remains the same: device files are accessed the same way as regular disk files.

Regular and Special Files

As mentioned previously, the UNIX file system contains three types of files: regular files, directories, and special files. A regular file is an unstructured, one-dimensional array of bytes stored on a disk or other mass-storage device. Directories are files that provide the mapping between the names of files and the files themselves. Special files are block or character devices or FIFO pipes.

A common naming syntax is used in I/O requests for all three types of files. Many I/O operations that read or write data can be performed with equal success on ordinary and special files. The data will be moved to or from a file in the first case and a device or pipe in the second. Directories are similar to regular files, but because they have a special meaning to the kernel, they cannot be written directly by user processes.

Directory Structure and the I-List

The directories in a UNIX file system are arranged in a tree with a single root. Every directory except the root appears in its parent and each subdirectory. Every directory can contain any number of subdirectories. When a user process opens a file, the kernel searches the directory tree until it locates the specified entry. A directory entry maps a file name to an entry in a table of file descriptors called i-nodes. The i-node table entry indicates whether the file is a regular or special file.

The i-node for a regular file contains addresses that directly or indirectly locate the file on the disk. The i-node for a special file contains the major and minor device numbers that locate its device driver. The i-node for the root of the directory hierarchy is at a known location on the disk. When a user process references a file by name the kernel uses this i-node to locate the root directory, which contains an identifier for the i-node for the next lower directory, and so on.

In a UNIX file system all directories appear in a single tree, which may span several devices. The root of the tree (the root directory) is always found on the bootstrap disk. If a second file-structured disk is attached to the system (mounted), its directory tree is attached to the tree on the bootstrap disk at a selected node.

By convention the special files that represent I/O devices are kept in the directory /dev on the root device.

· System Data Structures for File Operations ·

The i-node is the primary data structure describing a file. The operating system maintains a table of i-nodes in memory for each file open in the system. Additional entries in this table are required to store i-nodes for files that are being executed or are the current working directory of some processes, as well as for other miscellaneous uses. The in-memory i-node table entry contains all the information from the i-node on the disk as well as some additional information used by the operating system. For example, only one process can write to an i-node at any given instant, so the in-memory i-node table entry contains a lock field to control access to the i-node. The in-memory i-node table also acts as a cache for commonly used i-nodes. This means that the i-nodes for directories such as /bin and /usr/bin, which are referenced frequently, do not need to be read in from the disk each time a directory name lookup is performed. (See Figure 2-3.)

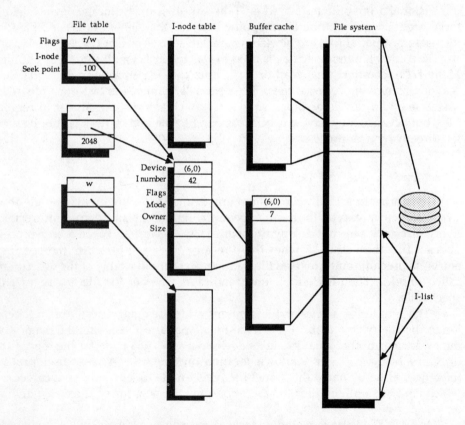

Fig. 2-3. File system data structures

In addition to the in-memory i-node, each open file descriptor is associated with an open-file-table entry (file structure). Each entry in this table refers to an entry in the in-memory i-node table and also has flag bits indicating whether the file descriptor was opened for reading, writing, or both, and contains the "seek point" for that file descriptor.

Open file descriptors for each process are maintained in the process's user structure. This is just a short table of pointers referring to entries in the system-wide open-file-table. The file descriptor used by system calls is just an index into this table inside the user structure.

Both the open-file-table entries and in-memory i-node table entries have reference counts to keep track of how many file descriptors refer to a file-table entry and how many file-table entries refer to an i-node. These reference counts are essential for proper operation of system calls such as fork, dup, and close.

The fork system call works by copying the address space of the parent process and also copying the system context of the process—the process structure and the user structure. Only the data and stack segments of the address space need to be copied. Since the text segment is never changed, the child process can share the same copy of the text segment as the parent process. Some versions of UNIX make use of the memory management hardware to avoid copying any data until either the parent or child process tries to make a change. Use of "copy-on-write" can be more efficient, especially for large processes, but is not essential to the operation of the fork system call.

When the user structure is copied by the fork system call, the open file table for the parent process is copied into the child process. This ensures that the child process can read or write any file that the parent process can read or write. Moreover, since the open-file-table contains pointers to file-table entries, the parent and child process will share the same "seek pointer" for all open files. To understand why this is important, consider what happens when the standard output has been redirected to a file instead of a terminal and a process creates one or more child processes. This is a common occurrence when redirecting the output of a *shell script*, a file that contains one or more shell command lines that are executed in sequence.

To be more specific, consider a shell script that executes a long directory listing and then uses the wc command to count the number of lines in each file. When this script begins executing, the seek pointer for the standard output will be zero. When the ls -l command executes it will write some number of characters to the standard output. The exact number of characters written depends on the contents of the current directory, but let us assume that 100 characters were written. If the ls command has its own copy of the seek pointer for the output file, the wc command would begin writing the output file from the beginning since the shell (the parent process of both the ls and wc commands) did not write anything to the standard output. This would cause the first part of the output of the ls command to be overwritten by the output of the wc command.

When the fork command copies the open-file-table, it must add one to the reference count for each file-table entry that the open-file-table entries refer to. This allows the operating system to know how many processes have a file open so the file-table entry will remain in use and the file will remain open as long as any process still has that file open. Continuing the previous example, when the ls command exits it will close all its open files. The close system call works by subtracting one from the reference count of the file-table entry pointed at by the open-file-table and removing that entry from the open-file-table of the process that is closing the file. The file itself is only closed if the reference count in the file-table entry has reached zero indicating no process has the file open anymore.

The dup system call works like fork except dup copies one entry in the open-file-table of a process into another entry in the open-file-table of the same process. The dup system call must add one to the reference count of the corresponding file-table entry to ensure that the file itself is not closed until both file descriptors for that file are closed.

If some other process (or the same process) opens the same file more than once, closing one of these file descriptors will remove an entry from the system-wide open file table, but the underlying file or i-node should remain open. Again, this is accomplished by using a reference count in the in-memory i-node table entries to keep track of how many file table entries are using that i-node. This is especially important for devices since closing a device invokes the device driver and often makes the device unusable until the device is opened again. This causes errors in the other process that has the device open, and from the point of view of this other process, these errors would be unpredictable.

▪ The Block Buffering System ▪

An I/O request that specifies a regular file or a block device is handled differently from one that specifies a character device. Requests for character devices are passed directly to the appropriate device driver with very little preliminary processing. Requests for block devices must eventually be passed to a device driver, but first a fairly complicated system within the kernel, known as the block buffering system, comes into play.

The UNIX I/O system maintains a pool of data buffers in primary memory. This pool is illustrated in Figure 2-4.

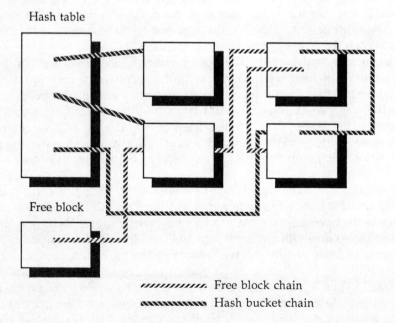

Hash table

Free block

╱╱╱╱╱╱╱╱╱╱ Free block chain

∾∾∾∾∾∾∾∾∾ Hash bucket chain

Fig. 2-4. The buffer pool

At any given time each buffer is either associated with a specific block device and device address (block number) or is unused. This buffer pool constitutes a data cache for the block devices. When a read is issued to a block device the kernel first searches the cache to see whether the requested block is present. If it is, no device driver action is required; a copy of the requested data is returned to the caller. If the desired block is not present it is read from the device by calling a driver routine. On a write request, an updated version of the output block is placed in the cache; if only part of the block is being written and the block is not in the cache, the driver is called to obtain a copy of the full block before the update is made. The data will not be written to the disk until the cache buffer is needed for other purposes. The buffers may also be written to the disk as a result of an explicitly requested flush operation by a user process (see sync(2) and fflush(3)).

This buffering system allows the execution of block device drivers to be asynchronous relative to user process I/O requests. Thus when a block driver performs a physical read or write, it always does so on behalf of the kernel and its block buffering system. Many of the I/O requests queued to a block device driver originate in the kernel during searches of directories. Requests issued by user processes may require no driver activity or may arrive at the driver much later, when a cache buffer must be made available to hold newly requested data.

▪ Device Drivers ▪

A device driver is a collection of subroutines and data within the UNIX kernel that constitutes the software interface to an I/O device. When the UNIX kernel recognizes that a particular action is required, it calls the appropriate driver routine. No other code within the kernel makes direct contact with the device. It is possible (but rare) for a user process to map device registers into its virtual address space, but only a device driver can respond to device interrupts.

Device drivers are an integral part of the UNIX kernel. They are written in the C language and compiled into object modules that are linked into the kernel image using the loader, ld. In order to add a new device driver or modify an existing one, a new kernel image must be linked and booted.

Driver Routines

The principal interface between a device driver and the rest of the UNIX kernel consists of a set of standard entry points. The names of the entry points and the operations they perform must conform to the rules given in subsequent chapters of this book.

The set of entry points provided can vary from one driver to another. Which entry points appear in a particular driver depends partly on the driver type (block or character) and partly on the nature of the device (a write-only device such as a printer will not have a read routine). The entry points that may appear in a driver include

- An initialization routine that is called during the boot procedure

- Open and close routines

- Read and write routines to initiate data transfers
- An interrupt handler to respond to device interrupts
- A general purpose I/O control routine
- A select routine to handle synchronous I/O multiplexing
- Other entry points specific to particular versions of UNIX

Execution Context and Control

Each driver routine has a context in which it executes. Important features of the driver context include the relationship to the current process, the distinction between system and user address spaces, and the need for coordination with other executions of the driver.

Some driver routines are always called on behalf of the current process. They read the structure u to obtain the information they need about the I/O request. Other driver routines are called to handle interrupts and have no direct relationship to the current user process. Routines of this type must not access the u structure.

Routines that execute in the context of the current user process often need to suspend execution of that process until some event takes place. Since I/O can be very slow relative to CPU execution speed, drivers must not loop waiting for a device to become ready; they must relinquish the processor and allow other processes to execute. The kernel provides a sleep routine for this purpose. When a driver routine calls sleep, the current user process is blocked from further execution until a corresponding wakeup call is made by some other routine (usually the interrupt service routine).

In the MASSCOMP RTU environment the kernel and the current user process each have their own virtual address space. Device driver routines are a part of the kernel; their code and internal data structures occupy system address space. But drivers frequently need to read or write data buffers in user process address space; to do this they call kernel routines to move data between system and user spaces.

Another important point about driver execution context is that some driver routines may have multiple executions in progress at the same time. A driver may suspend itself and the calling process while waiting for a hardware operation to complete; during that time the routine may be called on behalf of another process. Driver code must handle all data and status flags carefully so that parallel executions do not interfere with one another.

▪ Flow of I/O Requests Through the System ▪

This section describes briefly the flow of typical read and write requests through the UNIX system (other requests such as open and ioctl will be discussed later).

A user process requests an I/O operation by issuing a system call. Device-independent I/O routines within the kernel determine whether the device on which the operation is to be performed is a block device or a character device.

If the I/O is to a character device:

- The read or write routine within the appropriate device driver is called

- The called routine initiates activity on the device and blocks execution of the calling process (and itself)

- The kernel passes control of the CPU to some other process

- At some later time the device completes its action and issues an interrupt request; the interrupt is serviced by calling the device driver interrupt handler

- The interrupt handler sets up status indicators and reactivates the driver routine that initiated the action

- That routine returns control to the user process that issued the service request

If the request is to an ordinary data file:

- The relative block number within the file is mapped to a physical block number on the block device. If the request is to a block device, this operation is skipped.

- The block buffering cache is then used to mediate the data transfer. The request may be satisfied without device driver action.

- When device I/O is needed, the kernel calls the block driver I/O routine. The driver adds the request to an internal queue that is processed asynchronously. Any required suspension and reactivation of user processes is handled by kernel routines outside the driver.

This is a simplified summary that overlooks many variations on the standard read and write operations that may occur. The following chapters give a more comprehensive and detailed view of the full range of operations that are possible.

▪ Overview of Device Drivers ▪

This section gives an overview of:

- Driver routines
- Structure of character and block drivers
- Driver execution context and data structures

Driver Routines

All drivers must have a set of routines that serve as entry points for the kernel. Drivers are not required to include all the possible entry points. A system configuration file specifies for each driver which entry points it includes. The configuration file is described in Chapter 4.

A driver's entry points must have names with a conventional form. In particular, the entry point names are formed by concatenating a unique alphanumeric driver prefix with a generic name that describes the routine. For example, the initialization routine in a driver whose prefix is pq would be pqinit. The following list shows the typical entry point names that a driver can potentially include. Note that your driver prefix would replace the xx_ in the example names.

xx_init	Initialize driver and device
xx_open	Open device
xx_close	Close device
xx_read	Read character or raw data
xx_write	Write character or raw data
xx_strategy	Read and write block data (required for block devices)
xx_intr	Handle device interrupts (required for all devices)
xx_ioctl	Perform special functions (character drivers only)
xx_select	Determine if a call to a read or write routine will block

In addition to the entry points listed, different implementations of the UNIX operating system may include entry points for other functions such as a function to perform initialization for devices and drivers that are not essential to the initialization of the kernel, a function to facilitate power fail recovery, or functions to suspend and continue current processing in favor of another process. The following paragraphs give a general description of the functions that are performed by each of the driver routines in the previous list. They also discuss some of the data structures that form the interface between the driver routines and the rest of the kernel. Subsequent chapters give more details.

Initialization Routine.   If a driver has an initialization entry point, it is called at system bootstrap time. This routine initializes the driver itself, by clearing flags and counts, allocating resources, and so on. A driver that manages DMA devices frequently allocates a group of I/O map registers permanently for its private use.

An important function of this routine is that of determining whether the devices managed by the driver are online. Drivers are supplied with a controller count, a device count, and the base address of each controller. The initialization routine should access each controller in turn to see whether it is indeed present in the system. The kernel provides a method that allows the driver to detect a bus timeout: if a device does not respond it must be declared offline by zeroing its base address (see Chapter 5). The kernel then does not include an offline device in an interrupt poll, and other driver routines can avoid accessing its registers.

Finally, this routine can issue initialization commands to prepare the devices that are online for subsequent I/O operations.

Open and Close Routines.   A driver's open routine is called whenever a user process issues an open(2) system call on the device handled. It can prepare the device for subsequent I/O. The open routine in a driver for a line printer, for example, might send a page eject to the printer.

Open and close routines are not mandatory. Many simple devices can get along without them. These routines are frequently used to implement exclusive access by setting a flag on the first call to open and clearing it on close.

The driver close routine is called only when the last process that has opened the device closes it. Therefore, drivers that do not enforce exclusive access cannot use open and close to maintain a count of processes that have the device open (in addition to not being called each time a file is closed, the device driver is not called when a file descriptor is duplicated by either fork or dup). Note that device here means a unique combination of major and minor device numbers.

The open routine in a block device driver is called only when a user process opens the device or when the device is mounted. The open routine is not called to open an ordinary file.

Character Driver Read and Write Routines.   In a character driver the read and write routines are called by the kernel whenever the current user process issues a read(2) or write(2) system call from or to a special file. This can occur only after the process has issued a successful open on the device.

These routines are always called on behalf of the current user process. They receive the minor device number as an argument and obtain the other information they need to describe the I/O request from the u structure. Read and write routines keep track of whether the device is busy. If the device is not busy, they write directly to the device. If the device is busy, they queue the operation until the device is free again.

Block Driver Read and Write Routines.   On some systems, including MASS-COMP systems, a block driver can also have read and write entry points. These optional routines are called to set up raw I/O transfers. Raw I/O is a special feature that improves file I/O performance. The kernel calls the driver raw I/O entry points if they exist and the following conditions are met:

- The size of the requested data transfer is greater than some threshold (2048 bytes on MASSCOMP systems)

- The transfer is to or from a contiguous section of the device

- None of the blocks in the request are currently in the block buffering cache

These routines act like character read and write routines and are identical to the raw read and write routines in device drivers that support both a block and character device. They act on behalf of the current user process and obtain the data that describes the I/O request from the u structure. In order to synchronize with other active I/O requests they prepare a buf structure to describe the request and then call the strategy routine as opposed to initiating device I/O directly. Then they call sleep and wait for the data transfer to be completed.

The reason for including raw I/O routines in a block driver is to enhance performance. These routines allow the operating system to make transfers directly to and from user process buffers. These entry points are optional. If they do not exist the kernel will copy the user data into system space cache buffers and call the strategy routine.

It is important to note that raw I/O on a block device is not the same as I/O to a character device in a block driver although in MASSCOMP systems, it is implemented using the same underlying driver entry points. Raw I/O will only occur on a block device when reading and writing to regular files located on a block device that is currently mounted. It can only occur if the device driver for the block device has been configured to support raw I/O independently of whether the device driver also supports a character device interface. For example, while magnetic tape devices usually support both a block and a character interface, raw file I/O is not supported on magnetic tape (the difficulty is that a reel-to-reel tape must be read using the same I/O transfer size as was used to write the tape while raw file I/O will use different transfer sizes in different circumstances).

Block Driver Strategy Routine.   The block driver strategy routine is called by the kernel to perform block read and write operations. When the kernel requires that a data block in its block buffering cache be read or written, it calls the strategy routine with a pointer to a data structure that describes the buffer and the block to be read. This data structure is called the buf structure. The buf structure contains flags and data that describe the request, a pointer to the data, and other information used by the kernel to maintain the block buffering cache. Block I/O requests are not necessarily related to the current process, so the strategy routine must never use the u structure. It finds all the information it needs in the buf structure.

The I/O requests sent to the strategy routine are processed asynchronously by the driver, which maintains a queue of outstanding requests. When strategy is called it adds the buffer pointed to by its argument to its queue and returns control to the caller. The required device activity may be initiated by strategy or later by the interrupt handler. When the requested action is completed the interrupt handler releases the buffer back to the kernel. The strategy routine must not sleep because it may be called from interrupt code.

The strategy routine is not required to execute the read and write requests in the order that they are presented to it. This allows it to make simple strategic decisions by ordering the requests in its queue of outstanding work (hence the name strategy). The most common example is that of a disk driver that orders requests according to their cylinder numbers so that the disk heads sweep smoothly across the disk.

Interrupt Service Routine.   Driver interrupt routines are called to handle device interrupts. The function of a interrupt routine is specific to the device. In general, the interrupt routine services the interrupting device (e.g., reading or writing some hardware registers) and notifies the processes associated with a device when a data transfer is complete.

There can be two types of interrupt routines: polling routines and vectored routines. On systems without vectored interrupts, the interrupt routine may be called during an interrupt poll. The handler must determine whether one of its devices issued the interrupt and return a value that informs the kernel whether it must continue to poll other drivers. System configuration data determines whether an interrupt handler is polled. The polling can be handled by a separate polling routine that then calls the real interrupt routine. This is useful if your driver is for a device that will be run on both MULTIBUS (without vectored interrupts) and VMEbus (with vectored interrupts) machines.

Assuming that the interrupt was issued by a device handled by this driver, the handler must take the necessary steps to process the interrupt. Devices usually issue interrupts when they have completed an operation that was initiated by some other driver routine. If the operation was a character or raw data transfer, the handler will probably need to call `wakeup` to reactivate a suspended read or write routine. If the operation was a block data transfer, it will probably need to call `iodone` to release the `buf` structure, and then initiate the next queued request.

The interrupt handler executes in a context that has no direct relationship to the current user process. It never reads or writes the `u` structure and never calls `sleep`. It always terminates by returning to its caller. In some cases it returns a value to indicate whether it handled the interrupt or whether the poll should be continued.

Character Driver Special Functions Routine. Character drivers may include a "special functions" entry point to perform operations other than standard reads and writes. This routine is called whenever a user process issues the `ioctl(2)` system call request. The driver ioctl routine is frequently used to set a device mode, either by setting internal driver software flags or by writing commands to device registers. It can also be used to return information to the user about the current device state.

The ioctl routine is called with four arguments: a file descriptor, a code to indicate the device specific function to be performed, a pointer to data to be used in performing the function, and a mode that contains values set when the device was opened. It is always called on behalf of the current user process, but the fields in `u` that are used to describe read and write requests will not be meaningful.

Select Routine. Device drivers can do synchronous I/O multiplexing using the select routine. This routine allows the user process to check to see if the device is ready for reading or writing. If a device is ready for reading or writing on the specified channel (e.g., the operation would not block), the select routine returns true.

Structure of Character and Block Drivers

Device drivers can be specified to be character drivers or block drivers. The choice of type determines which entry points must be included in the driver.

Drivers that perform only character I/O include either a read or a write routine or both, but neither is mandatory. They do not have a strategy routine. When a user process issues a `read` or `write` system call on a character device, the kernel calls the driver routine of the same name. The driver routine always executes on behalf of the current user process; it obtains all the information it needs about the request from the current process user structure `u`.

Drivers that perform only block I/O must include a strategy routine that handles both read and write operations on the device. Pure block drivers can optionally include read and write entry points; if these routines exist they will be called to perform raw I/O under the circumstances described. When the strategy routine is called it adds an I/O request block (a `buf` structure) to an internal queue. When the read and write routines are called to perform raw I/O they extract information from the `u` structure, prepare an appropriate `buf` structure, and call the strategy routine.

A driver can include routines to do both character and block I/O. A driver for a block device might also support that device as a raw device. For example, device drivers for disks generally support raw I/O so file system maintenance operations such as creating backup tapes can be done more efficiently. A driver that supports both block and character I/O must have read and write routines and a strategy routine.

In general, a dual-type driver handles I/O for each raw device. Each logical device has its own special file with its own major/minor device number. A driver of this type has only one read and one write entry point. If the block device supports raw file I/O, the same read and write entry points must also be used for raw device reads and writes.

Only a character driver can have a special-functions (ioctl) routine. However, many block drivers are also defined as character drivers so that they can support a raw device. This makes it possible for the device driver to have an ioctl routine, which can be used to deal with special functions supported by the device.

Only a character driver can have a select routine for synchronous I/O multiplexing. All other driver routines—init, open, close, and intr—can appear in both character and block drivers. They perform the same functions in both cases. Only devices that generate processor interrupts will require an intr routine (but that includes almost all devices). One-way devices (input-only or output-only) will require only one of read and write. Many simple devices may not need open and close routines.

Driver Execution Context

Each driver routine executes in a context that determines which data structures it can access and which synchronization methods it can use. Because device drivers are an integral part of the kernel, the system cannot protect itself from errors in driver code. Improper use of kernel data and functions by a driver will cause system failures that can be very difficult to trace.

Driver Top and Bottom Halves.   The terms *top half* and *bottom half* are often used to denote the driver routines that are called at I/O request time and at interrupt time, respectively. Read, write, and ioctl are in the top half of the driver. Strategy and the interrupt handler and any routines that it may call are in the bottom half.

A method commonly used in block drivers is to include a start routine that can be called internally to initiate device I/O. Doing so allows you to isolate the device-specific code into one routine. This routine is not a driver entry point. It is called either by the driver strategy routine or by its interrupt handler depending on whether the device is busy or not. Because it may be called in interrupt context it is considered to be a bottom-half routine.

By convention a block driver maintains an active flag to indicate whether a data transfer is in progress. The strategy routine checks this flag whenever it adds a buffer header to the driver queue. If the flag is off it calls the start routine. That is, the start routine is called from the strategy routine if the device is not busy. If the device is busy, the start routine is called from the driver interrupt handler when the current operation is completed. As long as there is some device activity in progress so that another interrupt is expected, the driver keeps the active flag set.

Additional information and examples of the use of start routines and active flags are given in later chapters.

Use of Data Structures. A principal issue related to the execution of driver routines is the relationship of the routines to the current user process, whose state is stored in the kernel data structure u. Although the user process cannot access the driver directly, some driver routines are always called on behalf of the current process. In effect, these routines have simply been called as subroutines by that process, which is temporarily executing in system state. They read the structure u to obtain the information they need about the I/O request, and they write final status back to that structure. These routines execute in system state in order to access things that a user process cannot. Note, however, that system state is not a superset of user state, it is an entirely different state. A user state process can access some things that a system state process cannot.

It is legal to access the current user process structure u from the top-half driver routines init, open, read, write, select, ioctl, and close. During calls to read and write routines this structure contains fields that give the size and location of the requested data transfer. These fields are not valid during calls to the bottom-half of a device driver.

The strategy and interrupt handler routines have no relationship to the current user process represented in the u structure. Even if they happen to be working on an I/O request that originated in a user process they cannot assume that it is the current process, and should not access the u structure.

The buf structures that are passed to a block driver strategy routine by the kernel are taken from the pool of the block buffer cache system. When the I/O operation is complete it is necessary for the driver interrupt handler to indicate properly the final status and release the buffer back to its owner. This is usually done by calling the kernel routine iodone.

Certain fields in u and buf structures are read-only for drivers and must not be disturbed; others must be updated in order for the caller to receive the correct I/O completion status. Specifications for the proper handling of the fields that are meaningful to drivers are given in Chapters 5 and 9.

Drivers frequently need to allocate space for data that is being temporarily buffered between top- and bottom-half routines. The driver can allocate this space in one of three ways:

- Static buffering

- Allocating blocks from the pool of cache buffers using `geteblock`

- Calling `wmemall` to allocate nonpageable memory in system address space

If the driver declares a static internal buffer then it must be careful to synchronize access to that buffer. Drivers are reentrant and may have multiple parallel executions. A routine that wishes to use a static buffer must wait until it is free and then mark it as busy. Standard methods for doing this are described in Chapter 5.

Synchronizing Driver Execution.   Drivers use two principal methods to synchronize their execution:

- Calls to `sleep` and `wakeup`

- Calls to routines that set the CPU priority

`Sleep` and `wakeup` are kernel functions that can be called by drivers to suspend and resume execution of the current user process. When a process is suspended by `sleep` its execution is blocked; it becomes ineligible for use of the CPU. A subsequent call to `wakeup` resumes execution. An integer argument (called a channel or event) is used to indicate which `sleep` calls are to be undone by the `wakeup`. (See Figure 2-5.)

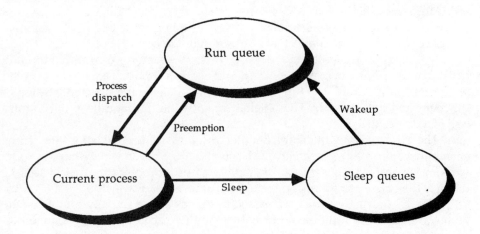

Fig. 2-5. Process transitions

A typical sequence of events in a character driver is as follows:

1. A read or write routine initiates an I/O operation on the device and issues a call to `sleep`.

2. The user process is suspended and some other process obtains use of the CPU.

3. Later the device issues an interrupt request that activates the driver interrupt handler.

4. The handler determines that the interrupt has signaled completion of the requested operation and calls `wakeup`.

Driver strategy and interrupt handler routines must never issue `sleep` calls since they do not execute in the context of the current process. If a user process must be suspended while waiting for I/O on a block device, a kernel routine outside the driver calls `sleep` after it has called the driver strategy routine.

Drivers also synchronize their execution by calling routines to set the CPU interrupt priority to specified levels. This is done principally to synchronize execution of top-half and bottom-half routines. When a top-half routine must access a data structure that is also accessed by the interrupt handler, it first raises the CPU priority to the device interrupt level. This prevents the interrupt handler from being called while the sensitive operations are in progress. In particular, the driver must always go to device priority level before writing device registers.

Synchronization between the top and bottom half of a device driver can be more complicated in a multiprocessor system. On MASSCOMP RTU systems all device driver routines are guaranteed to run on a single processor. Therefore, single processor synchronization techniques will work even on a dual-processor system.

C H A P T E R

∎ ∎ ∎ ∎ ∎

3

I/O HARDWARE AND
DEVICE DRIVERS

∙ I/O Architecture ∙

This chapter describes the hardware context for device drivers. There are a number of system hardware features that affect how you write the device driver. From the driver writer's point of view the key hardware topics are:

- CPU access to I/O bus address space
- Device access to system memory
- Processor interrupts

This chapter gives an overview of I/O architecture, using MASSCOMP systems as examples, and then treats the above topics.

Overview of I/O Architecture

In MASSCOMP architecture the CPU, system memory, and some high-speed devices such as the floating point processor are attached to the proprietary memory interconnect bus. Devices are attached to the system by an I/O bus (MULTIBUS or VMEbus). The I/O bus is connected to the memory bus through a hardware Bus Adapter (MULTIBUS or VMEbus), which is resident on the CPU board. A system may have either a MULTIBUS or a VMEbus. A system may have multiple MULTIBUSes or multiple VMEbuses. The terms *I/O Bus* and *I/O Bus Adapter* are used here wherever the information applies to both MULTIBUS and VMEbus.

The MULTIBUS.   The MULTIBUS is an industry standard device interfacing bus that supports 24 address bits, 16 data bits, and 8 levels of prioritized interrupts.

On the MC68000 family of processors all I/O device registers are memory mapped. That is, there are no explicit I/O instructions. The processor does not distinguish between memory and peripheral devices. Whenever software must read or write a device register, it uses the same instructions used to read and write memory. Specific physical addresses are reserved for device registers. The MULTIBUS was designed for the Intel 8080 family of processors, which have two separate address spaces. That type of processor has separate instructions for reading and writing from memory and transferring data to and from devices. Therefore, the MULTIBUS has two overlapped address spaces: I/O space and memory space. Separate bus control lines are used to select one of the two address reference types. Most MULTIBUS I/O devices respond to I/O accesses while memory controllers respond to memory accesses. The choice is up to the board designer, and some boards in fact respond selectively to both types of references.

MULTIBUS controllers that respond to I/O references decode only the lowest 8 or 16 bits of the address used. Therefore, there are 64 kilobytes of MUL- TIBUS address space available for I/O devices. However, 8-bit devices use addresses in the range 0–255. If you have a 16-bit device, take care not to assign it an address whose lower 8 bits match a value used by an 8-bit device.

The details of MULTIBUS operation are defined by IEEE Standard 796. Detailed specifications of MULTIBUS operations can be found in the *Multibus Data Book*, which is available from the Intel Corporation.

The VMEbus.   The VMEbus is an industry standard device interfacing bus that supports 6 levels of prioritized processor interrupts, and either 16, 24, or 32 address bits with either 16 or 32 data bits. Unlike the MULTIBUS, the VMEbus does not distinguish between I/O and memory space and it supports multiple address spaces. These address spaces respond to 16-, 24-, or 32-bit addresses. This is more flexible than the MULTIBUS, allowing you to put the 16-bit devices in 16-bit space, the 24-bit devices in 24-bit space, and the 32-bit devices in 32-bit space. When you are writing a device driver it is important to know which of these address spaces your device uses so that you can make an appropriate entry in the system configuration file (see Chapter 4 for more details on configuration).

The details of VMEbus operations are defined by IEEE Standard P1014/D1.2 (also known as IEC 821 BUS). Detailed specifications of VMEbus operations can be found in *The VMEbus Specification*, Rev C.1, which is available from Micrology.

CPU Access to Devices

Most systems have a range of physical address space allocated for system RAM memory for system local devices, which the driver writer should not alter. The physical address space also has one or more address ranges in system I/O space through which the CPU can access devices on the I/O Bus. These address ranges are referred to as I/O spaces. The CPU translates references within these I/O spaces into addresses on the corresponding I/O bus. This translation is different for the MULTIBUS and the VMEbus.

The size and division of physical address space and I/O spaces and the specific device addressing conventions vary from system to system. The examples used here are for MASSCOMP systems.

Translation of References in I/O Space.   Each MULTIBUS has areas that are designated I/O and memory. MULTIBUS I/O space is always 64 kilobytes, but the amount of MULTIBUS memory is system specific. The MASSCOMP system treats all MULTIBUS space as I/O space. The CPU translates references within memory bus I/O space directly to the MULTIBUS.

Each VMEbus requires three 16-megabyte I/O spaces (one for the 16- and 24-bit address spaces and two for the 32-bit address spaces). Each I/O space is divided into one or more I/O windows. Each I/O window has a specific address.

Device Access to Memory

Some devices have the ability to become bus master and issue addresses on the I/O bus in order to perform DMA data transfers. Though in some cases a DMA device will need to transfer data to or from I/O bus memory, it is more common for these devices to access system memory on the memory bus.

When an I/O bus device issues a DMA reference to system memory, the address used is passed to the memory bus by the I/O bus adapter. The address is either translated and mapped to the memory bus by the I/O map in the bus adapter (MULTIBUS or VMEbus), or the address is direct mapped (passed directly) to the memory bus (VMEbus only).

The I/O map is necessary for the following reasons:

- Some MULTIBUS devices issue 20-bit addresses; these must be translated into 24-bit addresses to permit the device to access all of physical memory.

- Some operating systems' virtual memory systems (e.g., MASSCOMP's RTU) map contiguous pages in virtual memory onto scattered, noncontiguous pages in physical memory. The I/O map permits devices to make long data transfers that cross page boundaries while using a contiguous range of addresses.

- Some MULTIBUS controllers read initialization data from fixed addresses in lower memory. These locations in physical memory may be reserved for other purposes.

The I/O Map contains an array of registers, each of which maps one page (4096 bytes) of memory. The MULTIBUS and the VMEbus I/O maps vary in the number of registers they contain and in the use of address bits during translation, but they function in the same general way. The address translation takes place as follows:

- The low-order bits of an address issued on the I/O bus by a device are mapped unchanged into the result address. These are the page offset bits, which select a byte within the page.

- The high-order bits form an index into the I/O map to select a mapping register.

- The low order bits of the mapping register contents are interpreted as a page frame number in physical memory. These bits become the high-order bits of the result address.

This I/O mapping scheme is shown in Figure 3-1.

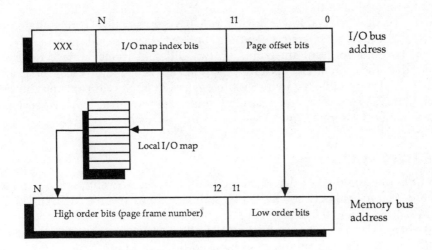

Fig. 3-1. Operation of the I/O map

Device drivers access the I/O map by calling kernel subroutines (`iomal-loc`, `iomapaddr`, `iomapvaddr`) and therefore do not need to know its physical location.

For devices that use 20-bit MULTIBUS addresses, the driver can specify when calling the register allocation routine that only registers in the first quadrant of the map are to be used.

The MASSCOMP VMEbus adapter has a direct-mapped area that allows a device to access system memory without going through address translation by the I/O map. This area is part of the 32-bit address space that is directly mapped to system physical memory. Direct mapping reduces the overhead of I/O transfers because I/O map registers are not used. Since I/O map registers are not used, I/O transfers are less likely to be limited by the number of free I/O map registers.

The memory pages allocated are not always contiguous for a corresponding range of virtual addresses. Therefore, the direct-mapped area is only useful to devices that do not require contiguous data and can use gather/scatter techniques to access discontiguous blocks of memory in a single transfer.

MULTIBUS adapters do not have a direct-mapped area. All MULTIBUS address references must be translated by the I/O map.

Processor Interrupts

The MULTIBUS provides eight processor interrupt lines, referred to as levels zero through seven. Levels one through six are used as prioritized interrupt levels, with level six having the highest priority. The VMEbus provides six processor interrupt lines, referred to as levels one through six. Again, level six has the highest priority.

Interrupt priorities are used in two ways: they are compared to the current processor priority and to the priorities of other interrupts. Software sets the CPU priority to a value in the range zero through seven; while the CPU priority is n, interrupts at levels n and lower are ignored. Interrupts at levels higher than n are allowed and cause an interrupt handling routine to be executed immediately.

If two devices issue interrupts on two different levels, both of which are higher than the current CPU priority, the interrupt at the higher level is serviced first. It is also possible for two or more devices to issue interrupts on the same level. In this case, as soon as a device is found to have interrupted, it is serviced.

Chapter 5 describes how to set device and processor priorities.

MULTIBUS Byte Ordering

The CPU Module (one of the MC68000 family processors) supports 8-, 16-, and 32-bit data transfers between the processor's data lines and the MULTIBUS data lines (MBUS DATA 00 L through MBUS DATA 15 L).

There is one peculiarity of the MULTIBUS that driver writers must take into account. The conventions for byte addressing (addressing bytes within words) are opposite for the Motorola MC68000 family processor and the MULTIBUS. The MC68000 processor puts the odd-numbered byte (higher address) as the right-hand byte within the dataword, whereas the MULTIBUS puts the even byte as the right-hand byte. Figure 3-2 illustrates the organization of memory words in each instance.

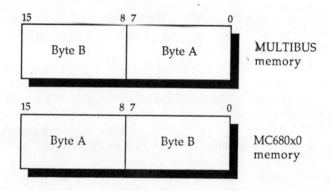

Fig. 3-2. Organization of memory words on MULTIBUS and MC680x0

To accommodate this reversal, the MULTIBUS adapter always reverses (swaps) bytes when transferring data between the MULTIBUS and the MC680x0 data lines.

Drivers may have a problem when they must write word-length values to memory-mapped device control registers. In some cases the driver must reverse the order of the bytes in memory before writing the device register. Some MULTIBUS boards have one or more switches to control the order of bytes within words for control and data I/O. Chapter 5 discusses ways of dealing with this issue.

▪ Characteristics of I/O Devices ▪

This section gives a general overview of I/O device characteristics including:

- Memory-mapped registers
- Processor interrupts
- Programmed I/O and DMA
- Controllers with multiplexed devices
- Character and block devices

Memory-Mapped Registers

The principal interface to an I/O device visible to software is the memory-mapped register. These registers are also known as Control and Status Registers (CSR). Device driver software can write to these registers to control the device (issue commands to it) and read from them to determine its current status.

As discussed earlier in this chapter, device registers appear in the upper two megabytes of physical memory (usually the upper 64 kilobytes). The mapping between the device registers and memory is set up by the UNIX operating system at system boot time. For the most part, software can treat these registers like any other memory locations. You can use assignment statements in C or other high-level languages to move values to and from the registers. However, registers do differ from ordinary memory in several ways:

- Registers may be active devices, not simple storage elements. A write to a register often has side effects, such as initiating device I/O activity. A read to a register may also have side effects, such as clearing an interrupt request or clearing an error condition.

- Registers may have timing characteristics that are different from ordinary memory. If a write to a device register is expected to produce a visible change in that or some other register, the software may have to introduce a pause (by executing no-ops or waiting for an interrupt) to give the device time to respond.

- A device register will not necessarily contain the value that is written to it. Some register bits are simply nonexistent (always zero or meaningless). Some are sensitive to the value written to them but do not return that value on a read. Sometimes the contents or meaning of a bit varies depending on values set in other registers.

- Device registers may be sensitive to the type of access (byte or word) made to them. They may respond properly to a word access but give a bus fault on a byte access. Also note that the type of access (byte or word) is difficult to control when using bit field operations in C. (In some cases, you can use the ANSI C type modifier `volatile` to control this.)

It is always necessary to study the hardware manual for the device you are writing the driver for in order to learn how its registers will behave.

Choosing Register Addresses.   Device registers usually appear in a contiguous area of memory whose base address is established by setting switches on the hardware board. When adding a new device to a system, you must be careful to assign it register addresses that do not conflict with those used by other devices. Remember in particular that addresses for 8- and 16-bit devices must not conflict. Check the system configuration file and the documentation on device addressing conventions for your system before you install a new device. See Chapter 4 for more information on system configuration files.

Programmed I/O versus Direct Memory Access

I/O devices can be separated into two main classes according to the manner in which they transfer data to and from primary memory:

- **Programmed I/O (PIO).** PIO devices rely on the central processor to perform the data transfer one byte or word at a time. For example, to do output the CPU first writes initialization commands to the device's CSR and then writes an output byte or word to a device register. When the device indicates that it is ready again, the CPU transfers the next byte or word. This cycle continues until all the data has been transferred.

- **Direct Memory Access (DMA).** DMA devices are able to read and write blocks of data in main memory without the aid of the CPU. Typically the processor initiates a DMA transfer by writing a base address and byte or word count to device registers. It then sets a "go" bit in the device CSR to start the transfer. After that the entire data block is moved to or from memory without the aid of the CPU. When the transfer is complete the device sets a "done" bit in its CSR and issues an interrupt.

DMA transfers are usually much faster because they do not require processor intervention for every byte or word transferred. The device can operate at bus speed, though it may have to contend with the CPU and other DMA devices for bus cycles. The CPU is free to perform other useful work. High-speed devices such as disks and magnetic tapes are usually capable of DMA operation. Slower devices such as interactive terminals and line printers are more likely to be PIO devices.

Device drivers handle PIO and DMA transfers in completely different ways. To the driver, PIO data transfers are identical to other CSR read and write operations. That is, an assignment statement is used to move a value from one variable or structure to another. For DMA transfers the driver does the preparation for the transfer and the device actually moves the data. The driver must usually

- Guarantee that the source or destination area in primary memory is locked down in physical memory. That is, the kernel's virtual memory system must be informed that the memory buffer cannot be paged or swapped out to secondary memory while the transfer is in progress.

- Load the I/O map with appropriate values so that the I/O bus addresses generated by the device are translated to the desired main memory addresses.

The driver calls kernel routines to perform these operations.

Processor Interrupts

Most I/O devices are able to issue interrupt requests when they require attention from the central processor (e.g., an error or the completion of an operation). The CPU responds to the interrupt request by calling an interrupt handling routine within the device driver.

There are several factors that can affect the priority of the device and therefore the time that elapses before its interrupt request is honored. The device may be attached to any of the interrupt levels one through six. If two devices request interrupts at the same time, the one attached to the higher level is serviced first. If two devices attached to the same level request interrupts at the same time, the order in which they will be serviced depends on the contents of system configuration data files described in Chapter 4. Finally, response to an interrupt can always be deferred for an indefinite time if the kernel software has raised the CPU priority to or above the device's interrupt level.

Usually, the older, low performance devices require the highest interrupt priority. For example, an interface to an interactive terminal may be able to hold only one or two input characters. If its interrupt is not serviced before another character arrives, an overrun occurs and a character is lost. Intelligent high performance devices usually have large on-board buffers and transfer data by DMA. They may be able to tolerate relatively slow servicing of their interrupts.

Your choice of an interrupt priority for a user device may also depend on system configuration. For example, you should not place a user device on interrupt level one in a MASSCOMP MC5500 dual processor configuration because the MULTIBUS level one interrupt line will interrupt both processors. You should check the hardware documentation for the system for which you are writing the driver for issues of this type before you choose the interrupt priority for your device.

Controllers with Multiplexed Devices

Frequently a single controller with a single set of device registers is used to control several I/O devices simultaneously. For example, a disk controller may control up to eight drive units. A controller may be able to execute some operations on several drives at the same time—disk head seeks and tape rewinds, for example. Other operations such as DMA data transfers may require exclusive use of the controller.

Effective use of overlapped operations can have a major impact on overall I/O throughput. More fundamental is the need for the driver to support multiple parallel executions. A driver may be in the process of initiating I/O to Device 1 on behalf of User Process A, when due to an asynchronous event, it is called to perform I/O on Device 2 for User Process B. The driver must be careful to maintain internal flags and other forms of synchronization to prevent its various executions from interfering with one another.

Character and Block Devices

The UNIX kernel requires that all drivers and devices be classified as being either the block or character type. This choice of type places specific requirements on the structure of the driver (as discussed in Chapter 2).

A block device is a mass storage device that can accept data, store it, and return it to the processor at a later time. Block devices have a logical structure that is known to and used by the UNIX kernel. The data is stored in fixed-size (512 byte) logical blocks. I/O requests are presented to the device driver in terms of the desired block number. Typical block devices are disks and magnetic tapes. Disk block devices can be mounted as a part of the UNIX file system.

A character device is any device that is not a block device. A character device accepts or supplies a stream of data on behalf of a user process. The kernel does not impose any structure on this stream. However, individual device drivers may place restrictions on how a device is accessed. Typical character devices are interactive terminals and graphics display devices.

4

SYSTEM GENERATION

Device drivers are code modules that are incorporated into the executable image of the kernel. The interface between the device driver and the rest of the kernel consists of driver entry points and driver-specific data structures. To incorporate a driver into the kernel, you must create these driver-specific data structures. This chapter describes these data structures and how they are generated. See Figure 4-1.

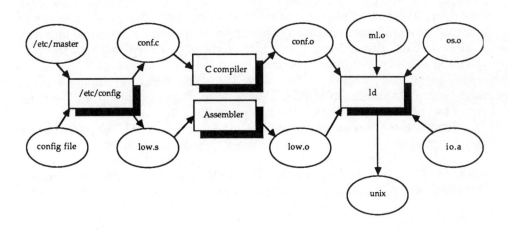

Fig. 4-1. System configuration

The process for incorporating a device driver into the kernel has the following steps:

1. Add descriptions of the device drivers and I/O hardware being added to the system to the system description files.

2. Execute a system configuration utility program (config) to generate source code files that form an interface between the device drivers and the rest of the kernel. The generated source code contains symbolic names for driver entry points and driver-specific data structures.

3. Compile the driver source and the generated interface files and link them with other kernel routines to form the bootable image.

4. Once the driver has been incorporated into the kernel, create a special file to provide the interface between the device and the UNIX file system.

This chapter does not give a comprehensive treatment of system generation and all the possible variations. Rather, it concentrates on the issues that directly affect the construction of drivers. For a more complete discussion, please refer to the system management documentation for your system.

· Kernel to Driver Interface Files ·

Two source files form the interface between device drivers and the rest of the kernel. One, conf.c, defines the kernel to driver interface, and the other contains information specific to the hardware to driver interface.

conf.c contains declaration statements that assign values to many parameters, create driver entry point tables, and specify driver-specific data structures used to pass information to and from the rest of the kernel, most important the block device switch table (bdevsw) and the character device switch table (cdevsw). It also contains global or external references to the driver entry points and block driver iobuf structure. The driver source code must define the entry points and block driver iobuf structure. Drivers that need to access the variables and data structures must declare them in extern statements.

The file that contains the hardware to driver interface information varies from system to system. On MASSCOMP systems, low.s contains the interrupt vector table and executable code for the interrupt handler(s).

Both of these files are generated by /etc/config, the UNIX kernel configuration program. There is no need to change these files manually.

Note that the names generated by config are built according to specific rules, described later in this chapter. The declarations, data tables, and executable code contained in conf.c and low.s use those names.

· System Configuration Data Files ·

The configuration program uses two input files that describe the characteristics of all the device drivers and all the devices that appear in the system. Their names may vary somewhat depending upon the system you are using, but they have the same basic purpose. This section describes the system description files used on the MASSCOMP RTU system. The system description files are:

- **Master Configuration File—/etc/master.** This file contains lines that describe in detail the structure and operating modes of each device driver in the system. Throughout this book, this file is referred to as the master file or the master configuration file.

- **System Configuration File—/usr/uts/SYSNAME.** This file contains lines that describe each hardware I/O device in the system. A version of this file is usually supplied with your system. The file supplied with a MASSCOMP system uses the type of the system as the filename, for example, /usr/uts/MC5500. Throughout this book, this file is referred to as the SYSNAME file, the system configuration file, or the configuration file.

Both files contain additional data that are not directly applicable to device drivers. Both files are ordinary ASCII files that can be modified with any text editor.

The master file describes device drivers but does not specify which ones are included in the generated kernel. The system configuration file lists the devices that are included in the system and thereby determines which drivers are included in the kernel. For every device listed in SYSNAME there must be a corresponding driver entry in master.

There is no penalty for having driver definition lines in the master file for which there are no corresponding devices in the SYSNAME file. The master file delivered with your system contains lines for all the standard drivers on your system. You must add a new line to the master file for each user-written driver.

Most installations make a copy of the supplied SYSNAME file using the name of the local system, such as HAWK, and edit it to describe the local configuration. An arbitrary name can also be used. Lines that are not needed can be commented out by placing a * in column one, and new lines can be added for nonstandard devices. When you add a new driver, make sure that you edit the local system configuration file.

The Master Configuration File—/etc/master

The format of the master file is described in the *UNIX Programmer's Manual* in master(5). This section expands on that description, using the MASSCOMP system to illustrate the details.

The master file has three parts. Part one contains a one-line description for each device driver that can be included in the kernel. These appear before the first line with a $ in column one. The entries in Part two form the Alias Table, and the entries in Part three form the Tunable Parameter Table.

Each driver entry line in Part one contains 11 mandatory entries and up to three additional optional entries. The entries for a driver appear on a single line and are separated by tabs and/or blanks. The following list describes the meaning of each entry.

Fields in Part one:

name devmsk devtyp prefix addrsiz csr_off intmsk bmajor cmajor unitcnt pri [str1 str2 str3]

Where:

name   Is a device name that corresponds to the device name in SYSNAME. Eight character maximum.

devmsk   Is a device mask (octal). Set the bit for each routine (handler) you have in your driver.

200000	cont handler
100000	stop handler
040000	exec handler
020000	fork handler
001000	select handler
000400	block read handler
000200	block write handler
000100	initialization handler
000040	reserved
000020	open handler
000010	close handler
000004	read handler
000002	write handler
000001	ioctl handler

devtyp   Is the device type indicator (octal). Set the bit for each type you wish to specify.

002000	VMEbus A32 device
001000	VMEbus A24 device
004000	VMEbus A16 device
000200	allow only one of these devices
000100	suppress count field in the `conf.c` file
000040	suppress interrupt vector
000020	required device
000010	block device
000004	character device
000002	16-bit CSR
000001	IRQ bits zero (for VMEbus devices, this is unused and must be zero)

prefix   Specifies the handler prefix used to form the routine and external variable names. Four character maximum.

addrsiz   Specifies the device address size in bytes (decimal).

csr_off   Specifies the offset from device base address of the control/status register for this device (decimal).

intmsk	Specifies the bit mask for any interrupt request bits in the device control/status register (hexadecimal). This field must be zero for VMEbus devices.
bmajor	Major device number for block-type device.
cmajor	Major device number for character-type device.
unitcnt	Maximum number of devices per controller (decimal).
pri	Maximum I/O bus interrupt priority level (one through seven).
str1 *str2* *str3*	These are optional fields that specify configuration table structure declarations and have a maximum of eight characters. See Chapter 10 for more information.

Fields in Part two:

alias   name

Where:

alias	Is the alias name of device. Eight character maximum.
name	Is the name of device as specified in the `name` field in Part one. Eight character maximum.

Fields in Part three:

param   PARAM   value

Where:

param	Is the parameter name as it appears in the `SYSNAME` file. Twenty character maximum.
PARAM	Is the parameter name as it appears in the `conf.c` file. Twenty character maximum.
value	Is the default parameter value. If no default value is given, then parameter specification is required. Twenty character maximum.

The System Configuration File—/usr/uts/SYSNAME

The entries in the system configuration file, `SYSNAME`, describe devices (controllers) that actually appear in the system. A device entry in this file causes data structures and a device driver to be included in the generated kernel. If you include entries for devices that do not exist, the kernel will still work correctly but will be larger than necessary.

In this file, it is important to note the distinction between controllers and drives. A controller is an I/O bus interface that has a block of registers and issues interrupts. A controller can have several drives or units attached to it. The system configuration file contains one entry for each I/O bus controller. The format of entries in the system configuration files may vary from system to system. For example, on MASSCOMP systems the fields in each line that describes a device are interpreted differently for MULTIBUS and VMEbus devices.

System Configuration File Entry Format for MULTIBUS Devices. The format for entries in the system configuration file for MULTIBUS devices is:

> *name addr pri devcnt*

Where:

> *name* Identifies the driver that handles this device. This field must match the name given in the *name* field of the `master` file entry for the device.

> *addr* Specifies the address in hexadecimal of the base of the contiguous block of controller registers. The *addrsiz* field of the driver entry in `master` gives the size of the block. This address is a system virtual address that is used to access physical MULTIBUS space.

> *pri* Specifies the device interrupt priority level. When an interrupt request is issued on the level given in this field, the device is included in the poll used to determine the source of the interrupt.

> *devcnt* Specifies the maximum number of devices that are simultaneously operated by this controller. This field is optional.

For MULTIBUS devices, the order of the controller entries in the system configuration file determines the order of interrupt polling. When an interrupt occurs on a particular level, all devices that have that level entered in the *pri* field are polled in the order in which their entries appear in the file.

System Configuration File Entry Format for VMEbus Devices. The format for entries in the system configuration file for VMEbus devices is:

> *name bus-id:addr devcnt vector pri [vector pri ...]*

Where:

> *name* Is the name of the device as it appears in the `name` field of the `master` file.

> *bus-id:addr* Specifies which VMEbus the device is on and the physical address of the device on that bus.

> *bus-id* is one of the following predefined symbols: VME1,

VME2, ..., VMEn. This field serves as an address extension to enable VMEbus A32 addresses on multiple adapters to be specified unambiguously.

addr specifies the physical address of the device on the VMEbus specified in the *bus-id* field. Instructions for choosing an address are provided in Chapter 7.

devcnt   Specifies the number of devices per controller.

vector pri   vector is an integer in the range 64 through 159 that specifies the interrupt vector assignment. The kernel uses the vector number to identify the source of the interrupt. Table 4-2 shows the arrangement of the vector table and assignment of vectors reserved by MASSCOMP.

Note that since there is only one vector table for all the I/O buses, you cannot specify the same vector on different VME-buses or on multiple controllers of the same type on the same VMEbus.

pri is an integer from one to six that specifies the interrupt priority level for the device when it interrupts with the vector assigned in the *vector* field.

You can specify up to 10 *vector, pri* pairs. The config program ignores any additional pairs and does not return an error.

Typically, interrupts for all vectors are handled by a single interrupt routine with the name dev_intr, where dev is the device prefix from the *prefix* field of the master file. The routine is called with the vector as an input parameter. However, by specifying multiple *vector, pri* pairs and using the vbind configuration file parameter, you can have various interrupt routines for the device.

The vbind parameter allows you to assign a vector to a particular interrupt routine, and thereby have different types of interrupts handled by different routines.

The format for the vbind entry is:

vbind   *handler vector*

Where:

handler   Is the ASCII name of the routine that will be called to handle the interrupt.

vector   Is a number in the range 64 through 159 that represents the vector to which the routine is bound.

The vbind entry can be placed anywhere in the file *after* the vector has been defined in a device entry.

The config(8) program installs the correct addresses in the exception vector table according to the device and vbind configuration declarations.

· Rules for Forming Names ·

The rules used by config(8) to generate driver entry point and data structure names are quite simple. You must follow these rules for names used in your driver.

The names are formed by concatenating the structure and entry point names with the driver prefix defined in the *prefix* field of the master file, as shown in the following paragraphs.

For clarity, some programmers prefer to use a driver prefix that ends with an underscore. Note that if you use a prefix that ends in an underscore with the names that have an underscore in the generic form, they will include a double underscore. References to the generated names in the assembly language file low.s always contain an additional leading underscore. This is because the C compiler attaches a leading underscore to all global symbols. Driver code written in the C language must not use the leading underscore.

Entry point names.   Entry point names are formed by concatenating standard names for routines with the driver prefix. No underscore is used. For example, for a driver with the prefix dev, the following entry point names are generated for the init, open, and close routines:

devinit	Initialization routine
devopen	Open routine
devclose	Close routine

The config program generates entry point names for each driver entry point specified in the *devmsk* field of the master file.

Definition names.   The file conf.c contains, for each driver, various definitions or initializations. The generic names for these items contain a leading underscore to set off the driver prefix. For example:

int dev_addr[]	Device address table
int dev_cnt	Device count

External reference names.   The conf.c file also contains an extern reference to the iobuf structure that must be declared in each block driver (see the file iobuf.h). This structure is usually referred to as the device table. The generic name for this item does not include an underscore:

devtab	Block driver iobuf structure, usually called the device table

Structure names.   If the `master` file entry for the driver includes entries in any of the *str* fields, those entries are used to generate both a structure type name and a structure array name. For example, if the name `yyy` appears in one of these fields, the following names are used in `conf.c`:

`yyy`   Structure type name

`dev_yyy[]`   Structure array name

For example, if `dev_cnt` is initialized to eight, the structure array name declaration in `conf.c` contains:

```
struct yyy dev_yyy[8];
```

• Configuration Table File—`conf.c` •

The configuration table file describes the kernel-to-driver interface. The file `conf.c` is a C language source code module that does not contain any executable code. It contains only variable declarations and value initializations. This section describes the portions of `conf.c` that are directly applicable to device drivers. These are:

- The device switch tables `bdevsw` and `cdevsw`
- The device address table and related structures
- The device count structures
- The per-device structure declarations
- The device intitialization table

The file includes some additional lines that are not discussed.

Device Switch Tables—`bdevsw` and `cdevsw`

`conf.c` contains two data tables called *switch tables* that are used by the kernel to dispatch work to device driver routines. They are:

`bdevsw`   Switch table for block devices

`cdevsw`   Switch table for character devices

The tables are defined as arrays of structures. The structure types `bdevsw` and `cdevsw` are defined in the header file `/usr/include/sys/conf.h`. See Figure 4-2.

```
┌──────────────────────────────┐
│   Device switch tables       │
│   (bdevsw and cdevsw)        │
├──────────────────────────────┤
│   Device address table       │
│   and related structures     │
├──────────────────────────────┤
│   Device count structures    │
├──────────────────────────────┤
│   Per-device structure declarations │
├──────────────────────────────┤
│                              │
│   Device initialization table │
│                              │
├──────────────────────────────┤
│                              │
│   Other system configuration │
│   information                │
│   (tunable parameters, system tables) │
│                              │
└──────────────────────────────┘
```

Fig. 4-2. Configuration table file contents

Note that the device switch tables do not include pointers to the driver initialization and interrupt handler entry points. Pointers to the initialization entry
points appear in a separate table in `conf.c` called `dev_init`. Calls to interrupt handlers appear in the executable code generated in the hardware interface
file `low.s`.

At least one of the switch tables has an entry for each entry in SYSNAME.
The position of each driver's entry in the array that forms the table is determined
by its major number. Null entries fill in the slots for unused major numbers.
Note that drivers appear in both tables whenever the *devmsk* field of the `master`
file indicates that the driver is both character and block type. This is usually
done to support raw character I/O on a block device.

The table entry for each driver includes an array of pointers to driver entry
points. The block driver switch table entries also include two other pointers.
Table 4-1 shows the order of values in the table entry row for each driver.

TABLE 4-1. Values for Block and Character Switch Tables

Switch Table	Value	Meaning
bdevsw	`int (*d_open)();`	Pointer to the open entry point
	`int (*d_close)();`	Pointer to the close entry point
	`int (*d_read)();`	Pointer to the read entry point
	`int (*d_write)();`	Pointer to the write entry point
	`int (*d_strategy)();`	Pointer to the strategy entry point
	`struct iobuf *d_tab;`	Pointer to the iobuf structure
	`struct char *d_name;`	Pointer to the driver name
	`int (*d_exec);`	Pointer to the exec entry point
	`int (*d_fork);`	Pointer to the fork entry point
	`int (*d_stop)();`	Pointer to the stop entry point
	`int (*d_cont)();`	Pointer to the continue entry point
cdevsw	`int (*d_open)();`	Pointer to the open entry point
	`int (*d_close)();`	Pointer to the close entry point
	`int (*d_read)();`	Pointer to the read entry point
	`int (*d_write)();`	Pointer to the write entry point
	`int (*d_ioctl)();`	Pointer to the special functions entry point
	`int (*d_select)();`	Pointer to the select entry point
	`int (*d_exec);`	Pointer to the exec entry point
	`int (*d_fork);`	Pointer to the fork entry point
	`int (*d_stop)();`	Pointer to the stop entry point
	`int (*d_cont)();`	Pointer to the continue entry point

The config(8) program generates a struct statement for each table. These statements include initialization values for all the pointers. The values used (except for the driver name, which is a literal string) are the symbolic entry point names generated according to the rules described below. They appear in extern statements also. When the kernel is linked, these references must be satisfied by declarations in the device driver itself.

Routines in the kernel call specific driver routines by indexing into the appropriate table with the major device number. A typical reference by code in the kernel to one of these tables is:

```
(*bdevsw[majno].d_open) (params ...);
```

This code calls the open routine for the block driver with the major number majno.

The values nodev, nulldev, and zero are used to initialize some fields in the switch tables. nodev is used in positions for which there is no driver, that is, for unused major numbers. The kernel routine nodev() always sets the error ENODEV into the user structure field u.error. The kernel routine nulldev() is effectively a no-op. It simply returns when called. nulldev() is used in positions for which there is a driver that does not supply that entry point and for which no action is required. A value of zero is used in positions that will never be accessed and also in the block read and write positions for drivers that do not support raw I/O.

Device Address Table and Related Structures

Each device entry in the system configuration file refers to one of the device driver entries in the master configuration file, but several device entries can refer to the same driver entry. For each driver that has one or more device entries in SYSNAME with nonzero device addresses, config(8) generates a device address table in conf.c. For a device with the prefix dev, the table is named dev_addr.

For VMEbus devices, each device address table has corresponding entries in conf.c. Assuming the prefix dev, these entries are:

dev_busid   Specifies which VMEbus the device is on

dev_vecs   Specifies the assignment of interrupt handlers to vectors

dev_addrtype   Specifies which address space the address is in

The following sections describe each of these structures in detail. In each section the driver prefix is assumed to be dev.

dev_addr[]. Each device address table, dev_addr, is an integer array. The array is initialized with the base address values in the order in which they appear in the system configuration file.

Each driver must define some method for translating a minor device number into an index into the device address table. If a one-to-one correspondence exists between special files and controllers, the minor number can be the index itself. In that case the minor device numbers used in mknod(8) commands to define the device special files must begin at zero and be consecutive. Other encodings are possible as well, such as using a subfield of the minor number as the controller number. This approach is useful when several device units are attached to a controller or when several special files are used to represent different operating modes of the same device. The kernel does not place any constraints on the use of the minor number by the driver.

The entries in the device address table are used at run time to indicate whether a device is online. The driver init routine, which is called at system boot time, checks to see whether the device is present and responsive. The actions taken by the init routine if the device is not present are different for MULTIBUS and VMEbus init routines:

- MULTIBUS init routines should zero out the corresponding entry in the driver's dev_addr array. The interrupt handler for the device will not then be called if a spurious interrupt occurs. The driver open routine can then check the table entry before opening the device and return a "device offline" indication if the address is zero.

- VMEbus init routines do not zero out the dev_addr entry; doing so does not make any difference to the kernel. If the vector comes in, the interrupt routine will still be called. Therefore, the VMEbus driver should be prepared to handle interrupts from a possibly malfunctioning device that does not respond at initialization time.

The device address table is also used in the interrupt service code generated by config(8) in low.s. For MULTIBUS devices only, when an interrupt occurs at a particular vector (level), the code polls all devices that interrupt at that level to determine which one generated the interrupt. MULTIBUS devices that have a zero entry in the address table are assumed to be offline and are not polled. This does not apply to VMEbus device drivers.

dev_busid (VMEbus devices only). The dev_busid structure is used to determine which VMEbus the device is on. The structure uses constants that are defined in the header file vba.h.

dev_busid contains a parallel array for each entry in dev_addr. Each dev_busid array is type int; the upper eight bits of the integer define the VMEbus.

config uses the value in the bus-id field of the SYSNAME file to generate the array in conf.c. For example, the following SYSNAME entries indicate that two zz devices are on VMEbus #1:

```
zz    VME1:824FC8600    70    2    71    3
zz    VME1:934FC8600    2    80    3    82    2    84    4
```

For these entries, config generates the following output into conf.c:

```
int zz_busid[] = {
    VME1 << VBA_SHIFT,
    VME1 << VBA_SHIFT,
};
```

dev_vecs (VMEbus devices only). For each device listed in the system configuration file, config generates a structure dev_vecs. Each entry of dev_vecs is of type struct vec, which is defined in the header file vba.h.

The values in each entry are taken from the *vector, pri* fields and from the vbind parameter entry if present. If no vbind entry is present, config generates the dev_vecs entry using the default interrupt routine, dev_init.

For example, consider the following SYSNAME entries:

```
zz    VME1:824FC8600    70    2    71    3
zz    VME1:934FC8600    2    80    3    82    2    84    4

vbind    82    errintr
vbind    84    testintr
```

The vbind entries bind vector 82 to the routine errintr, and vector 84 to testintr. The other vectors are not bound to a specific routine, so config assigns to them the default interrupt routine zzintr. From these entries, config generates the following dev_vecs structure entries in conf.c:

```
struct vec zz_vecs[] [10] = {
    {
        { 70, 2, zzintr },
        { 71, 3, zzintr },
    },
    {
        { 80, 3, zzintr },
        { 82, 2, errintr },
        { 84, 4, testintr },
    }
};
```

dev_addrtype (VMEbus devices only). The dev_addrtype structure tells the driver the addressing type of the device. This structure is a parallel array to dev_addr and dev_vecs. Valid values for dev_addrtype are VBA_A32, VBA_A24, and VBA_A16, as defined in the header file <sys/vba.h>.

config generates dev_addrtype from the devtyp field in the master file. For example, the value 2004 in the *devtyp* field of the following master file entry indicates that the device is a VMEbus A32 character device:

```
zz   137   2004   zz   7015   0   0   0   40   4   5
```

Assuming that the SYSNAME file contains one entry for a zz device, config generates the following output into conf.c:

```
int zz_addrtype[] = {
    VBA_A32,
};
```

Device Count

Two other variables and their initialization values also generated in the conf.c file are a controller count and a device count. For a driver with the prefix dev the variable names used are:

dev_ccnt   The number of controllers served by the driver, as determined by the number of entries in the system configuration file.

dev_cnt   The number of devices served by the driver, as determined by the sum of the maximum device fields for each entry in the system configuration file.

Per-Device Structure Declarations

Up to three per-device structure declarations can also appear in conf.c. If any of the *str* fields in the driver's master file entry line contain non-blank entries, config(8) generates corresponding struct statements. For example, if the *str1* field in the master line contains the string zzz and the driver prefix in the `prefix` field is `dev`, the following line will appear in `conf.c`:

```
struct zzz   dev_zzz[n];
```

The *n* is the generated initialization value of the driver device count `dev_cnt`. This facility is used to generate the `tty` structures used in drivers that support interactive terminals.

Driver writers can use the *str* fields in the `master` file to generate per-device data structures of arbitrary types. In order for this to work, you must define the type name used in one of the header files referenced directly or indirectly by `conf.c` in `#include` statements. Otherwise, `conf.c` does not compile. Because software updates from your vendor may overwrite `io.h`, you may want to define the structure in a private header file and add an include reference to it in `io.h` rather than inserting your structure definition into `io.h` directly. Examine `/usr/include/peri.h` for an example.

Device Initialization Table

`config`(8) also generates in `conf.c` a table of pointers to all device driver initialization entry points. The generated values for these pointers are symbolic names formed by concatenating the driver prefix with the string `init`. The names also appear in `extern` statements, and these references must be satisfied by declarations in the driver code.

If a device driver definition entry in the `master` file indicates that the driver has an initialization routine, this routine is called once at system boot time.

• Hardware Interface File •

The hardware interface file generated by the `config` program on MASSCOMP systems is called `low.s`. It is an assembly language file that generates the lower core portion of the kernel image. It defines the exception vector table and the setup code for the interrupt handlers.

Exception Vector Table

The exception vector table that is found in page zero of the image is defined in the first part of the file. The exception vector table is a list of vectors, each of which corresponds to one of the 256 exception types defined by the MC68000 family. Each vector slot contains the address of the driver routine to be called to handle that particular interrupt.

The vector table contains both system and user-definable vectors. The system vectors include the seven MULTIBUS vectors, one for each of the interrupt levels one through seven. VMEbus vectors are user definable, and can be assigned to any slot in the range 64 through 159. Table 4-2 shows how these vectors are assigned on MASSCOMP systems.

TABLE 4-2. Interrupt Vector Table

Vector	Assignment	Type
0		
·	Reserved for system	System vectors
·		
63		
64		
·	Reserved for customer assignment	User definable
·		
159		
160		
·	Reserved for MASSCOMP	User definable
·		
255		

The CPU uses interrupt vectors to find the source of interrupts. Each interrupt is accompanied by a vector number that defines the source of the interrupt. The code used by the kernel to find the source of the interrupt is known as the *skip chain*. Once the source of the interrupt has been determined, the CPU responds to the interrupt request. It loads the program counter with the address of the interrupt routine from the vector table slot indexed by the interrupt vector and then executes the setup code for the interrupt handler that will service the interrupt.

Interrupt Handlers

The setup code for interrupt handlers is contained in the hardware interface file, low.s.

MULTIBUS and VMEbus devices require different skip chains and interrupt handlers. These are described in the following sections.

MULTIBUS Interrupt Handlers.   MULTIBUS interrupts are not fully vectored in MASSCOMP systems. That is, devices do not necessarily have unique vectors, so an interrupt cannot cause a direct jump to a device handler. There are only seven hardware vectors, each of which corresponds to the seven interrupt priority levels. Several devices can be attached to each level. Therefore, when an interrupt occurs it is necessary for the kernel to poll all devices attached at that level to determine which one generated the interrupt. The interrupt level polling code is the MULTIBUS skip chain.

The skip chain is contained in the file low.s. The autovector interrupt slots of the vector table in page zero contain the symbols level1 through level7. These symbols appear later in the file, each preceding the code that performs the polling operation for that level. Each interrupt level has an independent polling routine. After the kernel dermines which device interrupted, it calls the interrupt routine for the interrupt priority level at which the device interrupted.

Polling proceeds as follows:

- If the *intmsk* field in the `master` file entry for the device driver is nonzero, that field is used as a hexadecimal bit mask to check for interrupt indicators in the device CSR.

- That mask is logically ANDed with the current CSR contents.

- Normally a nonzero result means that the device has generated an interrupt and the device driver interrupt handler is called. The sense of this test can be reversed (i.e., to test for a zero result) by setting the `1` bit in the *devtyp* field of the `master` file entry for the device driver.

- If the entry in the *intmsk* field of the `master` file for a particular driver is zero, then the CSR test is omitted and that driver's interrupt handler is definitely called.

- The devices attached to the active interrupt level are polled in the order in which their entries appear in the system configuration file. If none of the polled drivers accepts responsibility for the interrupt, a stray interrupt is declared.

- On systems with both MULTIBUS and VMEbus, VMEbus devices are always polled before MULTIBUS devices.

Note that the CSR that is checked is defined to be offset by the number of bytes given in the *csr_offset* field of the `master` file entry from the base address that appears in the system configuration file.

When the CSR test is omitted, the interrupt handler must use its return value to indicate whether its device was responsible for the interrupt. A nonzero return value indicates that the driver has handled the interrupt, so the polling terminates. A zero return value indicates that the interrupt was not generated by a device handled by this driver, so the polling continues.

Using a nonzero entry in the *intmsk* field of the driver `master` file entry is more efficient. Doing so eliminates a call to the interrupt handler when the interrupt belongs to another driver. Use a zero in the *intmsk* field only when a simple bit test on the CSR cannot determine whether the device has generated an interrupt.

Note: Zero and nonzero values in the *intmsk* field cause different arguments to be passed to the interrupt handler.

VMEbus Interrupt Handlers.   VMEbus interrupts are fully vectored. When a device interrupts, it generates the vector specified in its `SYSNAME` file entry. The kernel uses the vector as an index into the vector table to find the address of the interrupt handler.

VMEbus devices can issue a different vector for different circumstances. For example, the device can interrupt with one vector for error conditions, and with another for nonerror conditions. Both types of interrupts can be handled either by the default interrupt routine `dev_intr`, or by a different routine as specified by the `vbind` parameter in the `SYSNAME` file.

Once the CPU receives the vector, polling in the skip chain proceeds. On MASSCOMP systems the polling sequence is as follows:

1. The CPU first checks for the presence of VMEbus adapter #1 (VME1). If VME1 is present but no interrupt at that level is pending, the adapter returns zero and the CPU goes on to the next VMEbus adapter. If an interrupt at that level is pending, the CPU requests a read to the IAR (interrupt acknowledge register) for VME1 at the priority level specified.

   The read request causes the adapter to perform an interrupt acknowledge cycle on the VMEbus to determine which vector to put into the IAR. The adapter puts the value in the IAR, and the CPU completes the read.

   The IAR is a window on the VMEbus adapter that is used by the adapter and the CPU to pass information between the memory bus and the VMEbus. Each VMEbus adapter has six IARs, one for each interrupt priority level.

2. If the IAR contains a vector number, the CPU uses it as an offset into the vector table. It jumps to the address of the interrupt handler setup code, which is specified in the vector slot. It executes that setup code, which calls the driver interrupt routine.

3. If the value in the IAR for VME1 is zero, the CPU checks for VMEbus adapter #2 (VME2) and repeats the actions described in Step 1.

4. If the value in the IAR for VME2 is zero, the CPU checks the MULTIBUS devices. If the skip chain detects no device interrupts, the CPU declares a stray interrupt.

▪ Building a New Kernel ▪

Once you have created the configuration table file and hardware interface file (using the config program), you must compile them and link them into the kernel.

Object Modules in /usr/uts

Most of the files that are used to generate a kernel are found in the directory /usr/uts. The only exceptions are master and config, which are found in /etc. The directory /usr/uts contains all the object modules that are linked together by the loader utility, ld, to form the kernel image.

The required object modules fall into four groups:

1. Your newly developed device driver modules, obtained by compiling driver source code

2. Standard driver modules, delivered with your operating system in the object library io.a

3. The two configuration modules, obtained by compiling conf.c and assembling low.s (or whatever the hardware interface file is on your system)

4. Other kernel modules delivered with the base operating system

The standard device drivers delivered with the MASSCOMP operating system are, for the sake of convenience, collected in an object library called io.a. The kernel build procedure, described in the next section, assumes that all drivers can be found in this library. Therefore, to use the standard approach, you must add the new driver object module to this library using the ar utility and then apply the strip and ranlib commands to it. See the *UNIX Programmer's Manual* for more information on these utiltities.

The configuration module .conf.o is obtained by compiling the conf.c file that was generated by config. low.s requires special treatment: before it is assembled the file assym.s, also found in /usr/uts, must be prefixed to it. Compilation and assembly of these files is handled automatically by the kernel makefile.

The Kernel Makefile—/usr/uts/uts.mk

Assuming that the driver object code has been added to io.a and that you have run config to generate the configuration source modules, you can build the kernel image using the following command:

```
make -f uts.mk
```

The dependencies listed in the makefile uts.mk will automatically recreate the conf.o and low.o files if config has been run to generate new configuration source files. They will not, however, compile the driver source, add the driver object code to io.a, or run config. You must do those things before you build the new kernel.

The Kernel Image File—/unix

The result of executing the make utility is a kernel image file named /usr/uts/unix. The final step required is to copy this file to the root directory and boot it. After it has been copied the reboot command can be used. It is possible, though not usually advisable, to boot the kernel image without copying it to the root directory.

· Creating the Device Special Files ·

Once the new kernel image has been booted, the driver is ready to run. However, it is first necessary to create the special files that provide access through the file system to the devices supported by the driver. These files do not have to be created every time a new kernel is built and booted. It is only necessary to create them when you first add the new device. There must be a special file for each device on your system.

Device special files are created by the utility program mknod, which is documented in Volume 1 of the *UNIX Programmer's Manual*. When you set up the special files you must specify the device type (character or block) and the major and minor device numbers. The major numbers must agree with those used for the driver in the master file.

Device special files are normally located in the directory /dev. Note that mknod does not do this automatically. You should specify the full pathname. For example:

```
mknod /dev/tty03 c 1 3
```

creates a special file for a terminal device named "tty03," which is a character special file. The device's major number is 1 and its minor number is 3.

5

RUN-TIME
DATA STRUCTURES

This chapter discusses issues related to run-time operations that are performed by device drivers. The principal issues treated are

- Address spaces and the movement of data between them

- Data structures used to pass information to and from a driver

- Standard methods used to pass information and synchronize execution of driver routines and other kernel and user process code

Driver run-time operations are heavily supported by standard routines (functions) supplied by the kernel. This chapter introduces many of the kernel support functions that are used frequently by driver routines. It contains general descriptions of what they do and where they can be used. Detailed specifications of the arguments, operations, and return values of all routines called by device drivers are found in Appendix B.

· Virtual and Physical Addresses ·

Device drivers deal with both I/O bus addresses and virtual addresses. RTU is a demand-paged virtual memory system. Therefore, the addresses used in source and executable code in device drivers and in almost all other kernel and user code are never physical memory addresses. They are virtual addresses that are translated by hardware at run time into physical memory references. The translations are made with the aid of address translation tables, called page tables, which are created and maintained by the RTU kernel.

Each user process executes in a private virtual address space that begins at location zero; the RTU kernel has its own zero-based virtual address space. Device driver routines are called on to handle data found in system address space, in the address space of the current user process, and in the address spaces of other user processes. An address presented to a driver points to a different item in each of these address spaces, and only one of them is the correct item. It is essential that driver writers have a clear understanding of the context that is implied whenever they manipulate address values, explicitly or implicitly.

I/O bus addresses appear in two places: in programmed reads and writes of device registers performed by the CPU and in DMA operations performed by devices. I/O bus addresses are translated by the MASSCOMP kernel and hardware in much the same way as virtual addresses. Drivers are sometimes required to call kernel routines to alter the I/O bus address translation tables; some frequently used translations are arranged in advance by the kernel and need not be repeated by drivers.

System and User Page Tables

Translation of virtual memory addresses to physical addresses is essentially transparent to device drivers; they never need to manipulate the address mapping tables explicitly. A simplified description of the mechanics of address translation is included here to provide a general understanding of the operations that take place behind the scenes.

The executable code, compiled data, and allocated memory segments for each user process occupy a contiguous range of virtual addresses that begin at zero and grow upward. The process stack and some other parameters occupy a contiguous range of addresses that begins at the largest virtual address (hexadecimal FFFFFF) and grow downward. Altogether a process can occupy up to 16 megabytes of virtual memory.

MASSCOMP RTU maps virtual memory to physical memory in 4096-byte units called *pages*. For each user process the kernel maintains a page table that defines a mapping of virtual pages to physical pages. When the process code references a 24-bit virtual address, this value is broken into two parts. The lower 12 bits select a byte within the virtual page. The upper 12 bits act as an index into the process page table; 12 bits are extracted from the value found at that location in the table to provide a physical page frame number. This value is combined with the byte-in-page value (which is not changed by the translation) to produce a complete physical address. The CPU maintains a high-speed hardware cache of recently used page table entries to speed the translation process.

The RTU kernel also supports the shuffling of individual virtual pages to and from secondary memory. This is done to allow the total virtual address space occupied by the kernel and the active user processes to exceed the amount of physical memory included in the system. When physical memory must be allocated for other purposes, the contents of specific pages mapped to user processes are copied to a disk file. The corresponding page table entries are marked to show that this has been done, and the page frame numbers stored there are replaced by disk addresses. If at a later time a reference is made to a virtual page that has been copied to disk, a hardware trap occurs, and code is executed to return the page to primary memory.

When a device driver initiates a DMA data transfer it must be able to guarantee that the target memory buffer will not be "paged out" (shuffled to disk) while the transfer is in progress. The kernel provides routines that can be called by drivers to lock user process virtual pages into physical memory. See **Locking Pages into Memory**, this chapter.

The RTU kernel occupies its own 16-megabyte virtual address space and has its own page mapping tables. The arrangement of code and data in system virtual space is somewhat different from that used in user process space, and system space is not subject to paging; system virtual pages remain in primary memory at all times.

Translation of MULTIBUS Addresses

The method used by the MC5500 hardware to translate MULTIBUS addresses is described in detail in Chapter 3. To summarize, CPU references to the upper two megabytes of physical address space (E00000–FFFFFF) are placed on the MUL-TIBUS, either as memory or as I/O references. MULTIBUS DMA device references to memory are translated into MASSCOMP physical memory addresses by the MULTIBUS Adapter I/O Map.

Device drivers execute in system virtual address space; in most cases the relationship of this address space to physical memory is unknown. In order to simplify driver coding, however, the kernel always maps the upper two mega-bytes of system virtual address space to identical values in physical memory. Drivers can therefore always access I/O device registers by using their physical addresses, without performing any special mapping operations. For devices that respond to MULTIBUS I/O, references the upper eight bits of the address must be one; that is, the base of MULTIBUS I/O device space is FF0000. This address generates a reference to address 0 in MULTIBUS I/O space.

Before initiating a DMA data transfer, the driver must usually call kernel routines to map a portion of MULTIBUS address space to the target memory buffer by storing appropriate values in I/O map registers. These routines work in terms of user or system virtual addresses so that physical memory addresses are transparent to the driver. The memory address that must be loaded in the device depends on what portion of the I/O map is used to set up the mapping. **Mapping and Performing DMA Transfers**, this chapter, describes DMA operations in more detail.

Note that device driver routines do not need to arrange the mapping of the system or driver data and bss segments because these segments have already been mapped when the system was loaded. These segments include variables allocated or initialized in device drivers but do not include all system data structures.

· Standard I/O Data Structures ·

This section describes the individual data items in standard data structures that are used to pass information between the kernel and driver routines. In these structures only certain fields are pertinent to driver operations; the other fields are not discussed.

Header Files and Data Types

The standard data structures that are used to store and pass data within the kernel and its device drivers are defined in so-called header or include files. These files are delivered with the baseline MASSCOMP software in the directories /usr/include and /usr/include/sys. Most header files used by drivers are in the latter directory. Driver source code must define structure field names by referencing header files in #include statements.

Header files that are frequently used by drivers include the following:

ast.h	Defines structures used with ASTs (MASSCOMP only)
buf.h	Defines the buf structure (for block I/O requests)
cblock.h	Defines the cblock structure (for use in clists)
dir.h	Defines the structure of a directory entry in the file system
elog.h	Defines the iostat structure
errno.h	Defines error codes
file.h	Defines flags passed to open and close
iobuf.h	Defines the iobuf structure (for block I/O requests)
param.h	Defines constants and macros used throughout RTU
proc.h	Defines the process structure
signal.h	Defines signal types
tty.h	Defines the clist structure
types.h	Defines standard data types used by the kernel
user.h	Defines the user structure
var.h	Defines the var structure for configuration parameters

Note that drivers that send ASTs must reference the version of ast.h found in /usr/include/sys. The shorter file of the same name found in /usr/include can be referenced by user programs.

Note that dir.h must be included before user.h. Also types.h and param.h are usually included before other header files.

The header file types.h uses typedef statements to define a number of special data types that are used widely within the kernel. In particular, many fields in the standard data structures are defined to have these types. The principal reason for the existence of these type definitions is to enhance the portability of kernel code. Drivers that store values in structure fields will have to declare a variable of that type or cast the value being stored. Table 5-1 lists the types that are frequently used by drivers.

TABLE 5-1. Defined Kernel Data Types

Defined Type	Usage
daddr_t	Block device block number
caddr_t	Virtual memory address, byte aligned
label_t	setjmp data block
dev_t	Major/minor device number
off_t	Byte offset in file
paddr_t	Physical memory address

There are many other system data structures, some of which may be useful in particular situations, but are in general not used by drivers. These data structures are listed below. These system data structures have not been mapped to the MULTIBUS by the system (see discussion in Translation of Multibus Addresses, this chapter).

buffers	Data for system cache of disk blocks (from block devices)
buf	struct buf headers for system cache of disk blocks
swbuf	struct buf headers for swapping and paging
swpf	Used for swapping and paging
inode	Table of in-memory i-nodes (for open files, mounted file systems, and directories during named file operations (struct inode))
file	Table of open files (struct file)
proc	Table of proc structures (struct proc)
text	Table of shared text descriptors (struct text)
cfree	cblock storage (struct cblock)
callout	Storage for system callouts ("timeouts" (struct callout))
swapmap	Resource allocation map for swap (paging) space (struct map)
argmap	Resource allocation map for swap space for exec arguments (struct map)
kernelmap	Resource allocation map for kernel page table space (struct map)
cmap	Table describing allocation of physical memory (struct cmap)

With the exception of buffers (which would normally be addressed as bp->b_addr for some struct buf), most of these data structures would not be accessed by a device.

Character I/O Descriptor Fields—user

When a driver is called to perform character or raw I/O at its read and write entry points, the I/O request is defined by fields in the current process user structure, u. It is also legal to access the u structure from the init, open, ioctl, and close routines, but the fields that define the size and location of a data transfer are not meaningful in those routines.

Table 5-2 lists the fields in u that are pertinent to device driver code. Note that the variable u is the name of the current process user structure, not a pointer to it. References to fields in the structure always have the form u.xxxxx, never u->xxxxx.

TABLE 5-2. Fields in the user structure used by drivers

Field Name	Data Type	Usage
u_base	caddr_t	Address of next user data byte
u_count	unsigned	Count of bytes remaining
u_offset	off_t	Byte offset on device or file
u_error	char	Error status code
u_segflg[†]	char	Address space type ID
u_procp[†]	struct proc *	Pointer to process proc table entry
u_qsav	label_t	Handler ID block for signals
u_tsav	label_t	Handler ID block for hardware traps
u_nofault	char	Flag to call trap handler, setjmp

† Read-only fields that must not be altered by drivers.

Each of these fields is described in more detail below.

u.u_base, u.u_count. During read and write calls these fields define the location of the next byte in virtual address space and the number of bytes remaining to be transferred. They are not fixed values. The driver should increment the pointer and decrement the count for each byte moved. These values are adjusted by some of the kernel routines that are called to move the data between user and system space. The return value of the system call seen by the user process is the initial value of u.u_count minus its final value.

u.u_offset. This field holds the current value of the seek pointer for the file being used to access the device. Devices that are incapable of random access I/O (such as terminals or printers) can ignore this field. For a randomly addressable device (raw disks, including the block read and write routines), use u.u_offset to compute the block number on the device.

The kernel routines (passc, cpass, iomove, physio) that increment u.u_base as they move data will increment u.u_offset by the same amount. The final value of u.u_offset is ignored when updating the seek pointer for the file after the device driver routine returns: the seek pointer will be incremented by the number of bytes transferred as determined by the initial and final values of u.u_count.

u.u_error. If the I/O operation is not successful the driver must store one of the error codes defined in /usr/include/errno.h in this field. The value stored here will be copied to the global variable errno, and a failure will be indicated in the system call return value. A success value is stored in advance, so nothing need be done on a normal completion.

u.u_segflg. A value of one in this field indicates that the kernel called a driver to perform I/O from its own address space. Routines that reference and update fields in the u structure use this field to determine the virtual address space in which the data resides.

u.u_procp. This field is useful in situations where data must be moved to or from user space by a driver routine that does not execute in current-process context. The kernel supplies routines that move data to and from an arbitrary process specified by a `proc` pointer; they are typically used in an interrupt service routine to read or write data bytes or to write status values on completion of asynchronous I/O. The driver will have saved the value of u.u_procp during execution of the read, write, or ioctl routine that initiated the operation.

u.u_qsav, u.u_tsav, u.u_nofault. u.u_qsav can be used as the argument in a setjmp call in places where the driver needs to intercept signals being sent to the process. u.u_tsav serves the same purpose for bus faults and addressing errors. u.u_nofault is a flag that determines whether the trap handler will be called. The use of setjmp to establish signal and trap handlers in a driver is described in **Multiple Executions of a Driver**, this chapter.

Block I/O Buffer Descriptor—buf

When a block device driver is called at its strategy entry point it receives as an argument a pointer to a `buf` structure. Fields in this structure completely define the requested I/O operation; they specify the device to be used, the direction of the transfer, its size, the memory and device addresses, and other auxiliary information.

Driver code refers to `buf` fields by way of a pointer. For example, if the name `bp` is used for the pointer, references to `buf` fields will have the form bp->xxxxx. Table 5-3 lists the `buf` fields that are read or written by drivers.

The table indicates the fields that are read-only for the strategy and interrupt handler routines that execute the I/O request. Block driver read and write routines that set up `buf` structures and pass them to the strategy routine will be required to write appropriate values in these fields.

TABLE 5-3. Fields in the buf structure used by drivers

Field Name	Data Type	Usage
b_dev[†]	dev_t	Major and minor device numbers
b_ioaddr[†]	caddr_t	Virtual address of the data buffer
b_bcount[†]	unsigned	Count of bytes to be transferred
b_ioblkno[†]	daddr_t	Device block number
av_forw	struct buf *	Forward pointer for active queue
av_back	struct buf *	Backward pointer for active queue
b_completion[†]	int (*)()	Routine called by iodone
b_error	char	I/O status value
b_resid	unsigned	Bytes not transferred due to error
b_cylin	unsigned	Cylinder number for disk request
b_proc[†]	struct proc *	Pointer to process doing I/O
b_flags	int	Binary status flags
b_iopb	char *	Pointer to I/O parameter block

† Fields that are read only for strategy and the interrupt handler.
(Note that b_resid and b_cylin are the same field.)

Each of these fields is described in more detail below.

b_dev. The major device and minor numbers are packed into this field. The macros `major` and `minor` can be used to extract the individual values. It is common for a driver to use the minor number to select one unit or drive when several are attached to the same controller.

b_ioaddr, b_bcount, b_ioblkno. These fields define the source and destination addresses and the size of the transfer. Which is the source and which is the destination depends on whether the transfer is a read or a write, as indicated by `b_flags`. `b_ioaddr` is the virtual address of the memory buffer. `b_ioblkno` is the starting block number on the device, and `b_bcount` is the transfer byte count (not block count). Note that on MASSCOMP systems the driver does not use the values in the fields `b_addr` and `b_blkno`, which are in the `buf` structure but are not shown in the table. Those fields are used by the kernel for a different purpose.

av_forw, av_back. The block driver strategy routine is not required to complete the requested data transfer before returning to its caller. Usually it adds the `buf` pointed to by its argument to an internal queue of requests to be processed; if necessary the interrupt handler will notify the caller when the transfer is complete. These two pointers can be used by the driver to maintain a doubly linked list of outstanding requests. Note that the driver must not use the fields `b_forw` and `b_back` (not shown in the table) for this purpose; these fields are used by the kernel to link the blocks assigned to a particular device in the block buffering cache.

b_completion. This field can be used to hold the address of an I/O completion routine. If it is nonzero, the routine at that address will be called by the `iodone` routine with a pointer to the `buf` as an argument.

b_error, b_resid, b_cylin. If a transfer cannot be completed the driver should store an error code in `b_error`. Error code values are defined in `/usr/include/errno.h`. It should also store the count of bytes that could not be transferred in `b_resid` and set the flag `B_ERROR` in `b_flags`. `b_cylin` overlays `b_resid` and is used by `disksort`. It contains the cylinder number for disk requests.

b_proc. When a driver performs raw DMA I/O from user space this field is used by the `iomaddr` routine to set up the I/O map registers. `b_flags` describes how `iomaddr` is to be interpreted. The driver read or write routine must copy this value from `u.u_procp` and set the `B_PHYS` flag (usually done by `physio`). See **Mapping and Performing DMA Transfers**, this chapter.

b_flags.   The individual bits in this field are binary flags that carry information about how the request is to be handled and what its current status is. The following flags are of interest to drivers:

<table>
<tr><td>B_READ</td><td>Set when the request is a read operation; otherwise it is a write. Defines the direction of the data transfer.</td></tr>
<tr><td>B_WRITE</td><td>A pseudoflag with a zero value. It can be used as an argument to routines that require a direction to be defined.</td></tr>
<tr><td>B_PHYS</td><td>Must be set if the target memory buffer is in user space. Used by the routine iomaddr.</td></tr>
<tr><td>B_DONE</td><td>Must be set by the driver when the I/O operation is complete; usually done by the iodone routine.</td></tr>
<tr><td>B_ERROR</td><td>The driver should set this flag if the operation could not be completed successfully.</td></tr>
<tr><td>B_BUSY</td><td>Set if the buf is being used and cleared when the activity is complete. For cache buffers this flag is manipulated by kernel routines. Driver routines that need to allocate a private buf temporarily should sleep until this flag is clear and then set it. See Multiple Executions of a Driver, this chapter.</td></tr>
<tr><td>B_WANTED</td><td>If this flag is set wakeup will be called when the buf is released. A driver routine that needs to allocate a buf that is busy should set this flag and sleep. See Multiple Executions of a Driver, this chapter.</td></tr>
<tr><td>B_CMD</td><td>If this flag is set, the buf is a command, not a data transfer request. This flag is used to pass information to the driver or to set a mode; see the following description of urgent mode as an example. This flag affects the activity of the disksort and iodone routines.</td></tr>
<tr><td>B_URGON
B_URGOF
B_URGNT</td><td>A buf with the flags B_CMD and B_URGON set is used to place a disk driver in urgent mode. While the driver is in that mode only requests with B_URGNT set are executed in FIFO order; all other requests are queued until a buf with B_CMD and B_URGOF set is received. This flag is used to give absolute priority to a real-time data acquisition task. If the command buf with B_URGON set includes a value in the field b_ioblkno, a seek will be done to the proper cylinder. (This is a description of the logic used in the MASSCOMP disk drivers.)</td></tr>
</table>

B_UAREA   These flags are alternatives to B_PHYS; they are used by
B_PAGET   iomaddr to determine which virtual address space the
B_DIRTY   data buffer is located in. These flags are only set by the
                 kernel.

                 When accessing the values in b_flags, you should use
                 constructs of the form:

                      bp->b_flags |= B_xxx|B_yyy

           or

                      bp->b_flags &= ~(B_xxx|B_yyy)

                 rather than assigning values to these fields directly
                 because kernel routines rely on bits in these fields.

Block Device Control Block—iobuf

Each block device driver must declare a single structure of the iobuf type. The structure must be given a standard name constructed from the driver prefix defined in the master configuration file. If the driver prefix is xxx the driver iobuf structure name must be xxxtab. The block device switch table, bdevsw, contains this symbol to allow the kernel to locate the driver iobuf structure.

The flags in b_flags from the buf structure are repeated on a per-driver basis in iobuf (the flags in buf are on a per request basis). The kernel checks b_flags for the flag B_TAPE to identify magnetic tape drivers, which are treated in a special way. See Chapter 10.

Table 5-4 lists the fields found in iobuf. Since each driver has a single fixed iobuf, references to its fields can take the form xxtab.xxxxx. It is also possible to define a pointer to the structure simply for speed (for example, the declaration register struct iobuf *dp;). Note that iobuf cannot be used to hold information that is specific to a particular I/O request; data of that type must be placed in the buf structure. iobuf holds static and dynamic information that describes the current global state of the driver.

Note that each of these iobuf structures contains only one I/O address, one queue header, and one I/O map base. Therefore, each iobuf structure only supports one controller. If you want to support multiple controllers, you must allocate additional iobuf structures.

The fields described in Table 5-4 are initialized by the tabinit macro in /usr/include/sys/iobuf.h.

TABLE 5-4. Fields in the iobuf structure

Field Name	Data Type	Usage
b_forw	struct buf *	Optionally used to head a free queue
b_back	struct buf *	Optionally used to head a free queue
b_actf	struct buf *	First buf in active I/O queue
b_actl	struct buf *	Last buf in active I/O queue
b_dev	dev_t	Major and minor device number
io_addr	physadr	Base address
b_active	char	Flag: controller is active
b_errcnt	char	Error retry count
b_flags	int	Device type and status flags
io_mapbase	short	Base index of I/O map registers
io_erec	struct eblock *	Pointer to error log record
io_nreg	int	Number of register to log
io_stp	struct iostat *	Pointer to I/O statistics block
io_s1	int	Place to store a value
io_s2	int	Place to store a value
b_proc	struct proc *	Pointer to entry in proc table

Each field is described in more detail below.

b_forw, b_back. These fields are used by the kernel to track which system buffers have been assigned to the major device.

b_actf, b_actl. The strategy routine usually does not synchronously execute each I/O request before returning to its caller. Instead it queues the buf structures passed to it and executes the requests asynchronously, possibly in a different order. These pointers are used to maintain the request queue; they point to the first and last requests in the queue.

b_dev. If the driver needs to know what its block major device number is, the value can be stored here. The value can be initialized at compile time by using the macro tabinit. Note that a literal value will have to be coded into the driver; there is no mechanism for passing the value from the master configuration file to the driver.

io_addr. The CSR address of a controller can optionally be stored here. This field may be read by an error logging routine.

b_active. This field is commonly used as a flag or state variable that is set nonzero by the driver start routine when it initiates a controller action. When all the queued requests have been processed, the interrupt handler clears the flag. When the strategy routine queues a new request it calls start only if the flag is clear. Otherwise, the interrupt handler will do that job.

b_errcnt.   An error retry count is stored here. The value is cleared when processing of a new request begins and incremented each time an error is returned by the device. When a stored retry maximum is reached the driver gives up and returns a fatal error on the request.

b_flags.   This field can be used to hold the same binary flags that are defined in /usr/include/sys/buf.h. One flag is checked by the kernel and must be set properly:

> B_TAPE   Must be set for magnetic tape controllers. Indicates to the kernel that this is not a random-access device.

The effect of setting B_TAPE is described in Chapter 10. The driver is free to set other flags to indicate device status. For example, if there is only one controller the B_URGNT flag could be set here to indicate that the driver is in urgent mode.

io_mapbase.   When the driver allocates registers in the I/O map, the return value from iomalloc can be stored here. The value is used in subsequent calls to iomaddr.

io_erec, io_nreg, io_stp.   These fields are used for error logging. See Chapter 10 for more information on error logging.

io_s1, io_s2.   The driver can store anything it wants here. Some drivers store a count of queued requests or a hardware status flag.

▪ Address Translation and Data Access ▪

This section describes the methods that are used to access data and to allocate, manage, and release system resources. In particular, it introduces many of the kernel routines that are used by drivers. These routines are described in a very general way here. Examples of their use are given in subsequent chapters, and complete specifications appear in Appendix B.

Moving Data between User and System Space

Character drivers and block drivers doing raw I/O call kernel routines if they need to move data to system buffers. This prevents them from having to deal explicitly with the system page tables. However, drivers do not usually need to move data to system buffers.

This section describes the data as being moved between user and system space, but character driver routines are sometimes called by the kernel to move data to or from system space. When this occurs the field u.u_segflg is set to one; some data-moving routines check this flag and automatically access the correct virtual address space.

There are three groups of routines that can be used to move data; their use depends on the execution context:

1. In the read and write routines the location and size of the data transfer are defined by the fields `u.u_base`, `u.u_count`, and `u.u_offset`. The following routines automatically manage these fields:

`cpass`	Gets one character from user space
`passc`	Puts one character into user space
`iomove`	Moves many bytes in either direction

2. In the ioctl routine data may need to be moved to or from the space of the current user, but the base, count, and offset fields are not applicable. In this context the following routines can be used:

   `fubyte, fushort, fuword`
   Fetches one byte, word, or long word from user space

   `subyte, sushort, suword`
   Sets one byte, word, or long word in user space

`copyin`	Copies many bytes from user space
`copyout`	Copies many bytes to user space

3. An interrupt handler or other routine that does not execute in the context of the current process can access the space of any process by using the following routines:

`pcopyin`	Moves many bytes from the space of any user process
`pcopyout`	Moves many bytes to the space of any user process

The Type one routines use the fields in u to locate the data in user space; as bytes are transferred they automatically update each field. Once the byte count field has been decremented to zero, they will not transfer any more bytes. If many bytes must be moved, it is much more efficient to use `iomove` than to call `cpass` or `passc` repeatedly.

The fields `u.u_base` and `u.u_count` are not set up when an ioctl routine is called. Instead, an ioctl routine that needs to access user data space can interpret the third argument to the `ioctl` system call as an address in the process virtual address space. The Type two routines can be used to transfer data to or from this user virtual address. Again, if many bytes must be moved it is more efficient to use a single call to `copyin` or `copyout` rather than repeated calls to `fubyte` or `subyte`.

The Type three routines can deal with any process, regardless of whether it is the current process, and are generally called from interrupt handlers. These routines take a pointer to the process table entry for the desired process as well as a virtual address in that process. Before `pcopyin` or `pcopyout` can be used, the data that will be read or written must be locked into memory using `vslock`. This must be done while running in the context of the current process. It is also necessary to save the pointer to the process table entry for the current process (`u.u_procp`) for later use by the interrupt handler. The interrupt handler will generally unlock the data buffers after the data transfer, using the routine `vspunlock`.

The Type three routines are typically used in two situations:

1. To implement asynchronous I/O, as described in **Asynchronous I/O,** this chapter.

2. To allow synchronous I/O to be interrupt-driven without forcing the driver to buffer the entire transfer in its own space.

Temporary Storage Within the Driver

All drivers need temporary storage areas in system space to store global state variables, private temporary values, and buffered user data. Several methods can be used, depending on the situation.

First, all drivers need to maintain global state information to coordinate the actions of driver routines with one another and with the kernel. An example is the block driver `iobuf` structure, which must be accessible by several different routines. Other variables of this type may be needed to record the state of the hardware and software. Variables of this type must be external, that is, declared outside of all driver functions. Driver routines that modify the values of external variables must be careful to coordinate their access to the variables with that of other routines and with other executions of themselves. See **Synchronization within the Driver,** this chapter, for a discussion of the synchronization methods that are available.

Second, most driver routines will need private storage for local temporary and intermediate values. Private variables should be declared as automatics, within the function. This will guarantee that a separate copy of the variable will be created for each execution of the routine; it will be deleted when the routine exits. The code must not attribute any global significance to these variables; no other routine will see them. Driver routines should never use external variables for storage of private temporary data. Finally, drivers frequently need space to store user data or descriptions of it temporarily.

The simplest way to accomplish this is to allocate storage statically by declaring external data variables (usually arrays or structures). This method incurs the least runtime overhead since no calls need to be made to allocate storage. It also results in a simpler device driver. It has the disadvantage of permanently reserving space that may not be needed. This is not a problem if the device will almost always be open. Most device drivers written to support special devices in dedicated systems or applications fall into this category.

Also, it is often a good idea to debug the first version of a device driver using statically allocated storage to allow you to concentrate on debugging interaction with the device rather than debugging storage allocation mechanisms.

If static allocation is not acceptable, we can distinguish three principal cases: small amounts of character data, buf descriptors for data in user space, and relatively large amounts of data buffering.

When they exist, block driver read and write routines are called to perform DMA operations directly on user-space buffers. They do not need to copy the user data into system space, but they do need a buf descriptor in order to queue the request to the strategy routine. The standard approach in this case is to declare a small queue (possibly one entry long) of such buffers. The raw I/O routine fills in fields of the structure to describe the I/O request, calls strategy, and calls sleep to wait for the I/O to complete. Again, it is necessary for the routines that use the external structure to synchronize their access to it; see **Synchronization within the Driver**, this chapter.

When a driver declares a private buf structure it does not allocate storage space for the user data, only for the buf structure. There may be cases where the data itself must also be buffered in system space; for example, the bytes may need to be swapped within each word or tab characters may need to be expanded into spaces. One possibility would be to declare a large block of unstructured external storage within the driver, but unless the driver were constantly active, that would be an inefficient use of system memory.

A preferred solution is to call kernel routines to allocate one or more of the blocks temporarily from the kernel block buffering system. The kernel ordinarily uses these blocks as a memory cache for block device blocks, but there is nothing to prevent kernel code (including driver routines) from using them for other purposes. The only requirement is that their use be properly coordinated. This is accomplished by using the following system routines to allocate and release the blocks as required:

geteblk   Returns a pointer to a buf structure associated with an unused block of memory.

brelse   Releases the buf and its associated memory block back to the kernel.

Each block obtained in this way is 4096 bytes in size; its address is found in the buf field b_un.b_addr. The driver must be careful never to write more than 4096 bytes to that location. Drivers should also not allocate many block buffers for extended periods. The total number of blocks available is defined by the configuration parameter NBUF. NBUF is normally set to 0, which causes RTU to reserve 25% of the remaining physical memory to be used as I/O buffers. The number of buffers actually allocated is stored in u.u_buf. The principal use for the blocks is to support the block device cache. If too many of them are used for other purposes, disk I/O performance will suffer. Also, if more than one buffer is required to complete an I/O transfer, the system may deadlock.

Up to this point buf structures and their associated memory blocks have been discussed in the context of block device I/O and block driver raw I/O. However, there is nothing to prevent drivers from using them in more general ways. For example, a device like an electrostatic plotter is technically a character device since it cannot act as part of the block-oriented file system. However, the device uses DMA to move blocks as large as 128 kilobytes during a typical write. There is no reason not to use a private `buf` structure or allocated kernel memory blocks in this type of character driver.

There is one additional method that drivers can use to obtain a temporary storage area in system address space; they can call the routine `wmemall`. The space can be released later by calling `wmemfree`.

For device drivers written for RTU, calling `wmemall` is generally preferable to calling `geteblk` since kernel disk buffers are generally a scarcer resource than physical memory pages. However, there are often other considerations. Device drivers written for other versions of UNIX are more likely to use `geteblk`. Drivers written using `geteblk` will be slightly more portable since many versions of UNIX do not support `wmemall` internally (`wmemall` is originally from 4BSD UNIX systems). If your device driver needs to make use of queues of data buffers, buffer headers can be used to implement the queues with `geteblk` being used to allocate both the queue elements and the data buffers.

See Appendix B for details on `wmemall` and `wmemfree`.

Temporary Character Storage—`clist`. Character drivers frequently need to buffer a few bytes of data in a temporary storage area. For example, a terminal driver interrupt handler may need to accumulate incoming characters until an end-of-line is received or some maximum number is reached. One method of accomplishing this is to use a *clist*.

The driver creates a clist by declaring a `clist` structure, declared in `tty.h`. This allocates space for the "anchor" or head of the queue. The elements of the queue are `cblock` structures (declared in `cblock.h`), which are taken as needed from a global pool maintained by the kernel. Each `cblock` structure stores up to 24 bytes. cblocks are automatically allocated and released by `putc` and `getc` as required. Figure 5-1 shows cblocks in a clist.

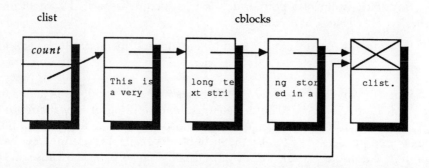

Fig. 5-1. Simplified clist structure

A clist is a FIFO string of bytes stored in system space that is dynamically allocated from a global pool. Characters added to the list by `putc` can be retrieved using `getc`. A driver can declare as many `clist` structures as it needs. Calls to `putc` and `getc` specify the particular clist to be used. A clist is accessible from any driver routine.

Groups of characters can be moved efficiently to and from a clist using the calls putcb and getcb. These calls transfer whole blocks to and from the clist. A call to getcf allocates a cblock. A call to putcb puts the cblock on the clist once data is stored in it. A call to getcb removes the cblock from the clist. After the data has been copied, a call to putcf returns the cblock to the freelist.

Storing and retrieving data in a clist can be relatively slow because of the overhead required. In addition, it is not guaranteed that there will be any space available; putc may fail to store the byte. The configuration parameter nclist (equal to 100 in the delivered system), defines the number of 24-byte blocks that will be available systemwide. Therefore, a clist should not be used in a driver that supports high-speed, time-critical operations, nor should it be used when space for more than a few dozen bytes may be required.

A variation on this approach can be used to avoid the possibility that a very large output record will exhaust the system clist space. The write routine can set an arbitrary limit on the number of bytes that it places on the clist at one time. When the interrupt handler has exhausted the clist and called wakeup, the write routine moves more data onto the list and continues the process.

Handling Block Buffers

This section discusses how buf structures and their associated data must be handled by block driver strategy and interrupt handler routines. The subject of how buf structures are prepared by raw I/O read and write routines is discussed in the next section. This section is also applicable to character drivers that queue requests in buf structures for asynchronous execution.

The standard approach is to use three driver routines with the following responsibilities:

strategy   Called with a buf pointer as an argument; adds the request to a queue.

start   Called to initiate device I/O on the request at the head of the queue.

intr   Called when the device issues an interrupt on completion of the I/O.

The start routine is not a driver entry point; it is called only from within the driver. In an asynchronous character driver the strategy routine is not an entry point; that name is used here only because it performs essentially the same operations as a block driver strategy routine.

To coordinate the activities of the three routines, drivers typically maintain a flag in the iobuf field b_active that can indicate at least two states, IDLE and ACTIVE (some drivers may use other states as well). The state is set to ACTIVE by the start routine when it starts a data transfer and is set to IDLE by the interrupt handler when the transfer is complete.

When the interrupt handler has completed all device operations related to the completed transfer, it removes the buf from the front of the queue and, if the queue is not empty, calls the start routine to start the next transfer. The strategy routine therefore calls the start routine only if the flag is IDLE; after that the queued requests will be processed in order until the queue is empty.

Disk drivers are free to queue the requests in any desired order. The kernel supplies a routine, discussed below, that queues requests in order of increasing cylinder numbers. If the driver manages the queue directly, it should manipulate the following fields in the iobuf structure and in each queued buf structure:

- In the iobuf structure b_actf holds a pointer to the first buf on the queue and b_actl holds a pointer to the last entry on the queue. When the queue is empty both pointers should have the value NULL.

- In each queued buf structure the field av_forw should hold a pointer to the next entry in the queue; the value in the last entry should be NULL.

Drivers are free to use the buf field av_back as a reverse link for the queue, but there is usually no need to do so. Queue maintenance in this style is not required by RTU, but by convention it is used in all disk drivers.

Instead of directly manipulating the queue, disk drivers can call the kernel routine disksort to queue the requests in order of increasing cylinder numbers. This is intended to improve I/O efficiency by causing the heads to make smooth sweeps across the disk. To use this routine the driver strategy routine must compute the cylinder number that corresponds to the value of the b_ioblkno field in each buf and store it in the field b_resid. Then the strategy routine calls disksort to insert the request at the proper point in the queue and, if the driver state is IDLE, calls the start routine to initiate the I/O.

disksort assumes that the cylinder value in the first request in the queue represents the current position of the heads. New requests with larger cylinder numbers are queued in ascending order after that request. New requests with values below the current cylinder are queued in ascending order after the request with the largest cylinder number. Thus as the driver works through the queue the heads will sweep up to the highest requested cylinder and then jump back to the lowest. When B_CMD is set, command blocks are queued in FIFO order. When a command block is queued it is placed at the end of the queue. Each succeeding B_CMD request resets the "elevator."

The division of labor among the driver routines is as follows:

1. The strategy routine queues the request, either directly or by calling disksort. If the driver active flag is IDLE the device start routine is called.

2. The start routine initiates physical I/O for the request at the head of the queue and sets the flag ACTIVE. It leaves the request on the queue so that in case of a retryable error the interrupt handler can simply call start again.

3. The intr routine clears the interrupt in the hardware, sets the active flag to IDLE, and stores status information in the request block. Then it removes the request from the head of the queue, calls the start routine to initiate the next request, and calls iodone to release the completed buf back to wherever it came from.

The kernel routine iodone does a number of things: it sets the B_DONE flag in the buf; optionally calls a completion routine (if b_completion in the buf structure is nonzero); and calls wakeup to activate any process that is waiting for this request to be completed. It performs other bookkeeping and error-checking tasks as well. The driver must call iodone for every buf structure that is passed to its strategy routine. This is normally done by the interrupt handler, but must be done by the strategy routine if preliminary checking causes the request to be rejected.

Mapping and Performing DMA Transfers

Before a DMA data transfer can be initiated, it is usually necessary to load translation data into a group of MULTIBUS adapter I/O map registers. This operation causes a contiguous range of MULTIBUS addresses to be mapped to the target memory buffer in virtual memory space.

The kernel supplies the following functions to perform the necessary operations:

iomalloc	Allocate I/O map registers. Returns an index that points to a block of registers that can be used to map a buffer of a specified size. These registers are for the exclusive use of the calling program until they are released.
iomaddr	Load I/O map registers to map a buffer described by a buf structure.
iomapvaddr	Load I/O map registers to map a buffer in the space of the current user process.
iomfree	Release I/O map registers previously allocated by iomalloc.

There are several approaches that can be taken to allocating the I/O map registers. The first approach is to allocate the needed registers once only, in the driver init routine. In this case iomfree will never be called; the driver keeps the allocated registers forever. This approach is appropriate for drivers for disks and other heavily used high priority devices that cannot afford the overhead of allocating the map at I/O time. The driver must either allocate enough registers to map the largest possible I/O, or it must be prepared to break large requests into a series of smaller transfers.

The second approach is to allocate just as many registers as are needed at the time the I/O request is made. When the transfer is complete iomfree is called to release the registers back to the system. It is important to note that if iomalloc cannot provide the required number of registers, it calls sleep until they become available. Therefore, iomalloc must not be called from a strategy routine or a driver bottom-half routine. The registers should be allocated and freed in the read or write routine. For block drivers, which only have strategy, start, and interrupt routines, the registers must be preallocated.

Some MULTIBUS devices are only able to issue 20-bit addresses on the bus; drivers for these devices must be assured of obtaining registers in the first quadrant of the map. iomalloc takes as an argument a flag that indicates whether 20-bit or more addresses are desired. If the flag argument is nonzero, the routine will definitely allocate registers in the upper three quadrants of the map.

iomalloc only allocates the registers; one of iomaddr or iomapvaddr must be used to actually load the address translation data. iomaddr is used when the buffer to be mapped is described by a buf structure; it uses flag values from the b_flags field to determine which segment of system or user virtual address space the buffer is in. This routine is normally called from a block driver strategy or start routine. iomapvaddr does not require a buf structure; it can be called by a character driver to map a buffer in the space of the current user process for immediate physical I/O.

Both iomaddr and iomapvaddr return a value that is the MULTIBUS address that corresponds to the base of the mapped memory buffer. This value must be loaded into the controller register that is suitable for the DMA base memory address.

There is one case in which no explicit I/O map operations are required. At bootstrap time the kernel maps its own data and blank storage segments (bss) through registers that produce MULTIBUS addresses that are identical to the system virtual addresses. These segments contain all external and static variables defined in kernel code. Therefore, if a driver needs to perform DMA on a private external array that it has defined, it can skip the iomaddr call and simply load the virtual address into the device register. The cache buffers used for block I/O are not premapped in this way and must be explicitly mapped by the driver.

The kernel supplies an additional routine, called physio, that is useful in block driver raw I/O read and write routines. This routine performs most of the operations needed to execute raw I/O. It prepares a buf structure to describe the request, locks the buffer into physical memory, calls the driver strategy routine, and calls sleep to wait for the I/O to be completed. If the requested transfer is too large to be carried out in a single DMA transfer, physio will loop and issue a series of shorter requests.

physio reads the current process u structure and modifies the fields u.u_count and u.u_offset. It can only be called from the read and write routines. See the listing of the template driver bkdriver in Appendix D for an example of the use of physio.

Locking Pages into Memory

Drivers that initiate DMA transfers from the space of a user process must first take steps to guarantee that the target memory buffers will be resident in physical memory for the duration of the transfer. Ordinarily there is no guarantee that any user process virtual page is memory resident. When the CPU makes a reference to a nonresident page, a hardware trap automatically holds up execution of the instruction until the page can be loaded. This transparent response to a page fault does not apply to DMA operations. The driver must explicitly lock the target buffer into physical memory before initiating the DMA transfer.

Drivers must also lock down user-process pages when their bottom-half routines are going to use pcopyin or pcopyout to access user space. Once the driver has completed the DMA or bottom-half programmed access, it must unlock the user pages to return them to their normal status.

The kernel supplies the following routines for locking and unlocking virtual pages:

vslock   Called with the address and size of a buffer in the current user
             process. Locks down all the addressed pages.

vsunlock   Called with the same arguments to unlock the buffer once the
             I/O is complete. A read/write flag is also supplied to indi-
             cate whether the pages have been modified.

vspunlock   Called to unlock pages in the space of a process that is not the
             current user process. Takes a pointer to a proc structure as
             an additional argument.

Both vslock and vsunlock are always called from a driver top-half routine
(read, write, or ioctl). Also, vsunlock is usually called after a call to sleep
has allowed the I/O to complete. vspunlock is called from a bottom-half routine after completion of asynchronous I/O. If a driver unlocks a user page that it
has not previously locked, the system will take a panic crash.

    Since the paging system must be informed when a virtual page has been
modified, the unlocking routines take an indicator flag as an argument. The
values that can be used for this argument are B_READ and B_WRITE as defined
in /usr/include/sys/buf.h. The flag value must correspond to the type of
DMA I/O operation that has been performed. That is, the value B_READ means
that the memory buffer has been written. This value must be used in a call to
vspunlock after a write of status information to the process space. Also, when
vsunlock is called with B_READ, it marks the pages that were entirely spanned
by base and count as globally consistent in all caches. Therefore, if DMA has not
occurred to all locations described by base and count (because of an error or
some other event), vspunlock on u.u_procp should be used. Note that if
physio is used to perform raw I/O it will lock and unlock the memory buffers
as required.

Access to Device Registers

The principal issues of interest in this area are

- Declaring variables that access the device registers
- Using the correct register access size
- Locating the base address for a particular device
- Determining the correct order of bytes within words

The driver source code should include a structure definition to create symbolic
offset names for the device registers. It is also a good idea to create symbolic bit
mask names for individual register bits and fields; the standard UNIX practice is
to define these names in uppercase. These offset and field names can be conveniently kept in a separate header file.

    The items in the device register definition structure must be an exact image
of the device registers, in size and order. This structure will determine for each
register its relative address (offset from the base address) and its access type
(word or byte). Many device registers must be accessed exclusively either as
words or as bytes; an attempt to write one byte in a word register or to read a
pair of byte registers with a word access will usually cause a bus timeout. The

compiler will generate an access that is consistent with the type of the structure member used to label the register.

Device registers should always be accessed through simple reads and writes; that is, in assignment statements that simply move a value from a non-device variable to a device variable or the reverse. Applying shifts and bitwise ANDs and ORs to device registers may have unpredictable results. To load a value in a word-length (16-bit) device register, you must assign a value to a variable that has the type short. The only way to determine the correct access length is to read the hardware manual for the controller. The manual will usually state clearly for each register "must be written as a word" or "must be written as a byte."

On some systems, for a statement of the form

```
reg = 0;
```

the C compiler generates an MC68000 CLR instruction, which causes the destination address to be read before it is written. Since this can cause side effects when applied to a device register, you may need to replace such a statement by

```
tmp = 0;
reg = tmp;
```

Note that the MC68010 CLR instruction does not do the read before write.

In case of trouble it may also be helpful to turn off the compiler optimizer by not using the -O option. If this helps, compare the code generated with and without the option to see whether the optimizer made an unacceptable change to a device register access. Another case where turning off the optimizer may be helpful is when the same physical location must be accessed twice to get a single piece of information. In this case, the optimizer may consider that the value at the location will not change, which is not necessarily true with a device.

The driver obtains the physical addresses of its devices from the address table defined in conf.c. If the driver prefix is xx, the name of the array is xx_addr[]. Drivers that support more than one controller must define a method for deriving a controller number from the minor device number. The minor number or a portion of it can be a simple index, or if there are multiple controllers each with multiple drives, a more complex scheme can be used. In any case, once a zero-based index has been computed, a pointer to the base address of the device can be obtained from a line similar to the following:

```
dp = (struct device *) xx_addr[unit];
```

This assumes that the source code has defined a structure type device to define symbolic names for the offsets to the registers. The cast is necessary because xx_addr[] is defined in conf.c as being of type int.

Driver writers must be aware of possible problems associated with the order of bytes within words. As was pointed out in Chapter 3, the MASSCOMP CPU and the MULTIBUS have opposing definitions of the order of bytes within words. Therefore, the MULTIBUS adapter interchanges the order of bytes as they move through the interface. If a 16-bit number is computed and stored in a device register, it may or may not arrive there in the proper orientation. Many MULTIBUS controllers include one or more switches that can be set by the user to control byte swapping on the board.

The kernel supplies macros named `lobyte`, `hibyte`, `loword`, and `hiword`, which can be used to extract the named portions from larger data in case it is necessary to reorder bytes before writing them to a device register. The kernel also provides functions `swab` and `swabl` for performing the most common byte reorderings. See Appendix A.

▪ Driver Interaction with the Caller ▪

This section discusses ways in which a device driver can affect the execution of a user process beyond simply performing the requested I/O operation.

Synchronization with Device Activity

A major potential side effect of issuing a `read` or `write` system call is that the calling process may have its execution blocked for an indeterminate length of time. Unless special steps are taken (see **Asynchronous I/O**, Chapter 10), UNIX I/O is logically synchronous. That is, when a user process issues a read or write system call, the call does not return until the data has been moved to or from the user buffer.

This standard form of I/O is called "logically" synchronous because on a `write` the data will not necessarily have been transferred to the device. It may have only been copied to the block buffering cache, or it may have been copied to a driver clist for interrupt-driven output to the device. Therefore, a successful return from a `write` call does not guarantee that the data has been (or will be) successfully transferred to the device. The presumption is made that there will be no device errors; if there are, it will generally not be possible to report them to the process that initiated the transfer.

On a block device the determination of whether the calling process is to be suspended while the I/O completes is outside the control of the device driver. It depends on the state of the kernel block buffering cache. For a character device the degree of synchronism between the caller and the device operation is a driver design choice. The driver can be written to be totally synchronous so that it suspends the caller until all device I/O is complete, or it can buffer large amounts of output data in system space and call `sleep` only if this space is exhausted. It could also lock in pages of the user process that contain the user buffers, return to the user, and allow the interrupt service to drive the transfer.

Returning I/O Status

Most driver routines return status to the caller indirectly, by storing values in data structures. Only in one case is it necessary for a driver routine to set its return value explicitly—in the interrupt handler for a driver that has a zero interrupt mask. Chapter 9 lists the status return actions for each driver entry point in detail. This section summarizes how drivers return status information to the calling user process.

Routines that are called in current user process context return status in fields of the `u` structure. They can declare an error by storing a nonzero error code in `u.u_error`. The value will be moved to the external variable `errno`, and the system call return value will be set to -1. Character device read and write routines also indicate the number of bytes transferred by decrementing the value of `u.u_count`. The difference between the original value of `u.u_count` and the value of `u.u_count` when the read or write routine terminates is used as the return value of the system call.

Drivers for sequential devices such as printers or terminals generally ignore the file offset pointer that is copied to `u.u_offset` since they are incapable of random access behavior. Character device drivers for random access devices (such as raw disk) will generally use `u.u_offset` to determine the device address to access. The file offset pointer is automatically updated by the system based on the final value of `u.u_count` and the contents of `u.u_offset` are ignored. The `physio` routine uses the current value of `u.u_offset` to compute the value of `b_ioblkno` in the buffer header it constructs and passes to the device strategy routine and also updates `u.u_offset` when I/O is completed on that buffer. This is done so that `u.u_offset` will be correct if a large transfer must be broken up into several smaller transfers by `physio`. Therefore, there is generally no need for device driver routines to explicitly adjust `u.u_offset`.

Block driver routines that handle `buf` structures declare an error by setting `B_ERROR` in the `b_flags` field and storing an error code in `b_error`. When they do this they must also store in `b_resid` the number of requested bytes that were not transferred. Block drivers always release `buf` structures back to the caller by calling `iodone`. If an error is detected in the request before the I/O is attempted, this should be done in the strategy routine. If device I/O is attempted and fails it must be done in the interrupt handler.

MASSCOMP RTU users can make asynchronous I/O calls that return control immediately but complete the data transfer and return status information at a later time. See **Asynchronous I/O**, Chapter 10, for a discussion of how status information is returned in this case.

Block device drivers that implement raw read or write entry points should obey the conventions for character device drivers for those entry points. The amount of data actually transferred by a call to these entry points is determined by the difference between the initial and final values of `u.u_count` and `u.u_offset`, which is recomputed when the device read or write routine returns.

The Special Functions Routine

A character or mixed-type driver can optionally include a special function or ioctl routine. Its execution context is the same as the read and write routines, except the fields `u.u_base`, `u.u_count`, and `u.u_offset` are not meaningful. This routine is used to perform operations that are not simple reads and writes of the device. It is typically used to set a device mode or to return information about the current device state. It can also be used to initiate an asynchronous operation.

The driver ioctl routine is called whenever the user process issues an `ioctl` system call. This system call takes three arguments that are passed unchanged to the driver routine:

1. A file descriptor

2. The device-specific function to be performed

3. A pointer to the data to be used in performing the function

See `ioctl(2)` in Volume 1B of the *UNIX Programmer's Manual* for more information on the `ioctl` system call.

If the requested operation requires that more data be passed between the user process and the driver than will fit in these two arguments, then the second argument should be a pointer to a data structure in user address space. The author of the driver should create a header file to define the structure and make it available to application programmers by placing it in the `/usr/include` directory. The user program declares a structure, stores driver input values in it, and passes its address to the driver. The driver reads and perhaps writes fields in the structure to satisfy the request. An example of such a structure is the one defined in `termio.h` for use with the terminal driver.

If the special operation can be completed synchronously by the ioctl routine, it can use functions like `copyin` and `copyout` to move data to and from user space. The routine may also be used to initiate asynchronous activity. In this case ioctl locks portions of the user address space and returns control to the caller. Other driver routines continue to access the process space by using the `pcopyin` and `pcopyout` routines. See **Asynchronous I/O**, this chapter, for further discussion of asynchronous I/O.

Asynchronous Interactions

This section discusses the ways in which a driver can interact with a user process outside of the serialized call-and-return mode. There are two possibilities: actions that interrupt the normal sequence of execution of the process and actions that simply alter the contents of its memory space. These mechanisms can be used to inform a process that an event has occurred (e.g., a device has gone offline) or to improve performance by overlapping I/O with process execution.

Signals. Signals are a standard feature of the UNIX operating system. Volume I of the *UNIX Programmer's Manual* documents how signals can be sent from one process to another (`kill(2)`) and how a process can control the handling of incoming signals (`signal(2)`). The notable feature of signals is that they interrupt the execution of the receiving process. This section describes how a device driver can issue a signal to a user process.

The most common examples of signals used by drivers are those sent by a terminal driver when a user types a Control-C or Control-Z. When the driver interrupt routine detects one of these characters in its input, it sends the corresponding signal (`SIGINT` or `SIGTSTP` respectively) to one or more processes associated with that terminal. As another example, a driver could be programmed to send a general purpose signal like `SIGUSR1` to a particular process when a device causes an interrupt by going offline. (The signal types are defined in `/usr/include/signal.h`.)

The kernel provides two routines that can be called by a driver in order to issue a signal to one or more user processes:

psignal   Send a signal to a process; arguments specify the signal type and a pointer to the process `proc` structure.

gsignal   Send a specified signal to every process in a specified process group.

The UNIX signal mechanism has many shortcomings that make it unsuitable for most asynchronous operations. Signals cannot be queued or deferred, and their default action is to terminate the receiving process. The only value delivered by a signal is its type; most types have predefined meanings, so only the types SIGUSR1 and SIGUSR2 are available for unspecified uses. Because of the importance of asynchronous interaction in real-time applications, MASSCOMP provides a more sophisticated mechanism known as the Asynchronous System Trap (AST).

Asynchronous I/O. Asynchronous I/O is a powerful technique that can greatly enhance overall performance by allowing a user process to overlap computation and data manipulation with input and output. It also allows the use of event-driven logic. However, these advantages are obtained at the expense of added complexity in both the device driver and user program.

The basic characteristic of asynchronous I/O is that when the device driver receives a read or write request, it initiates the device I/O operation but returns control to the calling process without waiting for the data transfer to be completed. When the transfer does complete, the driver interrupt routine notifies the process that initiated the request. Two notification methods are possible: the driver can write status information in a user-space buffer, or it can send an AST to the process.

A commonly used technique is called "double buffering." To choose an example, a process may need to write a stream of data to an output device. It defines two output data buffers, fills the first with data, and issues a request for asynchronous output to the device driver. The driver initiates a DMA output operation and returns control to the user process. The process fills the second buffer with the next batch of output data and issues a write request for that buffer. At that point it must wait for an indication that the first output has completed before writing new data into the first buffer. The indication arrives in the form of an AST sent by the device driver.

Another type of situation is the one in which a process needs to issue read and write requests simultaneously on several devices without knowing the order in which the requests will be completed. After issuing all the requests the process suspends its execution and then allows its AST handlers to be called in an unpredictable order.

A typical sequence of events within a driver goes as follows. A character driver top-half routine is called to initiate asynchronous I/O. An argument to the routine is a pointer to a data structure that defines the request; one of the items in the structure is a pointer to an AST descriptor block. The top-half routine moves the AST information into its own space and declares the AST by calling `dclast`. It also stores the value of `u.u_procp` and locks into physical memory the user buffers that will be read or written. It always locks the buffer that holds the data to be transferred and typically also a smaller buffer where the completion status will be written. Then it initiates the device I/O or queues the request for asynchronous processing. Then instead of calling `sleep` it returns control to the calling process.

When the data transfer is complete the driver interrupt service routine calls `vspunlock` to unlock the user space data buffer. If there is a user space status buffer it uses `pcopyout` to write the status and then unlocks that buffer. Then it calls `delast` to cause the AST to be delivered. The AST is posted to the process immediately, but it will not interrupt the process execution unless and until the process AST priority drops below the priority of the posted AST.

A driver that implements a full range of I/O options will allow the user process to choose between synchronous and asynchronous I/O and, in the latter case, will allow it to specify that final status information be written, that an AST be delivered, or both. `read` and `write` system calls should be used to request synchronous I/O and `ioctl` calls used to request asynchronous I/O. The `ioctl` function argument could select a read or write operation, and the second argument could be a pointer to a data structure containing a full description of the request.

▪ Synchronization within the Driver ▪

This section discusses the ways in which device drivers synchronize their execution. Driver writers must be familiar with the correct ways to synchronize

- Driver software with device hardware
- One driver routine with another
- Parallel executions of the same routine

RTU provides several synchronization and timing facilities. The following sections describe these facilities and give examples of their use.

Using `sleep` and `wakeup`

The kernel functions `sleep` and `wakeup` are used in drivers both to synchronize software with hardware and to synchronize one routine with another. When a driver routine calls `sleep`, its execution is blocked until a corresponding call to `wakeup` is made. The `wakeup` call is made by another process or by an interrupt handler.

The effect of a call to `sleep` is to block execution of the current user process. Therefore, `sleep` must be called only from routines that execute in current user process context; these are the open, read, write, ioctl, and close routine. You must never call `sleep` from the `init` or `strategy` routines, or from a driver bottom-half routine. Within the calling routine the effect of `sleep` is simply to delay execution of the next line of code until after the associated `wakeup` call has been made.

Driver routines call `sleep` whenever they must delay further execution until some asynchronous event has occurred. There are two situations in which a delay of this kind is necessary:

1. The driver has initiated a device operation and must delay until that operation has been completed or aborted.

2. The driver requires access to a hardware or software resource that is currently busy; that is, marked for exclusive access by some other process.

In either case the routine must suspend execution until the situation changes. It then depends on a routine that executes asynchronously outside the context of the current process to issue a `wakeup` call to allow it to resume execution.

When a driver routine calls `sleep` it specifies the particular event that it is waiting for in an argument that is commonly called the *channel*. The channel argument must be accessed identically from `sleep` and `wakeup`. Therefore, to avoid possible conflicts we use a system virtual address with type `caddr_t`. Execution will be blocked until a `wakeup` call is issued using the same channel value. The routines that call `sleep` and `wakeup` must use an agreed-upon convention to associate events with channel values. Typically the channel value used is the address of a data structure associated with the event. For example, in order to wait for completion of an I/O request in a `buf` structure that has been queued to a strategy routine, the caller uses the address of the `buf` as the channel value. The interrupt service routine that completes the I/O must issue a `wakeup` call using the same value.

It is not uncommon for several processes to `sleep` on the same channel. They may be competing for the same resource, or they may be waiting for different reasons that have been associated with the same channel value. In this situation a single `wakeup` call on the common channel will cause all the sleeping processes to become executable; the actual order in which they are executed will depend on their scheduling priorities. A driver routine must not assume that it can proceed after a return from a `sleep` call. It should check to see whether the event it was waiting for has actually occurred; if it has not it should sleep again, and repeat this cycle until the awaited event has actually occurred.

In principle it would be possible for a driver routine to wait for a device operation to complete by executing a tight loop that repeatedly tests a status bit in the device CSR. This method, called "busy wait," is often used in simple single-process computers. However, busy wait should never be used in a UNIX device driver since it would make the CPU unavailable for other work for long periods of time. In the unusual case of a device that does not issue interrupts, the driver should call `sleep` using the address of `lbolt` as the channel argument. The kernel issues a `wakeup` call on this channel once per second. See **Timing and Timeout Routines**, this chapter, for a further discussion.

Some kernel routines call `sleep`. For example, `iomalloc` calls `sleep` if there are not enough I/O map registers available to satisfy the caller's request, and `geteblk` calls `sleep` if a buffer must be written. Driver writers must be aware of the kernel routines that may call `sleep` and be sure to call them only in the proper context.

Calling `iomalloc` or `ioa_malloc` from a driver init routine is legitimate. However, calling `sleep` in this context is not. Use of `iomalloc` or
`ioa_malloc` is possible because they call `sleep` only when they run out of I/O
map space. That usually occurs only on a system error condition.

Scheduling Priority

When a driver calls `sleep` it also specifies the scheduling priority to be attached
to the suspended user process. When the process is reactivated (by a `wakeup`
call) this value determines its priority relative to other executable processes. The
scheduler always runs the process that is not suspended and has the highest
priority (higher priority corresponds to smaller numerical values).

A process' scheduling priority has a second important use: it determines
whether the process can be awakened by a signal or an AST. If a process sleeps
at a priority numerically less than or equal to `PZERO` (defined in
`/usr/include/sys/param.h`), it will not be awakened if it receives a signal or
an AST. The process will be reactivated only by a `wakeup` call and will process
the signal or AST at that time. A process that sleeps at a priority numerically
greater than `PZERO` will wake up immediately if it receives a signal or AST; if it
continues executing, the I/O operation that was in progress is aborted. The I/O
system call returns a value of −1 with `errno` set to `EINTR` unless `SNUSIG` is
set. If `SNUSIG` is set, RTU is compatible with the 4.1BSD new signal mechanism,
which will restart `read`, `write`, and `wait` system calls but will abort all other
system calls.

`SNUSIG` will be clear unless a `signal` system call has been made using the
expanded functionality provided by the new signal mechanism. These include
holding a signal, catching a signal with `DEFERSIG`, atomically pausing after setting a signal, or emulating a user-mode RTI at the completion of the signal system call.

The most commonly used signals are those that stop or kill a process. They
can be sent by another process in response to a shell command or by the terminal
driver in response to control characters. If a process is sleeping at a priority less
than or equal to `PZERO` it will not respond to these signals until the I/O operation completes.

Typically it is desirable to allow I/O in progress to a fast device to complete
before signals are processed. Thus the priority, `PRIBIO`, normally used for block
I/O is smaller than `PZERO`. For I/O to slow devices (like terminals) or to devices
that may be blocked for long periods (terminals or pipes) it is preferable to allow
interruption by signals. Drivers for these devices usually sleep at priorities
greater than `PZERO`.

The following priorities are defined in `/usr/include/sys/param.h`:

`PSWP`	0	Used by the swapper
`PINOD`	10	Used to read and write i-nodes
`PRIBIO`	20	Used for other block I/O
`PZERO`	25	Lowest non-interrupt sleep priority
`PPIPE`	26	Used for pipe I/O
`PWAIT`	30	Used for calls to `wait`
`PSLEP`	40	Used for user calls to `sleep`
`PUSER`	50	Active process stays near this value

Character drivers normally use values greater than PZERO. The exact value chosen effects overall system performance, but the effect is usually not a major one. Terminal drivers usually sleep at priorities PZERO+3 (defined as TTIPRI in /usr/include/sys/tty.h) and PZERO+4 (TTOPRI) for input and output respectively. A fast DMA device should perhaps sleep at priority PZERO+2; a line printer, which is less time-critical than a terminal, should probably sleep at a value greater than PZERO+5.

Device and Processor Priority

The MASSCOMP CPU maintains a hardware priority value that can be set by kernel software to a value in the range zero through seven. This hardware priority must not be confused with either the process scheduling priority or the AST priority, both of which are implemented entirely in software. The direct effect of the CPU priority is to enable and disable device interrupts. A device interrupt request issued at a priority level equal to or less than the current CPU priority has no immediate effect; it remains pending until the kernel software lowers the CPU priority to a value below the level of the request. When this happens the executing routine is interrupted immediately after execution of the instruction that lowers the CPU priority, and the interrupt handler begins to execute.

Drivers call the following routines to change the CPU priority:

spl0, spl1, ... spl7	Set CPU priority to constant value
splv (*pri*)	Set CPU priority to *pri*; where *pri* is a value returned by spl0,... spl7, splv
splx (*pri*)	Reset CPU priority to the value that it had before the last spl command; where *pri* is a value returned by spl0,... spl7, splv

Each of these functions returns the value of the previous CPU priority. A typical action is for a driver routine to raise the CPU priority to its device interrupt level while saving the previous value; after sensitive code has been executed the priority is returned to its old value. The following code could be used in a driver whose device interrupts at level five:

```
oldpri = spl5();      /* raise priority to device level */
/*
access shared data structures
...
*/
splx(oldpri);         /* return to previous priority */
```

Driver routines manipulate the CPU priority in order to synchronize their execution with that of their own and other interrupt handlers. Whenever a driver routine alters a data structure that can also be altered by an interrupt handler, it must first raise the CPU priority to or above the device interrupt priority. This action guarantees that an interrupt handler below or at that level will not be executed while the active routine is in its sensitive section. In particular, the driver must raise the CPU priority before taking any action that alters or reads the contents of the device registers.

An example is a block driver strategy routine which adds buf structures to a queue that is being processed by the driver interrupt handler. The queue could become damaged and inconsistent if execution of the two routines were intermingled. The strategy routine must prepare the buf structure, raise the CPU priority to the device interrupt level, add the structure to the queue, and then return the CPU priority to its original level. Driver interrupt handler routines do not explicitly manipulate the CPU priority. When an interrupt request is honored and the handler begins to execute, the CPU priority is automatically set to the device interrupt priority; when the handler exits, the CPU priority is automatically reset to its previous value.

Routines such as geteblk and brelse that move kernel data structures on and off of linked lists also must coordinate their actions with interrupt handlers that manipulate the same lists. All the routines of this type raise the CPU priority to six or seven in order to block all device interrupts while they are working with the kernel lists and restore the CPU priority when they are done. Drivers do not need to raise priority before calling these routines.

Multiple Executions of a Driver

There are two ways in which a driver top-half routine can temporarily lose control of the CPU:

1. A device interrupt is issued at a priority higher than the current CPU priority.

2. The executing routine calls sleep, voluntarily giving up the CPU.

In the first case the interrupted routine will regain the CPU when the interrupt handler exits. The kernel will not make a context switch and schedule another process in this situation.

In the second case, however, execution of the process that called the driver is blocked, and some other process begins to run. That process may issue a system call that executes the same driver routine that just suspended itself. Thus it is possible that there will be two or more parallel executions of the same routine. Driver routines that are subject to parallel instances—that is, routines that call sleep—must be careful to synchronize their several executions with one another.

As an example consider a character driver whose write routine stores values in device registers in order to initiate DMA output and then calls sleep to wait for the transfer to complete. During the sleep the write routine may be called by another process to perform I/O through the same controller. It would be an error to write new values to the device registers without waiting for the transfer in progress to be completed.

To manage this situation the driver must maintain a flag to indicate whether the controller is in use by some process. A separate flag is used to indicate whether the controller is busy performing a data transfer. The write routine delays by calling sleep until the controller is not in use. The device is marked as "in use" while the driver initiates the data transfer. The device is marked as busy and the write routine sleeps. The interrupt handler is run when the I/O is completed. It clears the busy flag and calls wakeup to restart the process that initiated the I/O. The write routine can then check for errors by examining the device registers. When it is finished accessing the device registers, the write routine clears the in-use flag and calls `wakeup`.

In the following example, the variable `dev_in_use` is the in-use flag and `dev_busy` is the busy flag:

Code in write routine:

```
while (dev_in_use)          /* wait till device is available */
    sleep(&dev_in_use, PSLEP);

dev_in_use = 1;             /* allocate the device */

/* initiate the I/O */
dev_busy = 1;
/* ... */
oldpri = spl6();

while (dev_busy)            /* wait for the transfer to finish */
    sleep(&dev_busy, PSLEP);

splx(oldpri);

/* check for errors */

dev_in_use = 0;            /* mark device as available */
wakeup(&dev_in_use);

/* finish and return */
```

Code in intr routine:

```
/* complete the I/O */
dev_busy = 0;              /* the device isn't busy anymore */
wakeup(&dev_busy);
```

Note that it is important for a process waiting for the controller to do so in a loop that checks the in-use flag. It would not be correct to sleep once and assume that the `wakeup` guarantees that the controller is free. If two processes are waiting for the controller, the `wakeup` will restart them both. The first one to run will obtain the controller; the second one will find the in-use flag on and have to sleep again.

Note also that processor priority is kept on a per-process basis. A call to `sleep` causes a context switch, and the kernel sets the processor priority appropriately for that process. When the original process is awakened and rescheduled, the processor priority is restored to the value that it had before the call to `sleep`.

It is necessary to examine the busy flag with interrupts disabled since otherwise the interrupt routine might clear `dev_busy` and call `wakeup` between the time the write routine checked `dev_busy` and called `sleep`. If this were to occur, the write routine would sleep forever since `wakeup` would never be called.

It is not necessary to examine the in-use flag at a high interrupt priority level since this flag is only set from the top-half of the driver and there is no possibility of another top-half routine executing between the check of dev_in_use and the call to sleep.

Driver top-half routines that do not directly access the the device hardware may still need to synchronize their access to data structures. A common example is a raw I/O routine that fills in a private buf structure to describe a DMA transfer and then queues it to a strategy routine. The queue of requests maintained by strategy serializes access to the device, but the raw I/O routines must synchronize their use of the shared buf structure through logic of the type shown in the previous example. In the case of a buf structure the flag B_BUSY in the field b_flags is normally used as the busy flag and the address of the buf is used as the channel value for sleep. These conventions must be followed if the iodone routine is called by the interrupt handler to complete the I/O.

Timing and Timeout Routines

The MASSCOMP RTU kernel provides several facilities that allow device drivers to measure elapsed times, delay for a specified amount of time, or be notified in case a device fails to issue an interrupt within a reasonable amount of time.

The kernel maintains a global variable named lbolt whose value is incremented 60 times per second. The value of lbolt is the integer number of clock ticks elapsed since the previous system bootstrap. The kernel issues a wakeup call with the address of lbolt as the channel value each second on the second. Therefore, a driver routine that needs to delay but is not expecting a device interrupt can call sleep using lbolt as the channel value. Note that this will not guarantee that one second will elapse before the wakeup, only that no more than one second will elapse.

When a driver initiates a device operation and sleeps waiting for a device interrupt, there is sometimes a possibility that due to bad input parameters or hardware failure the interrupt will never occur. A driver can protect itself against this situation by first calling the kernel routine timeout. Arguments to timeout specify an elapsed time in clock ticks, a routine to call, and a value to pass to the routine as an argument. After the specified number of ticks have elapsed, the routine is called with the specified argument. The called routine would typically set a flag to indicate that a timeout has occurred and then call wakeup using the same channel value that the driver interrupt handler would have used. In the normal case where the interrupt does occur, the interrupt handler should call a second function, cantimeout, to cancel the pending call to the timeout routine. timeout returns a unique identifier that is used in the cantimeout call. Therefore, drivers can establish several timeouts in parallel, perhaps associated with several active devices.

Catching Bus Faults and Signals

There are situations in which a driver must be able to intercept bus and memory faults or signals being sent to a process. Specifically:

- In the init routine the driver should probe the CSR for each device to determine whether the device is installed. A nonexistent device is detected by the bus fault that results; the driver must be able to regain control when this happens.

- When a driver temporarily allocates system resources such as buf structures or I/O Map registers, it needs to be notified before the calling process is aborted by a signal so that it can release the system resources.

The kernel functions setjmp and longjmp allow drivers to handle these situations. These functions are analogous to the library routines of the same name that can be called from user processes. A call to setjmp establishes a return point for a subsequent call to longjmp. The driver code does not call longjmp. The kernel calls this routine when the fault or signal occurs.

The initial call to setjmp always returns a zero value; a nonzero return from setjmp is a sign that longjmp has been called. The following example shows the use of setjmp:

```
if (setjmp(save_area) == 0)
  {
    /* normal in-line return ...
       probe registers, allocate resources,
       etc.,
       ...
    */
  }
else
  {
    /* fault or signal occurred ...
       do something about it,
       ...
    */
  }
```

The argument to setjmp is a pointer to a structure of the type label_t. The structure is used by the kernel to store information that defines the return point for longjmp calls. The user structure u contains two structures of this type that are used by the kernel to handle the two situations that we are discussing:

u.u_tsav   If u.u_nofault is nonzero, the kernel calls longjmp with this argument when a bus or memory fault occurs.

u.u_qsav   The kernel calls longjmp with this argument when the process receives a signal.

We can now give a more concrete example of an init routine for a driver that supports a single device. The driver prefix is xx, so the address of the device CSR is stored at xx_addr[0].

```
if (setjmp(u.u_tsav) == 0)
  {
    u.u_nofault = 1;     /* enable fault handling */
    temp = *xx_addr[0]; /* probe the CSR */
```

```
        u.u_nofault = 0;      /* fault didn't occur, continue */
}
else
    xx_addr[0] = 0;      /* fault occurred, mark dev missing */
```

An example of the use of `u.u_qsav` would be a driver that allocates a system resource in its read or write routine and sleeps at a priority larger than PZERO. An incoming signal will cause this I/O request to be aborted by the kernel; the driver must be able to regain control of the CPU temporarily so that it can release the allocated resource. This kind of situation should not arise too often. It is usually better to allocate resources in the open routine rather than in read and write.

6

EXAMPLES OF DRIVER LOGIC

This chapter provides examples of the concepts discussed in Chapter 5. Some of these examples are code fragments and some are complete driver routines that demonstrate frequently used techniques. Chapter 8 and Appendixes C and D describe complete example drivers that can be loaded and executed on any MASSCOMP system.

Most of the examples in this chapter use a hypothetical output device that accepts a stream of characters. This device might be a line printer, a graphics terminal, or a communication device. These examples do not deal with what the device does with the characters that are written to it.

Definition of the Device, this chapter, describes a set of device registers that might be found in a hypothetical output-only device. The device is capable of either programmed or DMA output and can generate an interrupt request when it completes an operation. **Device Data Structures**, this chapter, shows how a data structure and other parameters would be defined to allow the driver software to access the device registers. The following sections present code examples from several drivers that might be written for this device. Two drivers that use programmed I/O to write the user's characters without any translation are described—the first is completely synchronous on a character by character basis, and the second uses a clist to buffer a few characters in system space. The third example gives a more elaborate example of a printer driver that examines and translates the output characters, stores the results in a system-space buffer, and uses the device DMA capability to generate the output. The fourth example describe drivers that use DMA to move the data directly from user space to the device. We show how this can be done both synchronously (the standard UNIX method) and asynchronously (a special feature of MASSCOMP RTU). The fifth example describes a driver that uses the `select` system call to do synchronous I/O multiplexing; the example in this section uses excerpts from a generic terminal driver rather than using the hypothetical device used in the other examples.

All the examples given in this chapter are for character drivers. The template block driver, `bkdriver`, described in Chapter 8 is a complete, working example of a block driver. It differs from a real block driver only in that it does not deal with hardware registers and interrupts. The examples of those operations given in this chapter are equally applicable to block drivers.

The examples given in this chapter are meant to be educational. They do not necessarily use optimal methods nor do they include all the required features and details, such as fully reliable error recovery. It is not recommended that anyone write a driver for a real device that is character-by-character synchronous in the manner of the first example. That example is included for the sake of comparison to show a hypothetical minimum solution.

• Definition of the Device •

This section defines the device used in the first five examples. We will first define a set of hardware registers typical of those found in real devices. The characteristics of the hypothetical device are:

- The device is output only

- It is capable of both programmed and DMA output

- It has one device unit per controller. The minor device number will specify the unit or controller number.

The controller has the following registers, each one byte in size:

CR   Command Register (write only)

              Bit 0   Reset controller

              Bit 1   Enable interrupts

              Bit 2   Start DMA transfer

              Bit 3   Clear attention

SR   Status Register (read only)

              Bit 0   Device ready

              Bit 1   Interrupts enabled

              Bit 2   Attention

              Bit 3   Error

DR   Data Register (write only)

              Bits 0 through 7
                    Output character for programmed I/O

DALB   Data Address, Low Byte (write only)

DAMB   Data Address, Middle Byte (write only)

DAHB   Data Address, High Byte (write only)

> For DMA output these registers specify the 24-bit MUL-TIBUS address of the memory data buffer.

BCLB   Byte Count, Low Byte (write only)

BCHB   Byte Count, High Byte (write only)

> For DMA output these registers specify the 16-bit count of bytes to be transferred to the device.

These registers appear in MULTIBUS I/O space in the order given, beginning at a base address determined by the settings of hardware switches on the controller board. We will assume that the device driver is installed with the prefix `xx_` so that the base register address can be found in the array `xx_addr[]`.

The device operates as follows. At power-up time or after a one is written to the command register "reset" bit, the device is inactive, interrupts are disabled, and the attention and error states are cleared. At this time the status register contains the value one, indicating that the device is ready for output. The device can be activated in either of two ways: programmed I/O can be initiated by writing a single byte to the data register, or DMA output can be initiated by writing values to the data address and byte count registers and then writing a one to the "start DMA" bit in the command register.

When a byte is written to the data register the device responds by clearing the "ready" bit and initiating output of the character. When output of the character is complete the "ready" and "attention" bits are set to indicate that the device is ready to accept another character. If the "enable interrupt" bit was set before the data register was written, an interrupt request will be placed on the MULTIBUS at the same time. Since the time required to output even one character is likely to be large relative to CPU instruction execution times, a device driver must not use busy-wait polling of the "attention" bit. The driver must enable interrupts and call `sleep` to relinquish the CPU while waiting for the output operation to complete.

When the device is operated in the DMA mode the data register is not used. Instead, an address and byte count describing a memory data buffer are written to the DA and BC registers. Writing these registers does not initiate device activity; to do that the driver software must write a one to the "start DMA" bit. The device then clears the "ready" bit and begins to move characters from consecutive increasing memory addresses, beginning at the specified address and continuing for the specified number of bytes. When all the characters have been transferred, the status bits are set and an interrupt generated in the same way as for the programmed I/O mode.

After an interrupt has been generated it is necessary for the driver software to clear that state (and its status bit) by writing a one to the "clear attention" bit. The "interrupt enabled" bit is automatically cleared by the hardware when the interrupt is generated. If for some reason the device is unable to complete the output request successfully, it halts and sets both the "attention" and "error" bits. In DMA mode this could happen if a programming error loads address and byte count values that cause the device to attempt to access nonexistent memory. In either output mode an error might also be caused by an internal hardware failure within the device.

The register configuration and modes of operation for this device are typical of many real devices, but probably simpler than most that will actually be encountered. It is common, for example, to place the command and status registers at the same MULTIBUS address. Another method frequently used is to provide a single byte register to accept a 16- or 24-bit value and require that the individual bytes of the value be written to the register in a prescribed order. A more troublesome situation arises if the controller provides a 16-bit register to accept a 16-bit value and requires that the value must be written by a single word-length operation. In that case it becomes necessary to look carefully at the byte swapping performed by the MASSCOMP I/O adapter and possibly by the device controller itself. It may be necessary for the driver to reverse the byte order in memory before writing the value to the register.

• Device Data Structure •

In order to refer to the device registers and their fields the driver must create a descriptive data structure. The following declaration is appropriate for the registers described above and will be used in the code examples that follow.

```
struct xx_device
  {
    char xx_cr;        /* control register */
    char xx_sr;        /* status register */
    char xx_dr;        /* data register */
    char xx_dalb;      /* data address -- low byte */
    char xx_damb;      /* "         "    -- middle byte*/
    char xx_dahb;      /* "         "    -- high byte*/
    char xx_bclb;      /* byte count -- low  byte */
    char xx_bchb;      /* "      "    -- high byte*/
  };
```

Since all the registers are byte length, there is no need to worry about alignment within the structure. For devices that have 16- or 32-bit registers additional care must be taken since the C compiler will align short and int variables on their natural boundaries. This may cause gaps in the structure that do not exist in the hardware.

As an example, consider a device that has three registers whose sizes are 16, 8, and 16 bits respectively. If these registers are defined in a structure in the natural way, the compiler will align the third register on a word boundary, causing its offset from the structure base to be incorrect. The solution to the problem is to define the structure for this device as follows:

```
struct zz_device
 {
   short  reg1;
   char   reg2;
   char   reg3_low;
   char   reg3_high;
 };
```

In order to write a 16-bit value to the third register the following code could be used:

```
short *sp;                  /* define pointer to short */
short value;                /* define short variable */
struct zz_device *zp;       /* define pointer to device */
...
zp = zz_addr[0]; /* set pointer to first device base address */
sp = (short *)&zp->reg3_low;  /* set pointer to register */
*sp = value;                /* store value in register */
```

Again, it would be necessary in this case to understand the device requirements for byte order within words and possibly reverse the bytes within value before writing the register.

Returning to our simpler example device, it is also good practice to define symbolic names for the individual bits within the device command and status registers. The driver would include the following definitions:

```
#define CR_RST   0x01      /* reset */
#define CR_EI    0x02      /* enable interrupt */
#define CR_GO    0x04      /* start DMA */
#define CR_CA    0x08      /* clear attention */

#define SR_RDY   0x01      /* ready */
#define SR_IE    0x02      /* interrupt enabled */
#define SR_ATTN  0x04      /* attention */
#define SR_ERR   0x08      /* error */
```

The device structure and bit definitions could be included at the head of the driver source code or in a separate header file referenced in an #include statement. Note that we do not recommend using bit fields for structures that are implemented by hardware device registers.

• Example 1: Synchronous Character Output •

This first example demonstrates the simplest possible method that could be used to drive the device described above in its programmed I/O mode. This method is an inefficient one since it does not allow any overlap of driver and device activity.

Since we are not presenting a complete example driver in this chapter, we will describe only the two routines that are directly involved in writing characters to the device: xx_write and xx_intr. The logic used by these routines is as follows:

1. `xx_write` uses the kernel function `cpass` to obtain one character from user space.

2. It then writes values to the device registers to initiate output of the character and calls `sleep` to wait for completion of the device activity.

3. When the device completes the output it generates an interrupt, causing `xx_intr` to be called.

4. The `xx_intr` routine clears the interrupt and then calls `wakeup` to reactivate the write routine.

5. `xx_write` then examines the device status register, and if a device error has occurred it aborts the output and returns an error to the caller. Otherwise, it repeats the output cycle until the request has been satisfied.

The driver does not pass data directly between the write and interrupt routines. However, the write and interrupt routines require the address of an external variable to use as the channel value in their `sleep` and `wakeup` calls. For this purpose they use the base address of the device registers found in `xx_addr[]`. This driver can control any number of devices, and it is assumed that the `xx_init` and `xx_open` routines have verified that the device being written to is in fact online. As will be seen, the code also assumes that the open routine enforces exclusive access by allowing only one process to open a controller at any time.

The complete text of the write routine follows. It is assumed that all `xx` devices issue interrupt requests at priority level four. Instructions that are executed at elevated priority are flagged by the use of `/***` to open their comments.

```
xx_write(device)
dev_t device;             /* minor device number */
{
    struct xx_device *dp;  /* pointer to device base register */
    int outbyte;           /* character being written */
    char status;           /* copy of device status */
    int oldpri;            /* old CPU priority */

    /* get device register pointer */

    dp = (struct xx_device *) xx_addr[device];

    /* process all user characters */

    while ((outbyte=cpass()) >= 0)
    {
        status = dp->xx_sr;       /* get device status */

        if (status != SR_RDY)     /* check for correct status */
        {
            dp->xx_cr = CR_RST;   /* bad status, so reset device */
            /* announce failure on console */
            printf("hardware error--xx controller %d\n",dev_index);
            u.u_error = EIO;      /* return error to caller */
                                                        (continued)
```

```
        return;
    }

    oldpri = spl4();        /*** device ok, so block interrupts */
    dp->xx_cr = CR_EI;      /*** enable interrupts */
    dp->xx_dr = outbyte;    /*** initiate output */
    /*** wait for completion */
    sleep( (caddr_t) &xx_addr[device],PSLEP);
    status = dp->xx_sr;     /*** check completion status */
    splx(oldpri);           /*** restore CPU priority */

    if (status&SR_ERR)      /* check for an error */
    {
        dp->xx_cr = CR_RST; /* got one, so reset device */
        u.u_error = EIO;    /* and return an error */
        return;
    }
}
return;                     /* normal completion */
}
```

This code is very simple, but a few comments are called for. Use of the minor device number as a controller index is a choice, not a UNIX requirement. Some drivers use a portion of the minor number (e.g., the lower four bits) as a controller index and use the remaining bits to select an operating mode. Since the calling process has exclusive access to the device and since the routine always waits for completion of device activity, it is considered to be a serious hardware error if the device is not in the "ready" state. If this happens the routine prints a warning on the system console and returns an error to the caller. It also attempts to clear the problem by issuing a device reset.

Because execution of this routine is completely synchronized with device activity, the code reads the device status register without raising CPU priority to block device interrupts. There should be no possibility of the device status changing before the output is initiated. The CPU priority is raised before the command register and data register are written, and it is important that it not be lowered until after the call to sleep. Otherwise the interrupt handler might execute before that call, and sleep would never return.

Note that the variable outbyte which temporarily holds the output character must be defined as an int rather than a char. The function cpass which fetches bytes from user space returns an integer value so that it can deliver any 8-bit value and return a –1 to indicate that the user byte count has been exhausted.

The code for the interrupt handler is very simple. It clears the interrupt in the hardware and issues a wakeup call to revive the write routine. In this example it is assumed that Field seven of the xx entry in the master configuration file is zero so that xx_intr is called in the polling mode. Because the "attention" bit always indicates whether the device has issued an interrupt, it would also be possible to use a nonzero mask in Field seven for this device. That approach is used in the second example discussed in the next section.

```
    xx_intr(devno,dp)
    int devno;                      /* controller index */
```

```
struct xx_device *dp;          /* pointer to base CSR */
{
    char status;               /* copy of device status */

    status = dp->xx_sr;        /* get device status */
    if (!(status&SR_ATTN))     /* interrupt from this device? */
        return(0);             /* no, so return that fact */

    dp->xx_cr = CR_CA;         /* yes, so clear attention and */
    wakeup((caddr_t)&xx_addr[devno]); /* wake write routine */

    return(1);                 /* indicate interrupt handled */
}
```

In both these routines when it is necessary to check the device status, the code copies the contents of the status register to a memory variable and then tests bits in that variable. Hardware idiosyncrasies in many controllers cause device registers to respond in unpredictable ways to complex instructions like logical ANDs and ORs. If possible device drivers should always access device registers with simple assignment statements.

• Example 2: Characters Buffered in a List •

The second driver example accomplishes the same result as the first one—it moves characters from user space to the device without translation. In this example the strict synchronization between the write routine and the device is relaxed by using a clist structure to queue a small number of characters for output. This intermediate buffering usually allows the interrupt handler to initiate the next device action immediately after the previous one completes, allowing more efficient device operation with fewer software context switches.

This method requires two external data items to coordinate the activities of the driver routines. A clist structure is defined to hold the buffered characters, and a status variable is used to indicate whether the device is currently active and whether it has experienced a hardware error. Whenever the write routine adds a character to the output queue it checks the status variable. If the device is inactive it calls an internal driver routine to initiate the device action. If the status variable shows that the device is already active, the write routine does nothing further. When the interrupt is generated on completion of the current activity, the interrupt handler initiates the next output.

Instead of calling sleep to wait for completion of each character output, the write routine adds characters to the output queue as rapidly as it can until some limiting size is reached. Then it calls sleep to wait for the interrupt handler to reduce the queue to some minimum size and issue a wakeup call. Thus reactivation of the write routine, which requires a context switch to reestablish the calling process as the current process, occurs much less frequently than in the previous example.

To implement this method we add a new driver routine called xx_start whose purpose is to initiate device activity by writing appropriate values to its registers. It can be called either by xx_write or xx_intr; it is not a driver entry point and is never called from outside the driver. Since it may be called in interrupt context it is a driver bottom-half routine that must not refer to user-context variables and must not call `sleep`.

As in the previous example we will not list the entire driver but will merely show the parts that are central to the output activity. At the head of the driver source file, outside of all functions, the following definitions will be needed:

```
#include <sys/tty.h>    /* get clist definition */

int xx_status;          /* define device status flags */
struct clist xx_outq;   /* define output queue */

#define XX_ACT 0x01     /* flag: device is active */
#define XX_ERR 0x02     /* flag: hardware error */

#define active (xx_status&XX_ACT)
#define error  (xx_status&XX_ERR)

#define Q_MAX 24        /* out queue maximum size */
#define Q_MIN 10        /* point to get more characters */
```

The first two `#define` statements establish symbolic names for the individual flags stored in `xx_status`, and the next two create simplified terms to make the subsequent code more readable. The last two `#define` statements set the upper- and lower-queue size limits at which `sleep` and `wakeup` will be called. Note that with the definitions given above the driver will only be able to manage one controller at a time. To support several controllers it would be necessary to maintain a separate output queue and status word for each of them by defining the two variables as arrays.

Because device drivers are linked into the UNIX kernel their external variables are global to the kernel. It is important, therefore, to give them unique names. A good convention to follow is to begin all names with the driver prefix. It would not be wise to define external variables with very general names like `temp` or `status`.

The status word and clist may be initialized in the `xx_init` routine as follows:

```
xx_status = 0;          /* clear active and error flags */
xx_outq.c_cc = 0;       /* indicate clist is empty */
```

Initialization to zero is not necessary because the operating system does this by default. Note that this initialization occurs once only at system bootstrap time; the driver must be certain to update the status flags whenever the hardware status changes. The clist character count will be maintained automatically by the `putc` and `getc` routines.

We can now show the text for the `xx_write` routine. As before we assume that the minor number specifies the controller number, that the device is known to be online, and that it issues interrupts at priority level four.

```
xx_write(dev)
int dev;
{
    int outbyte;        /* temporary store for character */
```

```
    int oldpri;          /* old CPU priority */

while ((outbyte=cpass() >= 0)     /* process all user bytes */
{
    while (xx_outq.c_cc >= Q_MAX  /* wait for room in queue */
          && !error)             /* or hardware error */
       sleep((caddr_t)&xx_outq,PSLEP);

    /* try to queue the byte */
    while (putc(outbyte,&xx_outq) < 0)
       /* if can't, wait a while */
       sleep((caddr_t)&lbolt,PSLEP);

    oldpri = spl4();         /*** block device interrupts */
    if (!active && !error)   /*** check the device state */
       xx_start(dev);        /*** idle, so start it */
    splx(oldpri);            /* restore CPU priority */

    if (error)
    {
       while (getc(&xx_outq) >= 0) /* empty the queue */
          ;
       u.u_error = EIO;            /* return error to user */
       xx_status = 0;             /* clear the device status */
       return;                    /* and exit */
    }
  }
}
```

Ordinarily this routine fills up the output queue to size Q_MAX and then calls sleep. In this example the address of the clist is used as the channel value. The routine will usually be reactivated when the queue size drops to Q_MIN, but the wakeup can also occur if a hardware error is detected by xx_start. If the error flag has been set, xx_write throws away any characters remaining in the queue and returns an error to the caller. Note that in this case the return value seen by the calling process will give the number of bytes transferred to the device driver, not the number actually transferred to the device.

Drivers that use putc to store characters in a clist must take into account the possibility that system clist space will be temporarily exhausted. This should be an extremely rare event, but it is possible for putc to return a failure. This driver deals with the problem by sleeping on the once-per-second alarm lbolt until putc succeeds; a different strategy might be needed in some drivers.

The routine xx_start takes the following form:

```
xx_start(devno)
int devno;
{
    struct xx_device *dp; /* pointer to base CSR */
    char status;          /* temporary device status */
    int temp;             /* temporary outgoing character */


    /* point to CSR base */
```

(continued)

```
dp = (struct device *)xx_addr[devno];

status = dp->xx_sr;        /* get device status */

if (status != SR_RDY)      /* hard error if not ready */
  {
    dp->xx_cr = CR_RST;    /* reset the hardware */
    xx_status = XX_ERR;    /* indicate error status */
    return;
  }

dp->xx_cr = CR_EI;         /* enable interrupts */

if ((temp=getc(&xx_outq) < 0)   /* get next queued byte */
    /* big problem if none there */
    panic("xx_start -- queue empty");

dp->xx_dr = temp;          /* write the byte */
xx_status = XX_ACT;        /* indicate device active */
}
```

This routine normally removes the character from the front of the queue and writes it to the device, but it can be stopped by either of two errors. As in the previous example, if the device is not ready it is assumed that there has been a hardware failure. In this case xx_start issues a device reset in hopes of clearing the problem, sets the XX_ERR flag, and returns without trying to start the device. If getc fails to obtain a character from the output queue, a more drastic action is taken since this situation is logically impossible. panic is called to halt the entire system.

The last routine to discuss is the interrupt handler. In this example we assume that in the master configuration file entry for this driver field six contains the value one (offset from the CSR base to the status register) and field seven contains the value four (mask for the attention bit). xx_intr will therefore be called with three arguments.

```
xx_intr(devno,csr,dp)
int devno;                 /* controller index */
int csr;                   /* status register after interrupt */
struct xx_device *dp;      /* pointer to base CSR */
{
    if (csr&SR_ERR)        /* if device error, reset it */
        dp->xx_cr = CR_RST;
    else
        dp->xx_cr = CR_CA; /* else just clear attention */

    if (xx_outq.c_cc)      /* if more in queue */
    {
        xx_start(devno);   /* start device */

        /* if queue at minimum size or if hardware error */
        if (xx_outq.c_cc == Q_MIN || error)
            wakeup(&xx_outq); /* waken write routine */
```

```
        }
    else
        xx_status = 0;          /* indicate device inactive */
}
```

If this routine sees that a device error has occurred, it resets the device but does not inform anyone of the error. The methods chosen for handling errors both in `xx_intr` and `xx_start` might or might not be appropriate in other drivers.

· Example 3: DMA Output from System-Space Buffers ·

The remaining examples will demonstrate the use of the DMA capability of our hypothetical device. In the current example we assume that this device is a line printer whose driver is required to examine and possibly translate each user character. This requirement makes it necessary for the driver to prepare the output in system-space buffers. Examples 4 and 5 assume that the device can accept the user data unaltered; no system-space buffers are required, and the DMA is performed directly from user space.

In order to make use of the device's DMA capability we must abandon the use of a `clist` to buffer the data and use some form of contiguous memory instead. In this example we use buffers from the kernel block buffering pool. This is a reasonable choice for a device that is used intermittently since the buffers can be released and used for other purposes while it is idle. For a device expected to be in constant use it might be more reasonable to declare private buffer space within the driver.

The logic of this driver is as follows. At system bootstrap time the `xx_init` routine permanently allocates a set of I/O map registers. When a user process issues an `open` call to the device the `xx_open` routine allocates two unused `buf` structures and their corresponding memory buffers from the system buffer pool. During a write operation `xx_write` moves individual characters from user space, examines them for possible translation or expansion, and stores the resulting characters in one of the two system-space buffers. When the first buffer becomes full it is placed on a queue of buffers waiting for DMA output to the device, and fetching and translation of characters continues using the second memory buffer.

The DMA queue is managed in much the same way as the output clist in the previous example. An active flag indicates whether the device is currently busy; if it is inactive when a buffer is added to the queue, `xx_write` calls `xx_start` to initiate the DMA transfer. If the device is already active, output of the newly queued buffer will be initiated by the interrupt handler. When the buffer that has just been filled is placed on the queue, it is possible that the DMA transfer from the other buffer is still in progress. If it is, the driver calls `sleep` to wait for that transfer to complete before processing of user characters is resumed.

The use of two system-space buffers instead of one allows the driver to overlap its character translation activity with the DMA activity of the device. This overlapped I/O is transparent to the user process, which sees each call to the write service as being fully synchronous. If the system-space buffers are larger than the user process `write` requests, several `write` calls may return before any device activity takes place. When DMA is done directly from user space the user process must cooperate with the device driver to accomplish overlapped I/O. See the example of asynchronous I/O in Chapter 10.

This driver requires considerably more logic than the first two. In order to keep the example as simple as possible, we do not include any error checking. In addition, the printer formatting logic included is much simpler than would be found in a real driver. Only two formatting actions are included:

1. A horizontal tab (\t) causes a move to the next column which is a multiple of eight.

2. If a line of text exceeds the width of the page, a newline is inserted to wrap the line.

It is assumed that the device can accept a continuous stream of characters and that it recognizes the newline character as a line separator.

The driver text begins with the following external declarations:

```
#include <sys/buf.h>    /* define offsets for buf structure */

struct buf *xx_bp[2];   /* pointers to output buf structures */
struct buf *xx_abp;     /* pointer to active buf */

int xx_col;             /* current printer column */
int xx_status;          /* device status flags */
int xx_base;            /* index of base I/O map register */
struct buf *xx_qhed;    /* DMA queuehead */

#define LINE_SIZE 132   /* width of printer page */
#define BUFR_SIZE CLUSTER*BSIZE   /* size of output buffer */
#define XX_ACTIVE 0x01 /* device active flag */
#define active (xx_status&XX_ACTIVE)
```

The parameter BUFR_SIZE is the number of bytes that can be stored in a block buffer from the system pool; in MASSCOMP RTU its value is 4096. With its variables defined as above, the driver will support only one device. A multidevice driver would place these variables in a structure and define one structure for each controller.

The initialization routine xx_init will include (among other things) the following code:

```
xx_status = 0;                   /* device is inactive */
xx_bp[0] = xx_bp[1] = NULL;      /* no bufs are allocated */
xx_qhed = NULL;                  /* no bufs are queued */

xx_base = iomalloc(BUFR_SIZE,1); /* allocate I/O map regs */
```

The second argument to iomalloc indicates that the device supports 24-bit MULTIBUS addresses.

Next we show the portion of the xx_open routine that allocates the system-space buffers and initializes the printer variables.

```
xx_bp[0] = geteblk();   /* get two unused buffers */
xx_bp[1] = geteblk();

xx_abp = xx_bp[0];      /* start with the first buf */
xx_abp->b_bcount = 0;   /* clear its byte count */

xx_col = 0;             /* printer at column zero */
```

The xx_write routine fetches characters from user space and executes a switch
to handle control characters. In this simplified example all nonprinting control
characters other than \t and \n are discarded.

```
xx_write(dev)
{
    int temp;               /* temporary character store */


    while ((temp=cpass()) >= 0)   /* process all user characters */
    {
        if (temp >= ' ')    /* just write the normal characters */
            xx_out(temp);
        else                /* handle non-printing values */
        {
        switch (temp)
        {
            case '\t':  /* horizontal tab (\t) */
                do          /* write one or more blanks */
                    xx_out(' ');
                while (xx_col%8);
                break;

            case '\n':  /* newline */
                xx_out('\n');   /* write it */
                xx_col = 0;     /* and reset the column */
                break;

            default:    /* discard all others */
                ;
        }
        }
    }
}
```

The driver routine xx_out adds characters to the current output buffer and
maintains the xx_col value. If the buffer becomes full it is queued for DMA
output; the routine xx_qio performs that action and at the same time selects the
other output buffer for storage of subsequent characters. This latter routine
waits if necessary for completion of DMA output in progress on the other buffer.

```
xx_out(temp)
int temp;       /* output character */
{
    /* store the character */
    *(xx_abp->b_ioaddr+xx_abp->b_bcount++) = temp;

    if (xx_abp->b_bcount == BUFR_SIZE)
        xx_qio();                    /* buf full, so queue it */

    if (++xx_col%LINE_SIZE == 0)  /* at edge of paper? */
    {
        xx_out('\n');                /* yes, so send newline */
        --xx_col;                    /* but don't change column val */
    }
}

xx_qio()
{
    int oldpri;                      /* old CPU priority */

    oldpri = spl4();                 /* block interrupt handler */
    xx_abp->b_flags &= ~B_DONE;      /* indicate buf is queued */

    if (xx_qhed != NULL)             /* anything queued now? */
        xx_qhed->av_forw = xx_abp;   /* yes, so link to it */
    else
        xx_qhed = xx_abp;            /* no, put buf at head */
    xx_abp->av_forw = NULL;          /* mark end of queue */

    if (!active)
        xx_start();                  /* start the device */

    xx_abp = (xx_abp == xx_bp[0])?
            xx_bp[1] : xx_bp[0];     /* switch to other buf */

    while (!(xx_abp->b_flags&B_DONE)) /* and wait for it */
    {
        xx_abp->b_flags |= B_WANTED;
        sleep((caddr_t)xx_abp,PSLEP);
    }
    xx_abp->b_bcount = 0;    /* reset its byte count */
    splx(oldpri);            /* restore CPU priority */
}
```

The xx_start routine loads the device registers to initiate the DMA operation.
It calls panic to close the system down if the I/O queue is empty. This routine
should also check the device status and report a·hardware error; the code to do
so has been omitted to simplify the example.

```
xx_start()
{
    struct buf *lbp;         /* pointer to output buf */
    struct xx_device *dp;    /* pointer to base CSR */
    paddr_t mb_addr;         /* Multibus DMA address */
```

```
    if (xx_qhed == NULL)
        panic("xx_start -- no buf");

    lbp = xx_qhed;              /* buf to be started */
    /* example assumes one controller */
    dp = (struct device *)xx_addr[0];

    /* load the byte count */
    dp->xx_bclb = lobyte(loword(lbp->b_bcount));
    dp->xx_bchb = hibyte(loword(lbp->b_bcount));

    /* load the I/O Map */
    mb_addr = iomaddr(lbp,lbp->b_ioaddr,lbp->b_bcount,xx_base);

    /* load the base address */
    dp->xx_dalb = lobyte(loword(lbp->b_ioaddr));
    dp->xx_damb = hibyte(loword(lbp->b_ioaddr));
    dp->xx_dahb = lobyte(hiword(lbp->b_ioaddr));

    /* start the transfer */
    dp->xx_cr = CR_IE | CR_GO;
}
```

To conclude the example we show the interrupt handler, again omitting any
error checking and reporting.

```
xx_intr(devno,csr,dp)
int devno;
int csr;
struct xx_device *dp;
{
    struct buf *lbp;

    dp->xx_cr = CR_CA;          /* clear the interrupt */

    lbp = xx_qhed;              /* point to completed buf */
    xx_qhed = xx_qhed->av_forw; /* remove from the queue */
    if (xx_qhed != NULL)
        xx_start();             /* start the next one */

    lbp->b_flags |= B_DONE;  /* indicate DMA complete */
    if (lbp->b_flags&B_WANTED)
    {
        wakeup((caddr_t)lbp); /* wake up waiting process */
        lbp->b_flags &= ~B_WANTED;
    }
}
```

One more piece of code is needed to complete the example. When the user process completes its output and calls the close service, one or both of the output
buf structures may be on the output queue, and there may be a partially filled
buffer that has not been queued. The xx_close routine will have to:

1. Queue the last buffer if it is partially filled

2. Wait for DMA to complete on both buffers

3. Release them back to the kernel pool

• Example 4: Synchronous DMA from User Space •

In the previous example the need to translate the user characters made it necessary for the driver to prepare its output in system-space buffers. In cases where the data in the user process buffer can be passed to the device unchanged the overhead associated with moving the data to system space can be avoided. An example would be a plotter for which the user process has prepared line-drawing commands or raster patterns that are already in the format required by the device.

We will provide two examples of driver logic that could be used with a device of this type. In the first example the output will be fully synchronous; the driver will not return from a call to the `write` service until all the data has been transferred to the device. Of course the CPU will be released for use by other processes while the device performs the DMA transfer, but the process requesting the output will be blocked while the transfer takes place.

In these final examples we will not repeat those parts of the code that are essentially the same as in the previous examples. The declarations, init, and open routines, and interrupt handler are all very similar to one or more of the examples given above. We will also continue to ignore the issues of multiple controllers and error handling; real drivers should, of course, handle these subjects more carefully.

The code needed to perform synchronous DMA from user space is similar to that used in the `xx_start` routine in the previous example, but it can all be placed in `xx_write`. The principal differences are

- The user-space data buffer must be locked into physical memory.

- The I/O map must be loaded by the routine `iomapvaddr`, which assumes that the buffer is in the space of the current process.

In the previous example it was not necessary to lock the data buffer into physical memory because under RTU, system space is not paged; it is always resident.

Assuming that the external variable `xx_base` has been defined and loaded as in the previous example, the `xx_write` routine for this example will be as follows:

```
xx_write(dev)
int dev;
{
    paddr_t mb_addr;
    int oldpri;
    struct xx_device *dp;

    vslock(u.u_base,u.u_count);   /* lock user data */
```

```
    /* load I/O map registers */
    mb_addr = iomapvaddr(xx_base,u.u_base,u.u_count);
    dp = xx_addr[(dev)];    /* point to CSR base */
    oldpri = spl4();        /* block device interrupts */

    /*** load the byte count */
    dp->xx_bclb = lobyte(loword(u.u_count));
    dp->xx_bchb = hibyte(loword(u.u_count));

    /*** load the base address */
    dp->xx_dalb = lobyte(loword(mb_addr));
    dp->xx_damb = hibyte(loword(mb_addr));
    dp->xx_dahb = lobyte(hiword(mb_addr));

    /*** start the transfer */
    dp->xx_cr = CR_IE | CR_GO;
    /*** wait for completion */
    sleep((caddr_t)&xx_base, PSLEP);
    /*** restore CPU priority */
    splx(oldpri);

    /* unlock the data */
    vsunlock(u.u_base,u.u_count,B_WRITE);
    u.u_count = 0;          /* show data was written */
    return;
}
```

The address of xx_base was chosen arbitrarily as a convenient channel value to use in the sleep call. vsunlock must be called to restore the user process to its fully pageable and swappable state. The driver must also clear the value of u.u_count so that the calling process will receive the correct return value (number of bytes actually transferred). Only a very simple interrupt handler is needed, similar to the one used in Example 1.

• Example 5: Synchronous I/O Multiplexing •

This example shows the use of a select routine to implement synchronous I/O multiplexing. The example is based on an idealized excerpt from the generic terminal driver.

The arguments passed to this function are:

- A minor device number

- A read/write flag (valued either FREAD or FWRITE) indicating the type of select being performed.

The select function should return one if the indicated operation is possible on the device and zero if it is not.

The address of the global int variable selwait is used by the select system call as a wait channel when it puts a selecting process to sleep.

The function `ttnread` returns the number of characters immediately available for reading on the specified tty device. The function `ttspace` returns the number of characters that may be written to it without blocking. Functions or in-line code appropriate to each driver should be substituted here.

The state information kept by the driver for each device should include the following variables:

```
struct proc     *xx_selr,
                *xx_selw;
char            xx_rcoll,
                xx_wcoll;
```

The `xx_rcoll` and `xx_wcoll` variables are only used to hold boolean values and may therefore be defined as single bit flags in another variable if that is more convenient (as it is in the example). The `xx_selr` and `xx_selw` variables are used to hold a pointer to the `proc` structure for a process doing a select on the associated device. The `xx_rcoll` and `xx_wcoll` flags indicate whether a select collision has occurred on the device. A select collision occurs when several processes are doing a select operation simultaneously on the same device.

```
extern int selwait;

ttselect(dev, rw)
short dev;
int rw;
{
    register struct tty *tp = &tt_tty[dev];
    register struct proc *p;
    register int nread, ret = 0;
    int s = spl6();

    switch(rw) {
    case FREAD:
        if (ttnread(tp) > 0)
            ret = 1;
        else if ((p = tp->t_selr) &&
                p->p_wchan == (caddr_t)&selwait)
            tp->t_state |= TS_RCOLL;
        else
            tp->t_selr = u.u_procp;
        break;
    case FWRITE:
        if (ttspace(tp) > 0)
            ret = 1;
        else if ((p = tp->t_selw) &&
                p->p_wchan == (caddr_t)&selwait)
            tp->t_state |= TS_WCOLL;
        else
            tp->t_selw = u.u_procp;
        break;
    }
    (void)splx(s);
    return ret;
}
```

Whenever the driver receives data from a device and makes it available for reading, code similar to the following should be included. This will normally be accompanied by a check to see if some process is waiting to complete a read operation from this device.

```
if (tp->t_selr)
{
    selwakeup(tp->t_selr, tp->t_state & TSRCOLL);
    tp->t_selr = 0;
    tp->t_state &= ~TSRCOLL;
}
```

Similarly, when a driver moves data out to a device, thereby making additional buffer space available, it should include statements similar to the following:

```
if (tp->t_selw)
{
    selwakeup(tp->t_selw, tp->t_state & TSWCOLL);
    tp->t_selw = 0;
    tp->t_state &= ~TSWCOLL;
}
```

The arguments to the `selwakeup` function are a pointer to a `proc` structure and an integer value which is either zero or nonzero. If nonzero, `selwakeup` is informed that it must awaken all processes that are in the midst of a select operation; otherwise, only the specified process is awakened.

C H A P T E R
7

DRIVER DEVELOPMENT
METHODS

This chapter describes procedures that can be used during the development and testing of a new device driver. Because drivers execute as an integral part of the UNIX kernel, the system is largely unable to protect itself against their errors. Addressing errors will frequently produce hardware traps and a system crash. In addition, the facilities that are available for tracing and error detection are primitive compared with those available for application programs.

In general, debugging driver code can be a very time-consuming and tedious process. The best approach is to do everything possible to avoid introducing errors in the first place. When coding and testing drivers you should take a very cautious approach:

- Do not take chances. Whenever there is any question in your mind about a syntax detail, a variable type, or any other issue, look it up and make sure you have it right.

- Make and test changes incrementally. Do not try to save time by making many changes all at once. You will come out ahead in the long run if you take the time to insert and test one or two things at a time and keep your feet on solid ground.

- Use trace output. Drivers can present you with many surprises, and the best way to learn what they are doing is to maintain complete visibility of the flow of operations and the values of parameters.

- Do not take anything for granted.

This section describes the facilities that are available to support driver testing and suggests ways of approaching the task. In general we recommend relying principally on liberal use of synchronous and asynchronous trace print as described in the next two sections. These methods have the advantage of being portable to nearly all UNIX systems and are simple enough to construct in your own driver. The facilities offered by crash dumps, system debuggers, and console debuggers varies widely among systems from very primitive to extremely powerful. However, even the most capable system debuggers are used to supplement synchronous and asynchronous tracing methods.

• Debugging Macros •

Making good use of the C preprocessor can allow you to incorporate many debugging aids in your device driver in a way that makes it easy to remove these debugging aids from the production version of the driver.

Synchronous Trace Data—`printf` and `uprintf`

The simplest way to observe driver activity and status information is to insert statements in the driver source code that generate printout on the system console. The routine `printf` can be used for this purpose. Many UNIX systems also support the routine `uprintf` which is similar, but prints on the controlling terminal of the current process. Since `uprintf` works by invoking another device driver, it should not be called from a bottom-half routine. The arguments to these routines are identical to those used for the library routine `printf` called by user programs. However, only a subset of the format options are available.

Output generated by `printf` is usually completely synchronous. The characters are not buffered by a device driver, but are sent directly to the device. Consequently no other kernel or user process activity takes place while the output is being produced. Thus overall system performance may be severely limited while trace output is being generated by this method, but that will usually not be an important consideration while a device driver is being debugged. (Output generated by `uprintf` is sent to a device driver and is reasonably efficient.)

In addition to serving as trace printers during debugging, `printf` and `uprintf` can be used in completed drivers to issue informational messages. For example, if a device is offline the driver can print a warning message to the console or user terminal and then sleep until a "ready" interrupt occurs or a fixed time elapses. Because the synchronous output from `printf` uses the system hardware very inefficiently, output of this type in production drivers should be kept to a minimum.

There is a tendency for more complex versions of UNIX to also send `printf` output through some form of device driver for a variety of reasons: on MASSCOMP multiprocessor systems, only one processor is physically capable of communicating with the console device; systems that support multiple windows on a graphics terminal often want to redirect `printf` output to one of these windows. The actual implementation is generally not too important since in these systems it is still possible to call `printf` from any context. However, if `printf` output is buffered in any way you need to realize that your driver code may have returned from the call to `printf` and executed many lines of code by the time the message has actually appeared on the console.

More troublesome is the direct effect that synchronous trace output has on the timing of operations within the driver (and other drivers). The output may be so slow relative to other device operations that interrupts are lost and system failures are introduced; it is frequently impossible to trace an interrupt handler synchronously. Conversely, a sequence of operations involving device activity may work reliably when the individual operations are separated by print activity, but fail when the print is removed. Thus synchronous trace print is not useful in some circumstances. The next section describes a different approach that can be used in these situations.

An additional limitation on the use of these routines is that when the output bypasses the standard device driver, it is not affected by X-OFF and X-ON (Control-S and Control-Q) commands. If the output is produced on a video screen there is no way to prevent it from scrolling at its own rate. It cannot be redirected to a file, but on MASSCOMP systems it can be directed to the system printer (/dev/tty1) by using the -printer switch when booting from the standalone shell. For example:

```
$$ /usr/drivers/uts/unix -single -printer
```

On other systems it may be possible to get the same effect by using an ASCII terminal with a hardcopy option as the system terminal.

One of the drawbacks to inserting explicit print statements in a device driver is that these print statements need to be removed in the production driver. The easiest way to accomplish this is to use a combination of C preprocessor macros, conditional compilation, and control variables to determine when to actually print information. The template drivers include some simple macros that use printf to generate trace information. These macros use a flag variable to determine whether or not to generate trace print. These macros are described in Chapter 8 along with the rest of the driver. The rest of this section will describe some more powerful methods for controlling print statements.

One way of controlling whether to print some trace information is to test a control variable before calling printf:

```
if (debugging)
    printf("Device driver read, device number (%d, %d)\n",
        major(dev), minor(dev));
```

Since printing is controlled by a variable, the value of the variable can be altered while the system is running, either by a special driver action (as is done in the template drivers) or by using a debugger. Finer control over what trace output is produced requires using more control variables, or equivalently, using individual bits of a control variable to control trace output. For example:

```
#define TRACE_OPEN  0x01
#define TRACE_CLOSE 0x02
#define TRACE_READ  0x04
#define TRACE_WRITE 0x08

int debugging = TRACE_OPEN|TRACE_CLOSE|TRACE_READ|TRACE_WRITE;
    .
    .
    .
    if (debugging & TRACE_READ)
        printf("Device driver read, device number (%d, %d)\n",
            major(dev), minor(dev));
```

The variable debugging can be set to all ones (-1) to enable all trace output or to zero to disable all trace output. If it is set to the value three, then trace output related to opening and closing the device will appear, but tracing will not occur for reading or writing.

We can take this one step further by using a preprocessor variable to control whether any code related to tracing is included in the driver:

```
#ifdef DEBUG
#define TRACE_OPEN   (debugging & 0x01)
#define TRACE_CLOSE  (debugging & 0x02)
#define TRACE_READ   (debugging & 0x04)
#define TRACE_WRITE  (debugging & 0x08)

int debugging = -1;
#else
#define TRACE_OPEN  0
#define TRACE_CLOSE 0
#define TRACE_READ  0
#define TRACE_WRITE 0
#endif
    .
    .
    .
    if (TRACE_READ)
        printf("Device driver read, device number (%d, %d)\n",
            major(dev), minor(dev));
```

If debugging has been disabled then `TRACE_READ` will be defined as the constant zero so the print statement can never be executed. Many C compilers will remove so-called dead code. The effect is similar to having surrounded the `printf` statement with `#ifdef DEBUG` and `#endif`. However, the use of ordinary conditional statements often makes the code more readable since the preprocessor statements break the indentation.

You can determine whether your compiler removes dead code by looking at the sizes of object code compiled both ways—if the code with `DEBUG` undefined is not smaller than the code with `DEBUG` defined, your compiler has not removed the dead code. If your C compiler does not remove dead code or prints warning messages when it encounters dead code you may want to put in explicit `#ifdef`s, or you can use macros similar to the ones in the template drivers and described in Chapter 8.

Assertions

A common cause of problems in device drivers (and indeed, in any program) is making assumptions that turn out not to be justified. These mistakes may arise from simply misunderstanding the interaction between various pieces of code or may be a result of using the device driver in a different environment. Any assumptions you make in writing your device driver should be documented somewhere in the driver itself, particularly if you know or expect the assumption to be false in other environments.

Describing these assumptions in comments will make it easier for someone else to understand the code (and will also make it easier for you if you have to go back and change the code some time later). However, the computer will not be able to check their validity unless you include some executable code to check these assumptions. This is simply a matter of including explicit checks in your code, even for things that "can not happen." If they *do* happen, it is much easier to debug your driver if it has printed an explanatory message and halted than if it simply proceeded on the basis of incorrect data.

For example, a very common cause of problems is using a NULL pointer as if it pointed to a real data structure. Depending on the memory management hardware of a machine and how it is used by the operating system, this may or may not result in an illegal memory reference. In any case, you can protect your code by testing pointer variables before they are used:

```
if (p == NULL)
    panic("Driver routine: p is NULL\n");
if (p->p_flags & BUSY)
    .
    .
    .
```

For simple assumptions like this, it is often easier to use a macro that will check a condition and print a standard message if this condition is not satisfied. There is a standard C library routine assert (actually implemented as a macro) that performs this function for UNIX application programs. The macro is defined in /usr/include/assert.h and can easily be adapted for use inside device drivers and other kernel routines. In System V.3 this macro is called ASSERT and is defined in /usr/include/sys/debug.h:

```
#ifdef DEBUG
#define ASSERT(condition) \
  if (!(condition)) {\
    printf("Assertion failed at line _line_ of file _file_\n"); \
    panic("condition\n"); \
  }
#else
#define ASSERT(condition)
#endif
```

Here _file_ and _line_ are special symbols recognized by the preprocessor that are replaced by the line number and source file where the call to ASSERT occurred. Using the ASSERT macro the previous code fragment becomes:

```
ASSERT(p != NULL);
if (p->p_flags & BUSY)
    .
    .
    .
```

An additional advantage of ASSERT is that it will automatically be ignored if DEBUG has not been defined. This makes it easy to remove the extra code to check these assertions from production device drivers. This makes it unsuitable for checking conditions that you feel ought to be checked even in production drivers. You can either include checking code as in the first example or define your own macro similar to ASSERT that always checks the condition, even if DEBUG was not defined.

Checking External Declarations with lint

One of the weaknesses of C as a programming language is its lack of type checking in all situations. In particular, most C compilers do not check the types of arguments to functions, nor do they verify types of variables that are defined in separately compiled files. Instead of being implemented by the compiler and linker, these type checking functions are implemented by a program named lint. This simplifies the compiler and linker and allows them to run somewhat faster, but requires more discipline on the part of the programmer to use strong type checking throughout the program.

In order to do its job, lint needs to process all the source code that is compiled and linked together to form a single executable program. While this is not feasible for someone adding a driver to a UNIX system without a source license, you do not need to check the entire system to ensure that type usage in your device driver is correct. lint can be instructed to check external declarations against a library of functions. By default, a lint library corresponding to the standard C library is used. However, you can write your own lint library declaring the functions you use in your device driver (see the documentation for lint that came with your system to see whether user constructed libraries are available and how to construct them).

A simpler alternative that works well for checking function usage in a single file uses conditional compilation to provide full function declarations for lint that are not normally part of the driver. lint works by processing normal preprocessor commands and also defines a special symbol, LINT, when it processes each file. You can optionally include additional declarations and definitions in your driver depending on the value of LINT. Since these function definitions will never be executed, they only need to declare the type of the function and the type of each argument. Functions should also include a return statement specifying a dummy value. For example, in order to make sure you always call the physio routine with the proper arguments you can include the following code in your device driver:

```
#ifdef LINT
void physio(strat, bp, dev, flag, minphys)
int (*strat)();
struct buf *bp;
short dev;
int flag;
unsigned (*minphys)();
{
}
#endif LINT
```

This declares physio to be a routine that does not return a value (if your version of lint or your C compiler does not recognize the keyword void, do not declare any explicit type for physio).

• Tracing Driver Actions •

Synchronous Trace Data, this chapter, described the limitations on synchronous trace print that make it inconvenient or impossible to use in some circumstances. An alternate method that can be used in these cases is to have the driver store trace information in a memory buffer from which it can be retrieved or printed at a later, more convenient time.

Some versions of UNIX support a special device /dev/trace for tracing the action of the operating system or other device drivers. This device is described in Section 4 of the *UNIX Programmer's Manual.* If your version of UNIX does not support this device, it is not difficult to implement a similar capability entirely within the driver being tested. In this section we will describe the method in a general way. We leave it to the reader to write the required code.

The most convenient place to store trace data temporarily within a driver is on a clist. You can define a clist for this purpose and write a routine that moves bytes onto the list by using the putc function. Arguments to that routine can specify the source address and byte count. In order to avoid the possibility of exhausting the system clist buffers, the routine should keep track of how many bytes are on the list and discard trace data rather than exceed some maximum size. Then place calls to that routine at points where you wish to save snapshots of trace data. These calls will, of course, be temporary and will be moved around as you debug the driver.

To complete the facility, provide a special way of calling the driver in order to remove the data from the list. This can be done by means of an ioctl function or by issuing a read to the driver using a special minor number. When the driver is called in this way it should remove bytes from the head of the list and move them into the space of the calling process; that process can then display the data on a terminal or printer. You will need to devise a code that identifies individual items in the list by size and perhaps by name.

A simpler alternative to a trace device is to store trace information in a circular buffer declared in the driver. This method assumes that you can use a debugger of some sort to access the buffer and also assumes that you do not need to capture all the tracing information produced by the device but are only interested in finding out what happened shortly before a crash or some other interesting point in time. The buffer itself will usually be declared as an array of structures. For example, the following code shows how you might trace the last 20 read, write, open, or close calls in a device driver:

```
#define NTRACE 20

struct trace {
    int        routine;   /* which routine was called */
    int        dev;       /* major and minor device */
    caddr_t    base;      /* values of u.u_base */
    int        count;     /* and u.u_count at time of call */
} dev_trace[NTRACE];

struct trace *dev_tracep = &dev_trace[0];
```

```
#define DEV_OPEN     1
#define DEV_CLOSE    2
#define DEV_READ     3
#define DEV_WRITE    4

dev_trace(routine, dev)
{
    /* save trace information in current entry */
    dev_tracep->routine = routine;
    dev_tracep->dev = dev;
    dev_tracep->base = u.u_base;
    dev_tracep->count = u.u_count;
    /* advance pointer to the next entry */
    /* wrapping around at the end of the buffer */
    if (++dev_tracep >= &dev_trace[NTRACE])
        dev_tracep = &dev_trace[0];
}
```

This would be called from the device driver using the definitions DEV_OPEN and so forth. The trace data would usually be examined by printing the entire dev_trace buffer (80 integers) and using dev_tracep to determine where the latest entry had been made.

Since this trace routine uses a circular buffer there is no problem with it exhausting system resources. The amount of data stored is limited but can easily be made larger.

Using Utilities to Examine Driver and Process State

There will be times when you will need to know what your device driver is doing but you will not have the benefit of tracing information: this might occur when running a production version of a driver that encounters a new bug or in a debugging version of the driver that gets into difficulties in an area not covered by tracing calls. There are still many tools that can be used to try to discover what the device driver is doing.

The ps Command.   The ps command is a standard UNIX utility that prints the status of some or all processes on the system. ps has many options that vary among different types of UNIX systems. However, nearly all ps commands have an option that prints the state of each process. For example, on MASSCOMP systems the process state is printed by either the -l or the -v options (most versions of ps will print state information if given the -l option). The state is a single character, which may be one of:

n   Active on CPU *n* (always zero on a uniprocessor system)

A   Active and in execution transition

R   Runnable, but not assigned to any processor

S   Sleeping, but can be signaled (priority > PZERO)

P   Waiting for page-in (any sleep in a page fault)

D   Sleeping, but cannot be signaled (priority <= PZERO, usually waiting for disk I/O)

I   Inactive (sleeping more than 20 seconds)

T   Stopped (by a debugger or by job control)

Z   Terminated

Most of the time ps will show the program using your device driver in the S, D, or I states depending on what priority the driver sleeps at and how long it has been sleeping.

You can get additional information about your process from the priority (PRI) and wait channel (WCHAN) fields of ps -l output. If the process is sleeping, the priority is the priority given to the call to sleep inside the operating system. More important, the wait channel is the event the process is waiting for. Very often the wait channel will uniquely identify a call to sleep in your device driver. Even when this is not true (e.g., the template character device driver sleeps using the output queue as a wait channel in both ch_write and ch_start), the wait channel will give you an idea of where to start looking in your source code for places to put additional trace calls.

The crash Command. If your system implements the crash utility (usually available only on systems derived from AT&T System III or System V) you can get much more information about the state of the system. You can use crash to examine a running system or to examine a *postmortem* memory image made after the system has crashed. We will briefly describe how to use crash on a running system in this section. It is used essentially the same way to examine crash dumps except the name of a file containing the crash dump must be given as an argument. See the manual page in the *UNIX Programmer's Manual* for more details on crash.

crash is an interactive utility for examining the physical memory image of an operating system. It knows how to print many important system data structures in a useful format. For example, it can print process table slots in a format similar to the ps command when given the proc command. It can also print additional information, but this is usually done for only a single entry in the process table to reduce the amount of output and avoiding scrolling information off the screen of a video terminal.

crash usually uses the index within a table to identify entries rather than using information in the table entry itself. For example, processes are identified by their index in the process table rather than their process identifiers, and inodes are identified by their index in the system inode table rather than their device and inode numbers. You will need to print these tables and examine the output visually to identify individual entries, although when crash prints table entries that link to other tables, it will print the index in the appropriate table rather than a raw pointer. For example, the file command, which prints the open file table, prints the index in the inode table for each open file (along with the open file flags and other information associated with an open file).

The trace command is probably the most useful command for debugging device drivers. This will print a *kernel backtrace* of the specified process. A backtrace is the list of currently active function calls and their arguments. A function call is active if it has not yet returned. For example, the backtrace of a process waiting for terminal input might look like:

```
crash>STACK TRACE: csh
_swtch(f82d9898) from _sleep+230 frame ffff9e68
_sleep(f82ba268,1c) from _canon+1de frame ffff9e94
_canon(f82ba268) from _ttread+1e frame ffff9efc
_ttread+1a(f82ba268) from duartread+50 frame ffff9f34
_duartread+4e(0) from _cdev_read+142 frame ffff9f4c
_cdev_read+140(f82d8800,-6dc8) from _read1+70 frame ffff9f74
_read1(-6dc8) from read+10 frame ffff9f8c
_read+c() from _syscall+1ec frame ffff9f98
_syscall() from trap32+14 frame ffff9fa8
trap32+e() from 25643b25 frame 7ffae28

crash>
```

In this example, the `sleep` routine was called from the `canon` routine. The wait channel (the first argument to `sleep`) was F82BA268 and the sleep priority (the second argument) was 30, indicating that the process can be signaled out of this call to `sleep`. Note that the backtrace stops at `syscall`, the kernel system call handler, and does not display any information about function calls in the user process.

`crash` can also display the contents of memory with the `od` command. `crash` knows about the external symbols in a device driver, but is not a source level debugger and does not know how to interpret the names of local variables in your device driver, nor is it able to specially format the values of arbitrary structure variables. If you are capable of machine-level debugging of compiled programs you can use the `u` command to print the user structure associated with a process (including the values of registers for that process) and the `stack` command to print the kernel stack.

Using `adb` to get Kernel Backtraces. If your system does not support `crash` but does support a debugger such as `adb`, you may still be able to get symbolic kernel backtraces. Some versions of `adb` have been enhanced to understand the memory management and page table structures of a particular machine and version of UNIX. These versions of `adb` usually use the flag `-k` to indicate that this "virtual memory" mode should be turned on. When used as a kernel debugger `adb` is invoked as

```
adb -k /unix /dev/mem
```

where `/unix` is replaced by the name of the system image that was actually booted. See the documentation that comes with your version of `adb` to see whether "virtual" mode is supported and what other special commands are available for examining the address space of a given process.

If your version of `adb` does not support the `-k` option, all is not lost, but you will have to do much more of the work. `adb` will print backtraces when given the `$c` command, but you will have to set up `adb`'s address mapping for the process and will have to locate the last stack frame for `adb`. In order to print a backtrace, `adb` only needs to examine the kernel address space of the process, not the entire user virtual address space. In fact, it is only necessary to examine the kernel stack of the process, although in most versions of UNIX the kernel address space of all processes are identical except for the user structure and the kernel stack, which are stored next to each other.

First, invoke adb to examine physical memory with the command:

```
# adb /unix /dev/mem
```

The mapping operations performed by adb are fairly simple: adb keeps separate maps for looking at its text file and its data file. Each map contains two entries that are examined sequentially. Each entry has a starting position or base, a length, and an offset. When adb examines an address it checks to see if it is greater than or equal to the base address of a map and less than the base address plus the length. If it is, the data is found in the corresponding file by adding the offset to the address.

You can use the $m command to adb to examine the address map currently in use. The address map for the text file uses the two map entries to refer to the text and data segment of the text file, skipping past the header at the beginning of the file. You will probably not need to change the length or offset for the text map entries, but may need to change the base addresses. adb normally assumes that lowest virtual address in the text file is zero. This is usually true for programs that are executed in user mode, but may or may not be true for the kernel itself. On the MC5500 the kernel uses virtual address zero, but on the MC5400 the kernel begins at virtual address 0xF8000000, and on the MC5600 the kernel begins at virtual address 0xC80000000. The linker needs to be told the base address of your system when it creates the executable file. You use this base address in setting new map entries for the text map with a command sequence:

```
?m 0xF80000000
?*m 0xF8000000+<b
```

In this example we assume that the header of an executable file is 32 bytes long and have used the adb variable <b to compute the base virtual address of the data segment. You should use the $m command before and after changing the maps to ensure that you have only changed the base addresses by adding 0xF80000000, and not the lengths or the offsets.

The address map for the data file uses the first entry to map the data segment of the program (which contains the data and bss segments of the executable as well as any memory dynamically allocated by the program using the brk or sbrk system calls) and uses the second entry to address the stack. adb will probably not recognize /dev/mem as a core file so the address maps for the data file will be empty. For examining kernel state we will use the first entry to map the user structure and kernel stack of a process and use the second entry to map the rest of kernel memory. The exact command to use depends on how virtual addresses are set up for each system. For MC5500 systems where kernel virtual addresses and kernel physical address begin at zero, the proper command is:

```
/*m 0 _end 0
```

For MC5600 systems where kernel virtual addresses begin at 0xC8000000 and physical addresses begin at 0x80000000 the command is:

```
/*m 0xC8020000 -1 0
```

Since the mapping performed by adb is fairly simple, you will not be able to map the user structure and kernel stack unless they are contiguous in physical memory. This is true for MASSCOMP systems and other systems with fairly large page sizes, and it is also true for UNIX systems that do not implement virtual memory. On these systems the process address field (ADDR) printed by the ps command contains the address of the user structure. Since the same field is used to contain the address of the user structure in physical memory if it is currently loaded into memory, or the disk address if the process is swapped out, you will need to make sure the process is not currently swapped out. This is indicated by a bit in the FLAGS field displayed by ps (refer to your system's documentation for ps to see which bit). You will also need to know the scaling factor that must be applied to the address. This is usually specified by the ctob macro in /usr/include/sys/param.h. For MASSCOMP systems, the address is kept as a physical page number and must be multiplied by the page size, 4096. This can be done by converting the page number to hexadecimal and adding three zeros. Finally, this is used as the offset in the first mapping. For example, if ps reports that the user structure of a process is at address 102, set up the mapping using the commands:

```
102=X
    66
/m u u+4096 0x66000
```

Note that we used the symbolic name of the user structure and a constant for the length of the user structure and kernel stack.

Having done all this setup, we are finally in a position to start looking for the top of the kernel stack. The user structure must contain a copy of the saved registers for the process, including the stack pointer and frame pointer. It is often stored at the beginning of the user structure, but you will need to examine the declaration of the user structure in /usr/include/sys/user.h to find out exactly where. Traditionally the registers are stored in a "label" variable named u.u_rsav in the same format used by setjmp and longjmp, but they may also be stored in a process control block (PCB).

If you find the value of the frame pointer for the top of the stack, you can use this value as an argument to $c. If done properly, you will get essentially the same backtrace as would be printed by crash, although the exact format may be different.

adb can also be used to examine any kernel data structures. You do not have to go through all the mapping stages given above and can short-cut them altogether by using the special device that corresponds to kernel virtual memory:

```
# adb unix /dev/kmem
```

Using adb instead of crash to examine variables has the advantage that adb's format strings can be used to display data structures with different lengths and types. However, crash is much more convenient for displaying those data structures that it does know about.

Debugging Panics

panic is a routine that can be called in order to halt execution of the UNIX system; it is called when it appears that there has been either a hardware error or a kernel programming error. It takes as its single argument a pointer to a string to be displayed on the console before the system is halted. The final version of a driver should call panic only if conditions arise that should be impossible.

A common result of a coding or logic error in a driver is a reference to an illegal address—one that does not map either to system memory or to a device register. An error of this kind produces a hardware fault and a trap through the system exception vector table. The trap handler prints some information about the current kernel mode (the contents of registers) and then calls panic.

The precise action of panic varies from system to system. On MASSCOMP systems the kernel can be configured to include a kernel debugger called kdb. Whenever an illegal memory reference occurs or panic is called, control passes to kdb. The commands to kdb are a combination of adb commands or crash commands preceded with a percent sign (%). Therefore, a backtrace of the current process is produced by either the command $c or %trace. Other commands can be issued to kdb to examine other tables or variables in the kernel.

You can also use kdb to set breakpoints in the device driver or other parts of the kernel and to execute the kernel one instruction at a time. In short, kdb provides all the interactive debugging capabilities for the kernel that adb provides for user programs. It is possible to configure kdb so that typing Control-P on the system console will activate kdb. If you have a MASSCOMP system, you can find more information on configuring and using kdb in the *System Management Guide* for your system.

If kdb has not been configured with your system, the contents of the processor registers is displayed on the console and the system enters an infinite loop. The information that is displayed on the console when a hardware fault occurs can be very helpful. The values that are of immediate interest include pc, the address of the instruction following the one that generated the fault, and fltaddr, the illegal address that was used. The contents of other processor registers also appear.

If your system includes a magnetic tape drive, you can obtain a crash dump of memory after a panic. The *System Management Guide* provided with your system should provide a description of how to make a crash dump on your system. After the system is rebooted, the crash dump can be copied to disk and examined using adb or crash. The name of the crash dump file and the name of the system file may need to specified as arguments to the adb or crash commands.

Using the Debugger—adb

Whenever possible we recommend using trace print to isolate driver problems, but there are times when a debugger like adb can be helpful. As described previously, adb may be useful in obtaining kernel backtraces on systems that do not have the crash utility. There are many other cases in which you might want to use adb. We will not attempt to give complete instructions for using adb here. See the manual page for adb in Volume 1A of the *UNIX Programmer's Manual*. We will give one example of how the debugger might be used.

Assume that a memory or bus fault has occurred and that you want to determine which line of code in the driver generated the fault. When the fault occurs you must write down the value of pc displayed on the console by the fault handler; that is, the address of the instruction following the one that generated the fault. When the system comes back up, run adb on the kernel file that experienced the fault (normally /usr/drivers/uts/unix). By asking for the symbolic address and contents of the program counter value that was displayed by the fault handler, you can locate the exact instruction that caused the fault.

For example, if the fault handler displayed pc = 2d61a, the following commands might be used:

```
% cd /usr/drivers/uts
% adb unix
10000 $s
0x2d61a?i
_ch_init+138            extw   d0
^
_ch_init+134       movb   a0@,d0
$q
%
```

The fifth line is printed by adb in response to the command just above it. It shows the address of the instruction following the faulty one, relative to the nearest preceding symbol found in the symbol table—in this case ch_init. It then shows the instruction itself in assembler format. The next command causes it to back up one instruction to the one that actually caused the fault. Using this information you can examine an assembly language listing of the driver generated by the compiler and determine exactly what part of the code was being executed when the fault occurred.

A similar sequence is used to analyze a crash dump. You may need to copy the crash dump from magnetic tape to a disk file first. A typical command sequence is:

```
% cd /usr/drivers/uts
% dd if=/dev/rmt0 of=core bs=4k
% adb unix core
?m 0xF80000000
10000 $s
0x2d61a?i
_ch_init+138            extw   d0
^
_ch_init+134       movb   a0@,d0
$q
%
```

Note that in general, it will be necessary to perform the mapping operation described in the previous section in order to examine the text and data sections of memory. If you just want to determine where a fault occurred, you need only to set up the mapping for the text file. Also, since the text of the kernel is read only, you would not have to read in a crash dump in this case either.

In some cases the value of pc displayed during a crash will not be properly aligned with a machine instruction. If that happens, instead of printing an assembler instruction adb will print ???. If that happens you can enter addresses that differ from pc by two bytes, four bytes, and so on until you align with a legal instruction.

adb can also be used to examine and perhaps alter the kernel that is running. To do this, specify the file /dev/kmem, which is a window into kernel virtual memory:

```
# cd /usr/drivers/uts
# adb -w unix /dev/kmem
```

This will allow you to examine dynamic variables within an active driver. Be absolutely sure that you use the currently running version of the operating system. You can check this by trying to examine the start of your device driver entry points.

Using the System Console Mode

If a system crash occurs you may want to examine the values of driver variables at the time of the crash. If you are not able to make a crash dump, or do not wish to take the time to make a crash dump and read it in, you can try using the system console mode to accomplish the same thing. Your system may refer to a system "monitor" or "PROM monitor" instead of "console mode," and the exact syntax may vary widely between systems. However, most systems have some ability to display memory and process registers, and often to set breakpoints or execute programs one instruction at a time. These monitors generally are unable to read symbol tables of the programs they are debugging so all values must be entered as absolute hexadecimal or octal numbers.

The console commands for MASSCOMP systems are described in the *System Management Guide*. For MC5500 systems, you can place the leftmost front panel switch in the CONSOLE position and push the RESET switch to the HARDWARE position. The console will display the >>> prompt. Type an M command in order to enable memory. You can then use the E command to examine specific locations in memory. You will need to have previously used adb or nm to determine the hexadecimal addresses of the variables of interest. A more powerful and flexible alternative is to have access to a terminal connected to another system (which presumably has not crashed) that has a copy of your source and object code. You can then use adb and other programs interactively on this other system to help you examine memory on the system with your device driver.

Usually, the most useful piece of information after a system crash is the backtrace of active function calls. We have already described how to get this backtrace using adb or crash. If you only have a debugging monitor available, you can still get the backtrace information provided you know enough about how code is compiled for your machine.

A complete description of compilers and the run time structure of compiled code is outside the scope of this book. However, we can give a very brief description based on the Motorola 68000 family of processors and typical C compilers. This description should suffice to let you create your own backtrace on these machines and many similar machines.

Variables in C belong to one of several *storage classes* that determine how these variables are accessed by compiled code. *External* and *static* variables are accessed using absolute addresses. The only difference between external and static variables is that external variables can be accessed directly from separately compiled files while static variables can only be accessed outside the file containing the static variable if some function inside that file passes a pointer to that variable to some other function or assigns a pointer to that variable to some other external variable. *Register variables* are stored directly in processor registers. Since there are only a limited number of registers, each function is responsible for saving the previous value of any register variables when that function is entered and for restoring those values when it returns. Arguments to a function are passed on the stack, and *automatic variables* are also stored on the stack.

The stack is organized as a series of *stack frames*, one stack frame for each active function call. In its pure form, data is written to the stack by "pushing" values—adjusting the *stack pointer* to point to the next entry and writing a value. Data is "popped" off the stack by reading the value addressed by the current stack pointer and then adjusting the stack pointer to address the previous entry. On MC68000s the stacks grow downward. That is, pushing data on the stack decreases the value of the stack pointer and popping data increases the stack pointer. The stack pointer itself is always kept in a special processor register, address register seven (also called A7 or SP).

While arguments and automatic variables could be addressed relative to the stack pointer, it is more common for compiler to set up explicit stack frames and use a *frame pointer* to point to the base of each stack frame. Most MC68000 compilers use address register six (A6 or FP) for this purpose. Each stack frame is set up by pushing the previous value of the frame pointer on the stack and setting the new frame pointer to the current value of the stack pointer. This is done using the `link` instruction. A typical stack frame looks like:

```
        argument n
        argument n–1
        .
        .
        .


        argument 1
        return address
FP-> previous frame pointer
        saved register variables
        automatic variables
SP-> automatic variable or temporary value
```

As can be seen, the saved frame pointers on the stack form a linked list of stack frames. The return address is stored in the word just after the saved frame pointer. Arguments to that function are stored after the return address. Automatic variables local to a function are addressed using negative offsets off the frame pointer.

On MASSCOMP systems, a sequence of console commands to construct a backtrace could be:

```
>>>E/I
<first pc>
>>>E/A 6
A 000001              <first fp>
>>>E/V/N:4            <first fp>
V <first fp>          <second fp>
V <first fp+4>        <second pc>
V <first fp+8>        <first argument to first function>
V <first fp+12>       <second argument to first function>
>>>E/P/N:4            <second fp>
V <second fp>         <third fp>
V <second fp+4>       <third pc>
V <second fp+8>       <first argument to second function>
V <second fp+12>      <second argument to second function>
```

And so on. Eventually you will reach a stack frame that corresponds to the system call and will reference a stack frame in user virtual address space. This occurs when the frame pointer is not on the same page as the user structure. Actually, on MASSCOMP systems a special "idle" stack is used in some circumstances so that the kernel stack frames may either be in the idle stack or on the same page as the user structure, but you should stop your backtrace when you find a stack frame on the same page as the user structure which points to a stack frame on another page. Also notice that the stack frames appear slightly out of sync if you only look at the data column (i.e., the second stack frame contains the frame pointer and return PC for the third function and the arguments to the second function).

On other machines, the format of stack frames may be somewhat different, and the monitor commands used to examine memory will almost certainly be different. However, the principle remains the same: the stack will consist of a series of stack frames, and each stack frame contains a pointer to the previous stack frame, the return address for this function call, and the arguments to this function call. You will need to refer to the documentation that came with your system (and possibly examine some machine language code produced by your compiler) to determine the exact format of stack frames on your system. The format of stack frames is often described in compiler reference manuals in a section describing the interface to assembly language routines.

8

TEMPLATE CHARACTER AND BLOCK DRIVERS

This chapter describes a template character driver and a template block driver. These drivers are intended to demonstrate basic driver principles and to serve as starting points for development of your own drivers. The character driver, chdriver, supports pseudodevices that behave like UNIX pipes. The block driver, bkdriver, supports pseudodevices that behave like small disks. The block driver also supports raw devices and raw I/O.

This chapter discusses the internal details of each driver. The following section describes the overall arrangement of the template drivers and some of the features that they have in common. **Template Character Driver—chdriver**, this chapter, gives a detailed description of the template character driver. **Template Block Driver—bkdriver**, this chapter, does the same for the block driver, but it is briefer since much of what was said about the character driver also applies to the block driver.

· Common Features ·

This section describes the characteristics of the template drivers that are common to the two. These include the ordering of the parts, the formatting of the code and comments, and the trace print macros.

These drivers are designed to serve as tutorial examples. They are unlike most device drivers in that they do not use any special peripheral hardware; they control pseudodevices that are implemented entirely within the driver software. They are not intended to be useful tools for system users; their features have been selected to demonstrate standard device driver methods and possibilities.

Layout of Code and Comments

As long as all the required declarations and entry points are included, the arrangement of the parts of a device driver is largely a matter of personal choice. Because these two drivers are being provided as examples and templates, they have been formatted in a very regular way with all their components clearly labeled and explained. If you use them as templates for new drivers, you can retain this explanatory layout as an aid to documentation and remove the parts of the code that are not useful in your application.

The overall ordering of parts that is used in both drivers is as follows:

1. The driver name and a brief description of its logic

2. References to include files and definitions of trace print macros

3. Definitions of special symbols and macros used by the driver

4. Declarations of external variables and data structures

5. The initialization routine

6. The top-half (user context) routines

7. The interrupt handler and other bottom-half routines

Each driver entry point appears on a separate page and begins with a boxed-in label and brief description. Comments are included to indicate points where code to deal with hardware must be added for drivers that control real devices.

Standard Include Files

There are three include files that define symbols and variables that are used in almost all drivers: `param.h`, `systm.h`, and `user.h`. Drivers must also include `dir.h` to satisfy a reference in `user.h`. All drivers must define the symbol `KERNEL`, which is used in several include files to declare kernel data structures conditionally. The template drivers define this symbol in their source code.

These required define and include statements are the first code that appears in each template driver. You should leave them in all the drivers you develop.

Macro Definitions for Trace Print

These template drivers use two simple macros called `TRACE_TXT` and `TRACE_VAL` to generate synchronous trace print on the console. The first macro prints a line of text, and the second one prints text followed by a value; the value is printed in octal, decimal, and hexadecimal. The print is conditional and appears only if a boolean trace control variable is nonzero. Both drivers set the trace print on in their initialization routines; `chdriver` allows it to be turned off by an `ioctl` call.

The trace print macro definitions have the same form in both drivers, but they use distinct control variables. Because all device drivers are linked into the RTU kernel, they share external variables. If two drivers use the same external variable name to control trace print (or for any other purpose) they will both refer to the same memory location.

More elaborate trace macros can easily be constructed. For example, it might be useful to cause certain values of the control variable to direct the print to the user terminal by calling `uprintf`. The principal drawback of synchronous trace print is that it cannot be paused by entering a Control-S. One solution is to boot the system from a hardcopy console or use the `-printer` option at boot time. Another is to use `uprintf` and activate the driver from a hardcopy terminal. Because `uprintf` uses clists with no limit checking, large volumes of output, or Control-S for long periods of time can cause the clist supply to run out. To avoid this, specify a large number in your site configuration file (`MC5500` on the MASSCOMP-shipped system).

• Template Character Driver—`chdriver` •

The template character driver, `chdriver`, supports pseudodevices that act somewhat like UNIX pipes. The `ch` devices are FIFO queues that buffer characters between their writing and reading processes. You can demonstrate the operation of the driver by using the `cp` utility to copy data from a file to one of its devices and from there to another file. The driver generates synchronous trace messages on the system console so that the details of operation are visible.

The driver is intended to serve both as an example and as a starting point for development of other drivers. Therefore it contains some code that is not strictly required to support its simple pseudodevices. In order to make them more typical, some of its routines are written as if they were dealing with real hardware. Parts of this logic will never be executed in the delivered template driver but may be directly usable in drivers adapted from it. Comments in the code and the explanations given below make it clear which parts of the code are arbitrary examples and which parts are standard driver methods.

Implemented Device Characteristics

Characters written to a `ch` device are placed on a clist that serves as the device's memory. A defined parameter `D_MAX` sets a limit on the size of this memory; if it becomes full, the driver output routine, `ch_start`, issues a `wakeup` on the clist address and calls `sleep`. It remains suspended until some other process reads some characters from the device. When that happens the driver read routine issues a `wakeup` call to alert the output routine that it can place more characters on the queue.

If a call to the driver read routine causes it to empty the device before the read is satisfied, it sends a `wakeup` to the output routine and goes to sleep. Therefore a large file can be written to the device and read from it; the write and read routines will alternate their activity until the entire file has passed through the device.

When the read routine empties the device, it needs a way of knowing whether a writer is waiting to send more data to it. Therefore a special end-of-file (EOF) character is used to mark the end of a transmission. Once this character is seen in the data stream all further reads and writes to the device are inhibited until all processes close the device. This logic makes the driver compatible with the `cp` utility as long as the file written to it ends with the EOF character. (Note that this is not an acceptable way to implement a production pipe driver.)

The `chdriver` template demonstrates some other features that are frequently needed in drivers. It assumes that its individual device units are multiplexed on controllers; each controller supports two device units. When a device is opened it obtains exclusive use of its controller. The other device attached to that controller cannot be opened until the first device is closed. (A more sophisticated form of exclusive use would allow both devices to be opened and cause a device to own the controller only while a write was actually in progress.)

The driver also demonstrates how a bit in the minor device number can be used to set a device mode. Only four bits in the minor number specify the unit number. If a fifth bit is set, the device converts all lowercase characters to uppercase.

Configuration Data

The system configuration data for chdriver is delivered in the files ch.master and ch.dfile. Each file contains a single line of data that can be added to the corresponding configuration data file.

The baseline MASSCOMP system configuration files include entries for both real devices and pseudodevices. Although the ch devices are not real hardware, the configuration data is prepared as if they were; this is done to make the examples more realistic. The configuration entries for bkdriver are constructed for a true pseudodevice.

The fields in the chdriver entry line for the master configuration file can be summarized as follows:

Driver name	Must be used in the device description file entries
Entry point mask	The standard value 137 is correct for most character drivers
Device type mask	Only the "character device" bit is set. For a true pseudodevice the "suppress interrupt vector" bit would also be set
Driver prefix	Must appear in the driver entry point names
Device address size	An arbitrary value consistent with the ch_device structure is used. The ch devices have no real controller registers
CSR offset	Arbitrary but consistent with the ch_device definition
Interrupt bit mask	Because this field is zero, ch_intr may be called during an interrupt poll
Block major number	Not used since the "block device" bit is not set in field three
Character major number	This value must be unique; change it if necessary
Devices per controller	Arbitrary but consistent with the driver code
Interrupt priority	Arbitrary for this pseudodevice; not used
Structure declaration	Generates a tty structure declaration for each device in conf.c

Though it is not strictly necessary to do so, it is good practice to use similar strings for the driver name, driver prefix, and device special file names. The special files created by `ch.files` are named `ch0`, `ch1`, and so on. The names of the special files have no meaning to the software; only the major device number links the special file to the device driver.

`ch.dfile` contains two lines to imply that there are two `ch` controllers in the system. Arbitrary nonzero controller addresses are used in order to make the demonstrations realistic. The driver init routine probes these addresses, gets a bus fault in each case, and declares the controllers offline. The other driver routines ignore this status. The designated interrupt priorities are also arbitrary, but they do determine which interrupt poll the driver will be included in.

Declarations and Macros

The code in the file `chdriver.c` begins with include statements and trace print macro definitions; these are described in **Common Features**, this chapter. The next few pages of the driver code contain additional declarations. There is also an include statement for the file `tty.h`, which defines the `tty` structure. This structure is normally used by interactive terminal drivers, but it has a suitable form for `chdriver` and allows us to demonstrate the generation of per-device data structures in `conf.c`.

The other defined macros are convenient abbreviations for operations used at various places within the driver. The defined symbols are bit masks, commands, and literal values; their specific meanings are described in comments in the code. The naming convention followed for flag masks is that names beginning with `CM_` apply to the minor device number, those with `CD_` refer to device units, and those with `CC_` refer to the controller.

The last page before the beginning of the executable code defines two data structure types. The `ch_device` structure is included as an example of a structure that describes a set of device registers. For this template driver there is no hardware, and the contents of the structure are fanciful. Note that no memory is allocated for structures of this type, even in drivers that control real hardware. The device registers are in MULTIBUS address space; in the driver a controller base CSR address is declared to be a pointer to a structure of this type. See the `ch_init` and `ch_intr` routines for examples.

The `ch_cstat` structure type is defined to hold dynamic controller status information. There is no mechanism for defining per-controller structures based on system configuration data, so the defined symbol `C_MAX` is used as the size of the array of controller status structures. It places an upper limit on the number of controllers that the driver can support. At run time the controller number is checked against both `C_MAX` and the actual controller count `ch__ccnt`. See Chapter 10 for more information about per-controller structures.

The extern statements that follow the structure definitions declare the driver variables that are defined in `conf.c`. Note that although the array `ch__addr[]` has the type `int` in `conf.c`, it is declared in the driver as an array of pointers to `ch_device` structures. (To be formally correct the driver should declare `ch__addr[]` to have type `int` and cast it to a pointer when it is used.) The size of the array is given at run time by `ch__ccnt`. The last external variable defined within the driver is `ch_trace`, the trace print control flag.

Entry Points and Driver Logic

The overall logic of `chdriver` is described in **Implemented Device Characteristics**, this chapter. In this section we will briefly describe the details of the code in each driver routine.

`ch_init`.   The initial for loop announces the address of each configured controller on the console and probes the controller to see whether it is online. The hardware probe occurs in the line that assigns a value to `temp`; a hardware fault at this point causes a return from `setjmp` with a nonzero value. Since there is no hardware the two configured controllers are declared to be offline. In a driver whose hardware is online, execution would continue in line after the probe. Note that `u.u_nofault` is set `FALSE` immediately after the initial probe. If a fault occurs during subsequent hardware initialization, it is presumably due to a software error or hardware failure.

Two additional loops initialize the device and controller status variables. Note that it is necessary to clear the count variable for the clist queues used to buffer characters to make the queues initially empty.

`ch_open`.   An open routine should always begin by using its `dev` argument to determine whether the device unit and controller numbers are within the legal range. Though the code is commented out in this template, a driver with real hardware should also check the address table to see whether the controller is online.

This driver also demonstrates one way in which "exclusive open" can be implemented. When a device is opened fields are set in the controller status structure to indicate that the controller is busy. An attempt to open the other device associated with the controller will fail until the first device has been closed. However, two or more processes can open the same device.

`ch_close`.   This routine clears the fields in the controller status structure that mark the controller as busy. Note that because neither `ch_open` nor `ch_close` calls `sleep`, there is no possibility that they will execute in parallel. Therefore they do not need to raise priority or use a mutual exclusion lock before altering the fields in `ch_cs`.

The routine also sets the pseudoflag `CD_RDY` in the device status flag to cancel the effect of an EOF character that may have been read. It does not zero the count for the device input queue; any characters stored in the device will remain there and can be read later. Remember that the close routine is called only when the last process closes the device.

`ch_write`.   This routine looks very much like an output routine for a real device; most of the interaction with the read routine is hidden in `ch_start`. Only the last line of code in `ch_write` is specific to the template example.

The routine moves one byte at a time from user process space to the device output queue, which is theoretically being serviced by the interrupt handler. If the queue reaches its upper limiting size, `O_MAX`, the routine sets the wakeup request flag `CC_WAKE` and goes to sleep. The interrupt handler issues the wakeup call only when the queue size has dropped to `O_MIN`. This means that the routine can add at least O_MAX-O_MIN bytes to the queue each time it wakes up, which is much more efficient than calling sleep after each character is written to the hardware.

In truth the template driver does not deal with hardware that issues interrupts. The ch_start routine completes the output synchronously, and characters do not accumulate in the output queue. The management of the output queue will work as described if the start routine is replaced by one that initiates device activity that leads to an interrupt at a later time.

Note that a call to putc can fail if the kernel temporarily has no clist space available. This event should be very rare, but drivers must be able to deal with it. In this driver whenever putc returns a failure, the code sleeps for one second and tries again.

The flag CC_ACTV is used to indicate whether the device is currently working on an output character. If it is not, ch_start is called to start it up. Note that the CPU priority is raised before the flag is checked so that the interrupt handler cannot be called while this code is being executed. In the template driver the flag is never on, and the start routine is called for every character.

If an EOF character is written to the queue, the driver sets the CD_EOF flag and returns to its caller. After that it will not write any more output until the device is closed.

ch_read. This routine reads characters from the device input queue to satisfy user requests. If the queue is exhausted and the device is not in the EOF state, it sends a wakeup to the start routine and sleeps until it gets a response.

ch_ioctl. Three special functions are implemented in this routine. The first two turn the trace print on and off, and the third returns to the caller the count of bytes currently stored in the device. The values of the command symbols are defined at the head of the driver. For a real driver it would be advisable to define the command symbols in a separate header file in the /usr/include directory that could be referenced by the driver and by user programs.

ch_intr. The template driver does not cause any interrupts to be generated. However, because the interrupt mask in field seven of the master configuration file entry is zero, ch_intr may be called during an interrupt poll. It always returns a zero to indicate that the poll should continue.

The routine also includes example code that is not executed by the template driver that would be needed to handle real interrupts. This code works in conjunction with the ch_write routine to manage the size of the device output queue. After the current interrupt has been dismissed it checks to see whether there are any more characters in the device output queue. If there are, it calls ch_start to initiate output of the next one. Then, if the output queue has dropped to its minimum size, it sends a wakeup to ch_write to cause it to refill the queue.

ch_start. The usual purpose of a start routine is to write the necessary values into device registers to initiate a hardware output operation. In this template version it completes the output (and input) synchronously; it merely moves the character from the output queue (t_outq) to the input queue (t_rawq). If the input queue has reached its maximum size, it sends a wakeup to the read routine and sleeps until it receives a response.

Note that the routine also makes some initial checks and calls panic to halt the system if the conditions found are supposed to be impossible.

Demonstration Cases

After the driver has been installed, the first evidence you will see of it will be its announcement of the two controller addresses when the system is booted. Unless your system happens to include hardware at one or both of those addresses, the console print will indicate that both controllers are offline. That is normal and will not prevent the driver from operating as expected. You should create three special files in the /dev directory named ch0, ch1, and ch2. They will have minor numbers zero, 17, and two respectively; the second number is larger because it has the CM_UPR flag bit set.

The simplest test of the driver is to copy a short file to one of the devices by using the cp utility:

```
$ cp xxx /dev/ch0
```

When you enter this command you will observe on the system console the various trace messages generated by the driver. In order for the command to complete and return a prompt on the terminal, two things are necessary: the file xxx must be shorter than D_MAX bytes, and it must end with an EOF character (a Control-D). In this case the file will be stored in the ch0 device, and you can retrieve it by typing

```
$ cp /dev/ch0 yyy
```

If the file is longer than D_MAX characters the driver will sleep until some other process reads from the device, and the cp command will not complete. To prevent this from happening you could type the following command before copying the file to the ch device:

```
$ cp /dev/ch0 yyy &
```

This command will run in background and alternate its activity with the copy to the device. Both cp commands will continue to run until an EOF is encountered in the file xxx.

In addition to listings of the template drivers, Appendix C also contains listings of two chdriver demonstration files. The first, named ch.test, is a shell script that performs a sequence like the one described above using itself as the file to be copied to and from the ch device. The last character in ch.test is an EOF. The second example is a C program named chex.c that demonstrates several features of the driver. It attempts and fails to open two devices on the same controller, writes to and reads from ch devices, and uses the three ioctl commands.

· Template Block Driver—bkdriver ·

The template block driver `bkdriver` is a complete, functioning block device driver. Like `chdriver` it does not use any peripheral hardware. It allocates a small fixed amount of system memory to act as the data storage area for the `bk` devices. To the kernel and user processes these devices look exactly like small disks; you can use `mkfs` to create a file structure on a `bk` device and then mount it as part of the UNIX file system. The driver also supports raw devices and raw I/O.

Like `chdriver` the block template driver includes some example code that is not really needed to support its pseudodevices. In its init routine it allocates a small group of I/O map registers, and in its start routine it loads values into them. A routine named `bk_trim` is included to limit the size of raw transfers queued by `physio`. The strategy routine places the `buf` structures sent to it on a queue that could be serviced asynchronously by an interrupt handler. These features are included as examples of code that is required in most block drivers.

Note that in its configuration data `bkdriver` is treated like a true pseudodevice. In field two of the line in `bk.master` the "suppress interrupt vector" bit is set. In `bk.dfile` the CSR address and interrupt priority are entered as zero. These fields must be changed if these files are reused with a driver for a hardware block device.

Driver Code

The declarations in the first few pages of the code are similar to those in `chdriver`. There are additional include statements that refer to the files `buf.h` and `iobuf.h`, which are needed in all block drivers. Defined symbols beginning with `U_` establish the characteristics of the driver and its devices. `U_MAX` is the number of device units supported; it controls the amount of device memory that is allocated. `U_BLKS` is the size in blocks of each unit, and `U_MAXXFR` is the size of the largest data transfer that can be made in one operation. The last value is an arbitrary example that was chosen for convenience to be larger than eight blocks (the size of the file system transfers made by the kernel) and smaller than the size of the devices. For real block device controllers this value is determined by the hardware; it is usually the largest byte count that can be stored in the controller register.

The driver also declares its required `iobuf` structure with the required name `bk_tab`. The macro `tabinit`, which is defined in `iobuf.h`, is used to initialize the structure. The first argument to the macro is the major device number, and the second is the address of an I/O statistics block. The literal value of the major number must be coded; there is no mechanism for passing the value from the master configuration file to the driver. A zero is used for the address of the statistics block because the template driver does not use this structure. The macro initializes all other `bk_tab` fields to zero. This is a required operation in all block drivers; the driver will behave unpredictably if its `iobuf` fields are not initialized.

The array `bk_store` constitutes the memory of the `bk` devices. The declared `buf` structures, `bk_rbuf`, are used in the read and write routines to support raw I/O. The following notes describe the code found in the individual driver routines.

bk_init. This routine turns on trace print and then allocates a small group of I/O map registers. (Since U_MAXXFR is equal to ten blocks, three registers will be allocated.) An init routine for a real device should include a test to determine whether the configured controllers are online. The example code used in chdriver will work equally well in a block driver.

bk_open and bk_close. The bk_open routine checks whether the unit number being opened is a legal one. A driver for a real device should also check the controller address table to determine whether the device is online. The bk_close routine does nothing; in most block drivers there is nothing important for it to do.

bk_strategy. This code first obtains the device unit number and offset (block number) and checks whether they have legal values. Note that it is not considered an error to attempt to read the next block past the end of the device. In this case the code sets the residual count equal to the requested transfer count to indicate that no bytes were read. This is a convention that allows a reading process to detect the end of a device without obtaining an error. Note also that the code checks only that the first requested block is legal. This is a sufficient test because I/O requests to a block device are always for an eight-block cluster and always begin on a cluster boundary. The bk and most other block devices hold an integral number of clusters. For raw transfers, which can have various sizes and alignments, both the first and last blocks are validated in the read and write routines by the physck function.

If the request is valid it is placed at the end of the active request queue whose head is in the bk_tab structure. It is up to the driver to choose the point at which to insert the buf in the queue; many disk drivers use the disksort function to insert requests in order of increasing cylinder numbers (see the description of disksort discussed in **Handling Block Buffers**, Chapter 5). In this driver there is no reason to do that; in fact, completion of the transfer request is synchronous, and there is never more than one buf on the queue. Note that the strategy routine raises the CPU priority before manipulating the queue. This step is not important in the template driver but is critical in a driver whose interrupt routine also alters the queue.

Note that the active request queue maintained by the driver is defined by the fields b_actf and b_actl in the iobuf structure and by the field av_forw in the queued buf structures. This queue is maintained by most block drivers, but it is a convention and is not accessed by any software outside the driver. Drivers must not alter the fields b_forw and b_back in either the buf or iobuf structures. These fields are used by the kernel to maintain other queues.

Finally, the code calls the bk_start routine if the b_active field in bk_tab is zero. Normally the start routine would set this field nonzero after starting some hardware operation that will eventually produce a device interrupt. The field would later be zeroed by the intr routine when the transfer had been completed or aborted. The convention used to guarantee that all queued requests are processed as soon as possible is

1. The strategy routine adds the new request to the queue and calls start if the b_active field is zero.

2. Start sets b_active nonzero whenever it initiates device activity that will result in an interrupt.

3. Intr zeros b_active when it dismisses the interrupt. If there is another buf on the queue it calls start.

In this driver the active flag is never set nonzero because the data transfer is always synchronous. Because the iobuf field b_active is a char variable rather than a binary flag, a driver can define various active states if it has a reason to.

bk_trim. This routine is supplied as an argument to physio when the driver performs raw I/O (see the next paragraph). Its purpose is to limit the size of a requested data transfer to the size that the device hardware can support. It checks the size of bp->b_bcount and, if necessary, makes it smaller.

Drivers are not necessarily required to include a routine to perform this function. They can use the kernel routine minphys as the argument to physio if the standard data transfer limit of 252 kilobytes is acceptable.

bk_read and bk_write. These routines handle raw I/O requests; they are very short since all of the work is done by the kernel functions physck and physio. These entry points are called when an I/O request is made on a raw device; that is, one of the character devices supported by the driver or when a large contiguous transfer is made on a block device under the conditions listed in Chapter 3.

physck checks to see whether the first and last block to be transferred (as determined from the values of u.u_offset and u.u_count) are legal device addresses. If the first block is illegal physck returns a zero and physio is not called. If the first block is legal and the last block is not, the value of u.u_count is adjusted to truncate the request at the end of the device.

physio reads data from u, fills in the necessary fields in the buf structure supplied as its second argument, and calls bk_strategy with a pointer to that structure to perform the transfer. The last argument to physio is a pointer to bk_trim, which limits the transfer size. physio will call bk_strategy as many times as necessary to complete the full transfer specified by u.u_count. After each call it sleeps if necessary until the transfer is complete. In the template driver the sleep call is never made since the I/O is always performed synchronously.

bk_ioctl. A template for a special functions routine is included, but no functions are implemented. The routine always returns the error EINVAL.

bk_intr. The template routine returns a zero as though it might be called during an interrupt poll. However, the system configuration data for bkdriver guarantees that no interrupt vector will be generated for this driver.

bk_start. This routine performs the actual transfer of data to or from the device storage area. In the template version the transfer is synchronous and is merely a copy from one memory area to another. In a driver for a real block device this routine would write to device registers in order to initiate a DMA transfer and would then return to its caller.

As an example, the routine includes a call to `iomaddr` to load the necessary values into the I/O map to allow a DMA transfer by the device. These values are not used by the template driver. The macro `paddr` which extracts the address of the data buffer from the `buf` structure is defined in `buf.h`.

In the template routine the actual transfer of data to or from the "device" is performed by inline code. The flag `B_PHYS` is checked to determine whether the data buffer is in user or system space. In the former case either `copyin` or `copyout` is used; otherwise, the data is moved by an assignment loop. Note that this is a limited implementation that does not check other flags such as `B_UAREA`, `B_DIRTY`, and `B_PAGET`. The `bk` devices cannot be used to hold a swap file.

The last few lines of code in `bk_start` would normally appear in the interrupt handler. They indicate that no error occurred, remove the `buf` from the queue of requests, and return it to the original caller of the strategy routine by calling `iodone`.

Demonstration Cases

Appendix D contains two files that demonstrate the operation of `bkdriver`. The shell script `bk.test` creates a file system on a `bk` device, mounts it, and copies a group of files to it. The C program `bkex.c` issues `write` and `read` calls to `bk` block and raw devices. First, it writes five individual blocks to the raw device; the driver trace output on the console will show that each call to the driver is for a single 512-byte write. Next the program reads the entire 16-block raw device with a single call to `read`. The trace print will show that the driver receives a single call to its read routine but that `physio`, acting under the control of `bk_trim`, breaks the read into two calls to `bk_strategy`.

Finally, `bkex` closes the raw device and opens the corresponding raw device. Then it reads the same five blocks that were previously written. Now, however, the kernel block buffering system mediates the reads and calls `bk_strategy` with requests for 4096 bytes. The `bkex` reads of blocks zero and 13 cause synchronous reads of the corresponding eight-block device clusters. The reads of blocks one, 14, and 15 are satisfied without calling the driver. The read of block 15 causes an asynchronous readahead of the next device cluster (which does not exist).

9

BASIC DEVICE DRIVER REQUIREMENTS

This chapter is a reference that gives a detailed specification of the inputs, required operations, and outputs of each driver routine.

• Required Entry Points •

The only hard requirement for inclusion of entry points in a driver is that a function with the proper name must be included for each bit that is set in field two of the master configuration file entry. In addition, an interrupt handler must be supplied unless the "suppress interrupt vector" bit is set in field three. If these rules are violated the driver entry point names declared in `conf.c` and `low.s` will not be defined and the kernel will not be linked.

There is no entry point that must be included in every driver, but in practice most drivers include most of them. The following considerations apply:

- Every block driver must have a strategy routine.

- Every character driver must have either a read or a write routine or both. Most block drivers include them both in order to support raw I/O.

- All drivers for devices that issue interrupts must have an intr routine.

- All drivers need an init routine.

An open routine is always useful to verify that the device being opened does exist. However, it is possible to make that check in the read or write routine. Many drivers have no real need for a close routine, and an ioctl routine is completely optional.

Probably the most reasonable approach is to include all the possible entry points in every driver (but note that an ioctl routine in a pure block driver cannot be called). If there is nothing for the close routine to do, for example, leave it in the code as an empty no-op function. This will make it easier to add functions in the future if a need arises. No-op routines in a driver do not add any execution overhead since the kernel will call the `nulldev` or the `nodev` (no device) routine in place of any missing driver routine. If you do not specify a handler, an error will be generated.

• Entry Point Arguments, Actions, and Returns •

The following sections provide a detailed reference for each driver entry point. The entry point names that are used assume that the driver prefix entered in field four of the master configuration file was `xx_`. The read and write routines are described on the same page since they act exactly the same except for the direction of the transfer.

Device and Driver Initialization—xx_init

```
xx_init()
```

Calling Conditions. Called once, at system startup time.

Calling Context. A limited form of current user process context. The fields `u.u_tsav` and `u.u_nofault` can be used, but nothing else in `u` is valid. This routine must not generate interrupts because the `xx_addr` fields have not been set up yet. Therefore, it is not safe to call `sleep` because no external event could occur to wake the process up.

Arguments. None.

Other Inputs.

`xx__ccnt`	Count of hardware controllers
`xx__cnt`	Count of device units
`xx__addr[]`	Table of CSR addresses

Required Actions. Probe each of the `xx__ccnt` addresses in `xx__addr[]`, and for each probe that produces a fault store a zero in the address table. It is also recommended but not required that you initialize all data structures and zero all queue listheads and clist counts. This initialization can be done automatically on the first read or in the open routine.

Return Value. None.

Other Outputs and Side Effects. A zero stored in `xx__addr[]` indicates to the kernel and to other driver routines that the corresponding device is not in the system. If this is not done, the system panics with a trap type two (bus fault) when any interrupt is received on the interrupt level that the nonexistent device was configured for.

Open Device—**xx_open**

```
xx_open(dev,flag)
int dev;
int flag;
```

Calling Conditions.   Called each time a user process issues the `open` system call on a device whose major number selects this driver. For a block device, called when a `mount` command is executed on the device but not when files on the mounted device are opened.

Calling Context.   Current user process context.

Arguments.

dev   The low byte contains the minor number of the device being opened (variables of type `dev_t` passed to driver routines always contain a zero in place of the major number).

flag   Contains 16 bits of open status as set by the `oflag` argument in the `open` system call. The flag bits are defined in `/usr/include/sys/file.h`, *not* in `/usr/include/fcntl.h`. These flag bits have the same functions as the ones in `fcntl.h` but the names are different.

Other Inputs.   Driver status indicators stored in static variables. For example, a driver can keep its own variable that indicates that the device is open and no one else can access it.

Required Actions.   Determine that the device is online. Verify that the minor number in `dev` is valid. Return failure through `u.u_error` if necessary.

Return Value.   None.

Other Outputs and Side Effects.   The `open` will fail if a nonzero error code is placed in `u.u_error`; the user will see a return value of –1 and find the stored error code in `errno`. If this is not done the `open` succeeds, and the caller will be able to issue `reads` and `writes` on the minor device.

Close Device—**xx_close**

```
xx_close(dev,flag)
int dev;
int flag;
```

Calling Conditions.   Called when a user process closes the device indicated by `dev` *and* no other process has that device open. For a mounted block device, called only when the `umount` command is executed on it.

Calling Context.   Current user process context.

Arguments.

> `dev`   The low byte contains the minor number of the device being opened (variables of type `dev_t` passed to driver routines always contain a zero in place of the major number).
>
> `flag`   Contains the lower eight bits of open status as set by the `open` and modified by the `fcntl` system calls. The status flags are defined in `/usr/include/sys/file.h`.

Other Inputs.   Driver status indicators stored in external variables.

Required Actions.   Cleanup actions may be required if there is unfinished I/O in progress; release resources, clear indicators, and so on.

Return Value.   None.

Other Outputs and Side Effects.   From the point of view of the process, the file is closed before the device driver close routine is called. Therefore, the device close routine should never indicate an error. In addition, the device close routine must either:

- Not sleep at high priority. (All `sleep`s should be at a sleep priority less than or equal to `PZERO`.)

- Trap signals using:

```
if (setjmp(u.u_qsav)) {
/*******************************
*                             *
* this code runs if the user  *
* receives a signal during the *
* close routine.              *
*                             *
*******************************/
}
```

Read and Write Data—xx_read and xx_write

```
xx_read(dev)
xx_write(dev)
int dev;
```

Calling Conditions.   In a character driver, called when a user process issues a `read` or `write` system call respectively. In a block driver that has the block read and block write bits set in field two of the master file, called when a user issues a `read` or `write` that meets certain conditions; currently those conditions are:

- Greater than 2048 bytes
- To or from a contiguous section of the device
- Not currently in the buffering cache

Calling Context.   Current user process context.

Arguments.

dev   The low byte contains the minor number of the device being opened (variables of type `dev_t` passed to driver routines always contain a zero in place of the major number).

Other Inputs.   The origin, destination, and size of the transfer are specified by

u.u_base	Virtual address of the data buffer
u.u_offset	Byte offset on the device
u.u_count	Number of bytes to transfer
u.u_segflag	Address space to which the transfer is taking place:

	zero	Points to user data space
	one	Points to system data space
	two	Points to user instruction space (same as user data space for MC5500)

u.u_fmode	Per-open file flags (returned by `F_GETFL`, `fcntl` system call)
u.u_offset	Current file offset (returned by the `lseek` system call)

The device driver routines must modify `u.u_count` to contain the number of bytes not transferred (`iomove` normally does this), because both the value returned to the user and the file offset are modified based on the value of `u.u_count`. The device driver routines may also update `u.u_offset` and `u.u_base`. This is not required by the `read` or `write` system call routines, but may be expected by various service routines such as `iomove` or `physio`. Note that any routine that expects `u.u_offset` or `u.u_base` to be updated will update these variables.

The driver may set u.u_error to indicate an error. Note that iomove also inspects u.u_segflag.

Required Actions.   Take action to initiate the data transfer, either by issuing device commands or by queing a request for asynchronous service. In a block driver a buf structure must be prepared and queued to the strategy routine. The UNIX standard is that these routines call sleep to suspend the calling process until the transfer is logically completed. The data must have been copied out of the user buffer although the actual I/O may not have completed.

Return Value.   None.

Other Outputs and Side Effects.   If the data cannot be transferred, a nonzero error code defined in errno.h must be stored in u.u_error. The user return value will be –1, and the error code will appear in the external variable errno.

Block Read and Write Handler—xx_strategy

```
xx_strategy(bp)
struct buf *bp;
```

Calling Conditions.   Called by the UNIX kernel to move blocks of data between a block device and the system block buffering cache. In a driver that supports raw block I/O or a raw character device, called from physio, which is in turn called from the driver read and write routines. The strategy routine is also sometimes called from iodone to complete a multipart I/O request.

Calling Context.   Unknown context. Should not refer to the u structure. Must not call sleep.

Because of the readahead and writebehind strategies of the system disk cache, the device strategy routine is usually called when the system is performing a system call for a process different from the process that requested the I/O (although the process calling the device routine is requesting I/O for *some* device).

For disk device drivers that will be used in conjunction with the MASSCOMP DA/CP for direct-to-disk data acquisition, the strategy routine will be called directly from the DA/CP interrupt handler. Strategy routines may also be called from interrupt level if the device is a mounted file system. As a result, the strategy routine must not access the current user structure and must not call sleep.

On the other hand, if the strategy routine is being used only to be called by physio (i.e., from a raw device read or write routine), it can access the current user structure freely. It is also acceptable to call sleep. However, sleep should be called at a priority less than or equal to PZERO or the strategy routine must trap signals. This is necessary so that virtual memory that was locked by physio before calling the strategy routine will be released. This will cause the error:

```
exit: process %d raw I/O lock %d
```

Arguments.

bp   Pointer to a buf structure that defines the I/O request.

Other Inputs. Driver status indicators stored in external variables. The routine must coordinate its actions with the driver interrupt handler.

Required Actions. If the request is valid, take steps to initiate the requested action. Usually this is done by placing the buf on an internal queue that is serviced asynchronously. Strategy usually returns to its caller without waiting for the request to be processed. If the request is invalid and is not queued, set error indicators and call iodone to release the buf.

Return Value. None.

Other Outputs and Side Effects. If there is an error in the request and it cannot be queued, these fields should be written:

- Set B_ERROR in bp->b_flags
- Optionally store an error code in bp->b_error; if the error code is zero the kernel will insert EIO
- Set bp->b_resid to bp->b_bcount to indicate no data transferred

Special Functions—xx_ioctl

```
xx_ioctl(dev, cmd, arg, flag)
int dev;
int cmd;
int *argp;
int flag;
```

Calling Conditions. Called whenever a user process issues an ioctl system call on a file descriptor opened by this driver.

Calling Context. Current user process context.

Arguments.

dev   The low byte contains the minor number of the device being opened (variables of type dev_t passed to driver routines always contain a zero in place of the major number).

cmd   A value that specifies the requested operation; its meaning is defined by the driver.

argp   An argument value or pointer; the driver defines how this argument will be interpreted for each value of cmd.

flag   Contains the lower eight bits of open status as set by the open and modified by the fcntl system calls. The status flags are defined in /usr/include/sys/file.h.

Other Inputs. Some fields in u are valid, but u.u_base, u.u_offset, and u.u_count are not. If you use ioctl to initiate asynchronous action, you must save u.u_procp in a driver external variable. If the function requires a single input, you can use argp as an immediate value. If additional inputs or outputs are required, argp can be used as a pointer to a variable or data structure.

Required Actions. The driver defines what actions will be performed for each value of cmd. UNIX does not place any restrictions on the use of this routine.

Return Value. None.

Other Outputs and Side Effects. In case of an error a nonzero error code can be stored in u.u_error. The caller will see a return value of –1 and the error code will be in the external variable errno.

Interrupt Handler—xx_intr

```
xx_intr(devno,csr,device)
      or
xx_intr(devno,device)
int devno;
int csr;
struct xx_device *device;
```

Calling Conditions. The driver's interrupt handler is called with three arguments if the following conditions are met:

- The driver has a nonzero interrupt mask in field seven in the master file

- An interrupt occurs on a level used by one of its devices

- The logical AND of field seven with the device CSR is nonzero (or zero if the low bit in field three is set)

The interrupt handler is called with two arguments if the following conditions are met:

- field seven is zero

- An interrupt occurs on a level used by one of its devices

- No other polled driver has accepted responsibility for the interrupt

Drivers are polled in the order in which they appear in the site configuration file (MC5500, as shipped on the system). There is no guarantee that all drivers with a nonzero CSR field will be polled before any driver with a zero CSR field.

Calling Context.   Unknown context, at interrupt priority level. Must not access u and must not call `sleep`.

Arguments.

devno   indicates which of several controllers issued the interrupt or is being polled. The first device supported by this driver in the device description file is zero, the next is one, and so on.

csr   the value read from the device CSR after the interrupt was seen; supplied in case reading the CSR changed its value.

device   The address of the device base CSR, `xx_addr[devno]`.

The `device` argument is shown above as being a pointer to a structure of the type `xx_device`, but it is up to the programmer to define that structure type. The type name is not imposed by UNIX.

Other Inputs.   The interrupt handler usually reads device status from its registers. It also examines driver external variables and request queues.

Required Actions.   Issue hardware commands to dismiss the interrupt. Remove completed items from the driver queue or clist. If more work is queued, initiate the next device action. If status flags indicate that a process is sleeping on the completed request, call `wakeup`. In a block driver, call `iodone` to release the `buf` for the completed request.

Return Value.   When called with three arguments, none. When called with two arguments, nonzero if the interrupt was handled by the driver, zero if it was not.

Other Outputs and Side Effects.   In case of error in a character driver, store an error code in a driver external variable associated with the request. In case of error in a block driver, set `B_ERROR` in `b_flags` and optionally store an error code in `b_error` in the associated `buf` structure before calling `iodone`.

CHAPTER
10

SPECIAL TOPICS

· Supporting Multiple Devices ·

When a hardware configuration includes several devices of the same or very similar types, it is of course desirable that a single device driver be able to support them all. RTU provides the necessary features to allow a driver to manage several devices at the same time.

The most general situation is that for a particular device type or class the configuration includes one or more controllers, each controlling one or more devices or units. The standard definitions of these terms are

- A controller is an I/O bus interface with memory-mapped registers at a unique set of addresses.

- A device is a functional unit, such as a disk or tape drive, plotter, or user terminal.

In some cases there is a one-to-one correspondence between controllers and devices; in other cases each controller may be capable of simultaneously managing more than one device unit. In the latter case a data transfer to or from a device will probably require exclusive use of the controller for its duration, however it may be possible for other operations like disk head seeks and tape rewinds to be in progress on several units at the same time.

The designer of a device driver must separate the variables and data structures that define the state of the system into four groups:

1. Per device. Parameters and state variables that apply to a particular device unit. For example, the number of blocks on a disk drive or the current position of a magnetic tape.

2. Per controller. Items of the same type that describe a particular controller. For example, an indication that a data transfer is in progress for a particular device unit and pointers to additional queued I/O requests.

3. Per request. Data items associated with a specific I/O request. For block drivers all information of this type is stored in a buf structure;

DMA character drivers may use a different structure for the same purpose.

4. Per driver. Global information, such as a count of controllers and their addresses. May include shared data structures that are temporarily allocated to process I/O requests.

A knowledge of the hardware is needed to determine which data items are associated with the device and which with the controller. For example, it is common for a disk or magnetic tape controller to contain DMA hardware that is shared by the attached drive units. This implies that only one data transfer operation can be in progress at any time and that the queue of outstanding I/O requests must be associated with the controller rather than the devices.

In order to handle the first two categories it is convenient to define two structure types called the "device status block" and "controller status block." Arrays of these structures can then be defined, and at run time the device number and controller number can be computed and used as indexes into the arrays. The prototype for a controller status block is the iobuf structure, which contains most of the fields that are usually needed. The basic items are

- Flags and dynamic status indicators
- Pointers to define the queue of outstanding I/O requests
- For DMA controllers, an index to the allocated I/O map registers
- Statistics recording fields

In many drivers it will be adequate to define an array of iobuf structures or to use the system configuration data files to define an iobuf per device.

config does support the generation of per-device data structures; see Chapter 4. The structure definitions appear in the file conf.c, so the structure types must be defined in one of the include files referred to in that file. A new structure type can be used as a device status block as long as its definition (or an include statement referring to it) is inserted in one of the cited files, such as io.h or peri.h.

The file /usr/include/sys/io.h is included in the conf.c configuration file. It, in turn, includes the file /usr/include/sys/peri.h. These files can be used to declare driver specific data structures. The difference between these files is primarily that io.h includes definitions or initializations for these data structure, while peri.h includes declarations for data structures that are allocated under the control of the master configuration file. Both files can make use of symbols that are defined by the config program as controlled by the local configuration file. For example, if a line of the form

```
dk  ffxxyy 4    8
```

appears in the local configuration file, the conf.c file generated by config will contain

```
#define DK_0 1
```

Then declarations or initializations added to io.h or peri.h should be enclosed by

```
#ifdef DK_0
. . .
#endif
```

If the device driver for DK is described in master as:

```
*name   devmsk  devtyp  prefix  addrsiz  csr_off
DK      737     214     DK      8        4

*intmask  bmajor  cmajor  unitcnt  pri
10        2       6       4        5      bar
```

then the conf.c file generated by config will contain the line:

```
struct bar DK_bar[8];
```

The file peri.h should contain a declaration for struct bar.

By making use of aliases in the master configuration file (note: there are no aliases in MASSCOMP's standard master configuration file), configuration specific initializations can be included in conf.c. For example, assume that the DK device is a disk controller which could support several different disk drives, but the drive types must be configured into the system. This could be handled by aliases of the form:

```
drive1 DK
drive2 DK
```

Then conf.c will contain either

```
#define DRIVE1_0 1
```

or

```
#define DRIVE2_0 1
```

instead of

```
#define DK_0 1
```

The code in io.h could use this to include the proper initialization of a data structure to indicate which disk drive was configured into the system.

config does not directly generate per-controller structure definitions, although if there is a one-to-one correspondence between devices and controllers the per-device structure can be used. Otherwise, the simplest approach is to set an upper limit on the number of controllers in the device driver itself and define an array of controller status blocks of that size. For example:

```
#define MAX_CONTROL 4
struct xx_control
{
    . . .
} xx_csb[MAX_CONTROL];
```

At run time the driver must check each controller number for which I/O is requested and verify that it is smaller than both MAX_CONTROL and xx_ccnt.

If this results in an unacceptable amount of unused space when fewer controllers are configured, it is possible to determine the number of controllers (up to some maximum) configured in /usr/include/sys/peri.h. For example:

```
#ifdef XX_0
#ifdef XX_1
#ifdef XX_2
#define XX_N 2
#else XX_2
#define XX_N 1
#else XX_0
#define XX_N 0
#endif

struct xx_control
{
    . . .
} xx_csb[XX_N];
```

In block drivers it is necessary to define at least one iobuf structure with a predefined name (xx_tab for a driver with the prefix xx_) regardless of whether it is used as a controller status block. The kernel uses two fields in this structure: b_flags to determine whether this is a magnetic tape driver (see **Magnetic Tape Drives**, this chapter), and b_forw and b_back to track which system buffers have been assigned to a device. Drivers should not access these fields. A driver supporting multiple controllers can maintain separate I/O request queues in each of several controller status blocks. A convenient approach is to use in the driver source file the definition

```
struct iobuf xx_tab[MAX_CONTROL];
```

Only the first structure in the array will be known to the kernel.

If a disk driver uses the disksort routine to order its I/O request queues it will call that routine with a pointer to the structure that holds the queuehead. disksort assumes that the pointer is to an iobuf structure; a different structure type can be used as a controller status block only if it contains fields b_actf and b_actl at the same offsets as they appear in the iobuf definition. Note that if several drives are attached to the controller it might still be reasonable to use disksort, but the effect will be to sweep the heads on all drives in unison. If the controller and drives are capable of simultaneous seeks on separate drives a different type of logic should be used in the driver.

At run time the driver must use the minor device number to identify the particular controller and device to which an I/O request is being directed. Any appropriate encoding scheme can be used. See the template driver chdriver, which defines the macros `dev_to_unit` and `dev_to_cont` to extract the device and controller numbers from the minor device number. That driver defines a `tty` structure per device and an array of privately defined `ch_cstat` structures to serve as very simple controller status blocks.

Drivers that support multiple devices must be careful to coordinate multiple parallel executions that may occur; see Chapter 5. The most common requirement is to make temporary use of a shared global data structure, such as a private `buf` structure used to queue a raw I/O request. Any structure used in this way should be equipped with `BUSY` and `WANTED` flags to synchronize their use by multiple driver executions.

• Error Retry Logic •

Disk and tape devices (and perhaps other types of hardware as well) are subject to random nonrepeating errors. Controllers for these devices use checksums to detect data transmission errors at the hardware level, but it is usually left to the software to retry the operation after an error is detected. Disk and tape drivers should include error retry logic to remove the burden of routine retries from the user.

The recommended method is to (1) include in the controller status block a field to hold an error retry count and (2) define for the driver an upper limit on retry attempts. The retry count is zeroed at system initialization time and whenever a data transfer is completed or aborted. When the interrupt handler checks the hardware status indicators after a transfer has been attempted, it must distinguish retryable errors (usually denoted "transfer error" or "checksum error") from fatal errors (such as "write protect error"). If the error is not fatal the driver should increment the retry count and restart the I/O operation as long as the retry limit has not been exceeded.

Assuming that the driver maintains a queue of outstanding I/O requests and has a start routine that is called to initiate execution of the request at the head of the queue, the following logic is appropriate. When start issues hardware commands to initiate a request, it leaves the request on the queue and returns to its caller. When the interrupt handler is activated it checks for errors. If there are no errors or if there is a fatal error or if the error retry count has been exceeded, it:

- Removes the current request from the queue and puts the current request at the start of the queue

- Zeroes the retry count

- Releases the request structure, possibly marked with an error

Note that it zeroes the retry count when the transfer is first queued rather than when a transfer completes.

If there has been a retryable error and the retry count has not been exceeded, the interrupt handler merely increments the count. Then, regardless of whether there has been an error, the device start routine is called to initiate the current request on the queue (if there is one).

A single retry may be successful in a great majority of cases, but it is common to use a value of eight for the retry limit.

Error Logging

RTU implements a method for device drivers to make error logging records available to be read from the special device /dev/error. The error daemon (/etc/errdemon) reads records from this device and saves them in a disk file. The errpt program can print out summaries of this error log or print the log as a text file.

The driver interface to the error logger is through the routines fmtberr and logberr. fmtberr should be called each time an error occurs. The first call to fmtberr will initialize the error record. This record contains selected information from the buffer header structure. If xx_tab.io_nreg is nonzero, then xx_tab.io_nreg bytes of device register contents are copied to the error record from the device address specified by xx_tab.io_addr. Note that xx_tab.io_addr can be set up to point to a software copy of the device registers if a byte-wise copy of the data registers will not work. If fmtberr is called again before a call to logberr, fmtberr simply increments the retry count in the error record.

Most drivers will only call logberr when the current I/O transfer is completed. The second argument to logberr is used to indicate fatal versus recoverable errors.

▪ Magnetic Tape Drivers ▪

This section describes the special requirements and features of magtape drivers.

Characteristics of Magnetic Tape Devices

The characteristics of ANSI standard half-inch nine-track magtape devices can be stated briefly as follows. This is a general description; some devices may operate differently in their details.

Data is written on magnetic tape in variable-length physical records. The size of the physical record that is written is determined by the byte count specified for the DMA data transfer. Most drives will theoretically permit a record to be as short as one byte, but some devices (and device drivers) enforce a minimum of about 14 bytes to avoid the possibility of mistaking random noise for a data record. The size of the longest possible record is typically 64 kilobytes, established by the size of the byte count register. Each physical record is followed by an inter-record gap that contains no data. The minimum length of the inter-record gap is three quarters of an inch. However, some streaming tape drives allow you to write longer inter-record gaps. Longer inter-record gaps may also be used to avoid a bad spot on a tape. In order to avoid having a large fraction of the tape occupied by these gaps it is usually desirable to have most data records contain at least a few thousand bytes.

Records must be written sequentially from the beginning to the end of the tape. It is not possible to read immediately after writing (without backing the tape up) or to back the tape up and rewrite an intermediate record without effectively destroying all the records beyond that point. When a read operation is initiated the tape always advances across one physical record. If the requested byte count is larger than the size of the physical record, only the number of bytes in the record is transferred to memory. If the requested count is smaller than the record size, only the requested number of bytes is transferred, and an error indication is set.

Magtape controllers will, on command from the software, write a special record called a "tape mark" which is normally used to mark the end of a file. A single reel of tape may contain several files separated by tape marks with each file containing an arbitrary number of physical records. The hardware returns a special indication if a tape mark is encountered on an attempt to read a data record and leaves the tape positioned after the tape mark. Two tape marks with no intervening data records indicate logical end-of-tape.

Magtape controller hardware does not maintain any knowledge of the current tape position other than indicating "beginning-of-tape" or "end-of-tape" if one of those conditions is true. Likewise it cannot accept a command to move the tape to a specified record number. Instead all tape positioning is accomplished by either rewinding the tape or by moving relative to the current position a specified number of records forward or reverse. Tape positioning commands (except rewind) stop at a tape mark.

Magtape Driver Logic

Magnetic tape storage devices have a mixed nature that does not fall clearly into either the block or character categories in the conventional UNIX sense of those terms. Magtape units are mass storage memory devices, and it is possible to implement device drivers for them that create or simulate addressable fixed length data blocks. Yet for many applications it is adequate to simply read and write data records in a serial fashion without providing any block addressing scheme.

The designer of a magtape device driver can choose to implement one or the other or both of these methods depending on the intended uses of the device. To be more specific, driver implementations that might be selected include:

- A pure character driver. Write physical records of the size specified by the user's requests in `u.u_count`. Ignore the value of `u.u_offset` and execute read and write requests from the current tape position.

- A standard block driver. Use fixed-size physical records. Use `bp->b_blkno` to determine the requested device address and move the tape forward or backward to the appropriate record before executing a read or write operation.

- Block driver with a raw device. This combined approach will permit both addressed and sequential I/O, but unless the raw write routine enforces a fixed record length, tapes written in that mode may be incompatible with addressed block access.

The third approach, which is the most general, is used by the MASSCOMP magtape driver (see section `mt`(4) in the *UNIX Programmer's Manual*).

The UNIX kernel block I/O system identifies magtape drivers by looking for the flag `B_TAPE` in the `b_flags` field of the driver `iobuf` structure (i.e., in the location `xx_tab.b_flags`, assuming a driver prefix of `xx_`). For drivers that have this flag set, the normal block I/O logic is modified as follows:

- I/O clustering is not used. Read and write requests are for `BSIZE` bytes at arbitrary device addresses. (For disks I/O requests are typically for `CLUSTER*BSIZE` bytes at device addresses of `n*CLUSTER`.)

- The delayed write feature is not used; a write request always results in an immediate call to the driver. (For disks the block may simply be marked to indicate that it should be written before being reused.)

Use of a magtape as a block device is limited by the nature of the device. Tapes must be written sequentially; after a block has been written no higher-numbered block can be read. Since writes cannot be delayed, short writes by a user program are grossly inefficient. If a program issues a series of one-byte writes, the driver will be called to write the same block over and over. Unless it maintains its own internal buffer it will be forced to repeatedly write a standard size physical record, backspace, and write it again.

To support addressed block access, a magtape driver must use a fixed record length whose size is a multiple of the UNIX block size `BSIZE`. The driver compares the device address `bp->b_blkno` to the current tape position to determine how many records to move the tape forward or backward before executing the data transfer. The simplest choice is to use `BSIZE` as the record size, but it may be desirable to write larger physical records in order to reduce the amount of tape wasted in inter-record gaps. Record sizes of one to eight kilobytes might be reasonable, but if a size greater than `BSIZE` is used it will be necessary for the driver to maintain an internal data buffer of that size. Read and write requests from the UNIX kernel will be for `BSIZE` bytes, so an internal driver buffer of this type would serve as single cluster cache.

It is also conventional to encode some magtape operating mode selections into the minor device number. Mode selection then becomes a matter of opening the proper special file. For example, selection of character density, streaming versus incremental, and choice of whether the tape should be rewound when the file is closed are coded into the minor number in the MASSCOMP magtape driver. This method of mode selection is particularly appropriate for choices that cannot be changed once the tape has been opened.

When a magtape is handled as a character device with variable length records, the user frequently does not know the true physical record length in advance. It is common to issue reads with a fixed byte count equal to the largest record that the program is able to accept; the read service is expected to return the number of bytes actually obtained. It is important, therefore, for the driver to exit with the correct value in the field `u.u_count`.

The original value of `u.u_count` must be decremented by the number of bytes actually stored in the user buffer; determination of the correct value will be hardware dependent. Typical magtape controllers require that a negative byte or word count be stored in a device register to specify the size of the requested read. If the read terminates because the physical record is shorter than the request count, the register will retain a residual count that determines the value that should be stored in `u.u_count`.

As mentioned previously, magtape hardware will not seek to a specified record: the tape may be moved forward or backward some number of records or can be rewound to the beginning. The device driver should keep track of the current tape position so it can calculate the distance from the desired record and the current record and move the tape in the required direction.

When a magtape is treated strictly as a block device there is no need to provide the user with explicit tape positioning commands. The lseek system call simply changes the current file offset without calling the device driver. At the next read or write system call this file offset is copied into the u.u_offset field before the device driver entry point is called. If the number of bytes per record is fixed, the device driver can calculate the record number to seek to based on the file offset.

For so-called raw magtape this is not feasible since the device driver does not know how large the various tape records are. Therefore, UNIX magnetic tape device drivers generally ignore the file offset for the character device interface. Instead, ioctl commands are used to allow a program to specify explicit tape positioning operations. The file /usr/include/sys/mtio.h defines an appropriate set of positioning commands.

Because it is not possible to read beyond the last physical record written, the driver must also retain the number of that record. (Note that the number to be retained is that of the most recently written record, not the largest record number written.) In block mode an attempt to read a record number larger than the retained value should return an error; an attempt to write a record more than one greater than that number should likewise be flagged as an error. In character mode an attempt to space beyond the last written record is also an error.

Multiple Files. It is common for a reel of tape to hold several files separated by tape marks. The magtape device driver must provide the ability to write multiple files, to access any file, and to detect an end-of-file condition and report it to the user. The convention usually followed is to place one tape mark after each file and a second one after the last file to indicate a logical end-of-tape condition. The driver can enforce this standard without requiring special actions by the user by implementing the following logic.

When a tape device is closed the device driver writes a pair of tape marks after the last record written to the tape. This may require repositioning the tape. If the norewind bit in the minor device number is set, the tape is positioned before the second tape mark by executing a "space-reverse" operation; if the device is subsequently reopened, additional records will overwrite the second tape mark and leave the first tape mark as a separator between the old file and the new file. If the norewind bit is not set, the tape is rewound after both tape marks have been written. No tape marks should be written if the tape was opened only for reading or if no data was actually written to the tape since the device was opened.

If no records have been written to the tape since it was last opened, the device driver will either rewind the tape or advance the tape to be immediately after the next tape mark depending on the norewind bit. This provides a mechanism for advancing the tape beyond a tape mark. For block-mode tape devices, this should be the only way to move past a tape mark. This may require spacing backward over a tape mark if one is encountered, or more sophisticated checking when the device is closed to see if a "space-forward" operation is required for `norewind` tape.

For raw devices it is expected that tape marks will be treated as zero-length records. That is, the residual byte count is set equal to the requested byte count which causes the `read` system call to return zero. User programs will interpret this as an end-of-file indication. Since the tape will be positioned past the tape mark, the next `read` system call will read the first record of the next file. A driver can as an additional convenience to the user supply `ioctl` commands such as "space-file-forward," "space-file-reverse," or "select-file-*n*." Some magtape controllers provide "space-file" commands in hardware; others require that "space-record" be executed with a large record count and terminate the tape motion when a tape mark is encountered. Multifile operations of the type discussed here are principally for use in character or raw mode. For block mode the driver should probably require that the file be selected once only, before any I/O takes place, and then not allow any further motion across file boundaries.

Error Retry Logic.   Because of the sequential nature of magnetic tape, the error recovery and retry logic for a magnetic tape device driver is generally more complicated than a disk driver. Tape drives typically have a read head after the write head so the drive is able to determine if the data was written correctly. If an error occurs, the device driver is responsible for all error recovery actions.

It is not sufficient simply to repeat the read or write operation since the tape is usually left past the record in error. The device driver needs to keep sufficient state information to reverse one record before retrying the operation since most tape controllers will perform only a single operation at a time.

If a portion of the magnetic tape has a defect, repeating the write operation any number of times will not eliminate the error. However, it is possible to leave an extra-long inter-record gap that covers the bad spot. This is usually done with a command to erase a short section of tape (e.g., three inches) or to write a record with an extended inter-record gap preceding it.

Another difficulty with magnetic tape involves the position of the tape following an error. Most tape drives and controllers leave the tape just past the record where the error was encountered. For these purposes, a tape mark is often treated like a record that causes a distinctive error. That is, a space-forward or space-reverse operation will terminate at a tape mark. On a space-forward the tape is positioned after the tape mark, while it is positioned *before* the tape mark (closer to the beginning of the tape) on a space-reverse operation.

Dealing with errors when the end of the physical tape is reached is also tricky. Standard half-inch magnetic tape uses a reflective strip to identify the end of the reel of tape. This is referred to as the EOT. You may need to experiment with each particular tape drive and controller to determine how this should be handled. The ANSI standard for half-inch tape states that an additional record and a pair of tape marks can be written following the physical EOT but the controller may prevent this operation. Failure to recognize EOT will result in the tape coming off the supply spool.

· Using Register Variables ·

The register declaration can be used in C programs to indicate to the compiler that if possible the declared variable should be stored in a CPU register rather than in main memory. It is intended for use with variables that are expected to be accessed very frequently in order to improve the performance of a program.

Since it is always important to work to optimize the performance of device drivers, the register declaration can be a valuable tool. For example, in a block driver strategy routine it makes sense to declare the argument to the routine as:

```
xx_strategy (bp)
register struct buf *bp;
```

since it is likely that this variable will be used frequently.

Although the register declaration can be attached to any number of variables, there are usually only a few registers (typically three or four) available for storing variables. Excessive uses of the declaration will be ignored by the compiler.

· Programming Cautions ·

If you are writing your driver in C, there are two programming cautions you should be aware of:

- The MC68000 CLR instructions perform a memory read before writing memory. This will cause problems for devices that have a side effect when a device register is read. Since the C compiler will generate CLR instructions for simple assignments of the value zero, it is necessary to assign the value zero to a temporary variable and assign this temporary variable to the device register. This problem does not occur with the MC68010.

- In some cases, the optimizer may eliminate what it believes to be redundant instructions. Since accessing device registers often have side effects, these instructions may not be redundant. In fact, the C peep-hole optimizer (/lib/c2, usually invoked by the -O switch to cc) attempts to account for possible side effects. However, if you suspect troubles of this sort, try compiling without the optimizer. If this makes a difference, you should report the problem to your UNIX vendor.

· ASTs ·

An AST is similar to a signal in that it can be sent by a process or the operating system to another process (including itself) at an arbitrary time. When the AST is received and processed it interrupts normal process execution. ASTs have the following advantages over signals:

- Received ASTs are placed on a queue and processed one at a time, in order of their priority

- An AST delivers a user-specified 32-bit value to a specified handler

- The receiving process can raise and lower its AST priority in order to defer processing of ASTs

AST priority is unrelated to the process scheduling priority and to the CPU hardware priority; a user process controls its AST priority by calling `setpri`. ASTs have all the features needed to support fully interlocked asynchronous communication between user processes and device drivers.

The kernel builds and stores ASTs in `cblock` structures as a doubly linked list. A driver that uses ASTs must define a two-element array to contain the first pointer and the last pointer. This structure serves as an AST queue head. For example:

```
struct cblock *ast_head[2];
```

This array must be initialized in the init or open routine by setting each of the pointers to the value `NULL`. If the driver needs to handle more than one type of AST it can define more of these arrays.

To cause an AST to be delivered to a process, the driver calls the following kernel routines:

dclast   Declare the AST; causes the AST block to be built and added to the queue named in an argument.

delast   Deliver the AST; it is removed from its queue and placed on a delivery queue associated with the receiving process.

`dclast` is called when a user process declares that it wants to receive an AST when a certain event occurs. This call causes a cblock holding the AST description to be queued. When the event occurs the driver calls `delast`, causing the AST to be dequeued and delivered to the user process.

Appendix B gives complete descriptions of these two functions and their arguments, but we will briefly summarize here how they are used with respect to a defined queue head array. The last argument in a call to `dclast` is a pointer to the first element of the desired array; it has the type `struct cblock **`. Using the example definition given above, the argument to `dclast` would be `ast_head`.

The only argument to `delast` is a pointer to the cblock holding the description of the AST to be delivered; it has the type `struct cblock *`. If a single AST were queued on the example array, the argument used to deliver it would be `ast_head[0]`.

Each time `dclast` is called a new AST is added at the *front* of the queue; `ast_head[0]` always points to the most recently queued AST. If this AST is delivered the previously queued AST pops up to the front of the queue.

A complete description of an AST includes its priority, the value that it will deliver, the address of the user routine that will be called to handle it, and the event that will cause it to be sent. Drivers do not send unsolicited ASTs; the user process must call `ioctl` or another driver routine to provide the required information and enable delivery. The file `ast.h` defines a structure that can be used to deliver the AST description to the driver.

Typically a user process will initiate an asynchronous operation with a `read`, `write`, or `ioctl` system call, supplying among other information a pointer to an `ast` descriptor structure. Using the information from that structure, the driver top-half routine calls `dclast` to store an AST block on a driver queue. The driver then initiates the requested operation and returns to the caller. At a later time the driver interrupt routine calls `delast` to deliver the queued AST to the user process.

ASTs are also useful for notifying the user of the arrival of unsolicited input, such as pressing a mouse button.

The following section gives a more complete description of a typical use of the AST mechanism to implement asynchronous I/O.

▪ An Example: Asynchronous DMA Using ASTs ▪

This example demonstrates how a user process can use ASTs to maximize its rate of output by overlapping its own execution with the DMA activity of the output device. We saw in Example 3 in Chapter 6 that if the user data is copied into system-space buffers, the device driver can accomplish this overlap transparently to the calling process. However, if the device is to obtain the data directly from user-space buffers, the user process must be aware of the overlap and cooperate with the driver to accomplish it successfully.

Briefly, overlapped or double-buffered output works as follows. The user process defines two memory buffers to hold output data. When a buffer is filled and ready for output, the process issues a `write` or `ioctl` call; the driver queues the output request but returns control to the caller without waiting for the I/O to complete. The user process repeats the output sequence, alternating between the two buffers. However, it does not write new data into a buffer until it receives an indication from the driver that the data previously stored there has been transferred to the device. That indication is delivered asynchronously in the form of an AST.

In addition to the buffer address and byte count that define an ordinary write request, the process must send the following information to the driver:

- An indication that the request is to be handled asynchronously

- The address of an I/O status buffer where a success or failure indication can be written when the I/O is complete

- Arguments that specify an AST to be delivered to the process when the I/O completes

The conventional way of passing this information to the driver is to define a data structure containing the required values or pointers to them and pass a pointer to that structure to the driver.

In the example code that follows we will assume that both the user program and the device driver utilize the following include file:

```
/*****************************************************************/
/*                                                               */
/*   xxast.h -- define asynchronous I/O request structures   */
/*                                                               */
/*****************************************************************/

    #include <ast.h>                /* get ast_spec definition */

    struct async_rq                 /* AST request structure */
    {
      char *baddr;                  /* data buffer address */
      int count;                    /* byte count */
      struct async_st *saddr;       /* I/O status block address */
      struct ast_spec *ast_desc;    /* ast descriptor address */
      int ast_mark;                 /* verification code */
    };

    #define RQSIZE sizeof(struct async_rq)
    #define RQMARK 0xabcdabcd        /* magic ID number */


    struct async_st                 /* I/O status structure */
    {
      short done;                   /* completion flag */
      short error;                  /* error code */
      int count;                    /* count of bytes transferred */
    };

    #define STSIZE sizeof(struct async_st)
```

Structure type async_rq contains the information needed by the driver to initiate asynchronous output, including pointers to an I/O status area and an AST specification. Structure type async_st defines an I/O status block; the driver clears all its fields when the output is initiated. On completion of the I/O its done field is set to one; the error field is set to a nonzero value in case of an I/O failure; and the count field is set to indicate the number of bytes actually transferred to the device. (Because the write service returns before the I/O is performed its return value cannot be used for this purpose.)

The use of an I/O status block is a convention followed in this example, not a requirement of the MASSCOMP AST facility. It would be possible, for example, to design an interface that returned a status value in the AST parameter.

Because the use of asynchronous I/O places an extra burden on the user, it will usually be desirable for the driver to support both the synchronous and asynchronous options. A UNIX-standard synchronous mode will be required if the driver is to be compatible with utilities like cp. There are two methods that a driver can use to distinguish between synchronous and asynchronous requests:

1. Define a single special file, such as /dev/xx0. Use the write call to request synchronous output, and use an ioctl call to request asynchronous output. The ioctl argument will be a pointer to a structure defining the request, like the async_rq structure shown above.

2. Define two special files with different minor numbers, one for synchronous I/O and one for asynchronous. They might have names like
/dev/xxs0 and /dev/xxa0. Use the write call for all output and
let the minor number determine the mode. For synchronous mode the
second argument in the write call is as usual a pointer to the data to
be written; for asynchronous mode it is a pointer to a structure that
defines the asynchronous request.

In order to keep the example reasonably simple the driver code shown below
supports asynchronous output only; a write call is used to supply it with a
pointer to an async_rq structure.

A driver that uses write calls to initiate asynchronous I/O should check
all requests to protect itself against a user who mistakenly supplies a pointer to
an ordinary data buffer in place of a pointer to a structure specifying an asynchronous request. For example, someone might type cp anyfile
/dev/xxa0. In the current example the structure field ast_mark and the
parameters RQSIZE and RQMARK are used for validity checks. First, the driver
requires that the byte count supplied be exactly RQSIZE. Second, it requires
that the field ast_mark contain the arbitrary value RQMARK. It is very unlikely
that an ordinary data buffer will meet both these requirements.

The following code is a complete user program that interacts with an asynchronous driver using the data structures defined in the header file shown above.
The while loop in the main program issues the write requests, alternating
between its two output buffers. The code that would create meaningful output
and detect an end condition is omitted; as shown the program writes zeros and
does not terminate. The function synchronize pauses if necessary to allow
output from a buffer to complete before new values are written into it. The function lasthandler is the local AST handler that is executed when the AST sig-
naling I/O completion is received from the driver. Note that its address is supplied to the driver in the ast_spec field param1; the field handler must contain the address of an external language-specific function. For programs written
in the C language this field should always contain a pointer to the function
named _asthandler.

```
/****************************************************************/
/*                                                              */
/* xx_test -- demonstration of overlapped asynchronous I/O  */
/*                                                              */
/****************************************************************/

#include <stdio.h>
#include "xxast.h"          /* define AST structures */

#define ASTPRI 10           /* AST delivery priority */
#define MAXWAIT 10000        /* longest wait (milliseconds) */

#define BUFSIZE (128*1024)  /* size of data buffers */
char buf[2][BUFSIZE];       /* two buffers for overlapped I/O */
int iocount[2] = {0, 0};    /* corresponding byte counts */

int lasthandler();          /* routine to receive AST's */
```

```
                    /* AST structures: */

struct ast_spec astblk = {_asthandler, lasthandler, 0, ASTPRI};
struct async_rq ioctlblk = {0, 0, 0, &astblk, RQMARK};
struct async_st iostatus[2] = {1, 0, 0, 1, 0, 0};


main ()
{
  int ionum = 0;              /* index of current data buffer */
  int done = 0;               /* flag: no more output */


  while (!done)               /* main output loop */
  {
    synchronize(ionum);       /* wait till buffer is ready */

    /* compute and fill output buffer here */
    /* eventually set 'done' non-zero       */

    ioctlblk.baddr = &buf[ionum][0]; /* set async parameters */
    ioctlblk.count = iocount[ionum] = BUFSIZE;
    ioctlblk.saddr = &iostatus[ionum];
    astblk.param2 = ionum;

    if (write(1,&ioctlblk,RQSIZE) < 0) /* issue write request */
    {
      perror("cannot write device");
      exit(-1);
    }

    ionum = (ionum)? 0:1;   /* switch to other buffer */
  }

  synchronize(ionum);         /* wait for both to finish */
  ionum = (ionum) ? 0 : 1;
  synchronize(ionum);
}




/**********/
/*
/*   lasthandler—receive and check AST
/*
/**********/


int lasthandler(param)

int param;
{
  if (!iostatus[param].done)    /* check AST consistency */
  {
    fprintf(stderr,"AST error: I/O not done\n");
```

(continued)

```
      exit (-1);
    }
  }




/**********/
/*
/*  synchronize—wait for I/O completion and check status
/*
/**********/

synchronize (ionum)

/* depends on FIFO delivery of I/O completions from the dev */

int ionum;
{
  setpri (ASTPRI);                    /* block AST delivery */
  if (!iostatus[ionum].done)          /* if not done yet */
  {
    astpause (ASTPRI-1,MAXWAIT);      /* allow ASTs and wait */
    if (!iostatus[ionum].done)        /* give up if not done */
    {
      fprintf(stderr,"I/O failure: AST timeout\n");
      exit (-1);
    }
  }
  setpri (ASTPRI-1);                  /* allow AST delivery */

  if (iostatus[ionum].error)          /* check for I/O error */
  {
    fprintf(stderr,"I/O failure: error is %d\n",
        iostatus[ionum].error);
    exit (-1);
  }

  /* check for correct count */
  if (iostatus[ionum].count != iocount[ionum])
  {
    fprintf(stderr,"I/O failure: count is %d\n",
        iostatus[ionum].count);
    exit (-1);
  }
}
```

When the device driver receives a request to initiate asynchronous I/O, it prepares a data structure describing the request and places it on an internal queue. It also locks the user-space output buffer and I/O status block into memory, clears the I/O status block to indicate that I/O completion is pending, and declares an AST based on the arguments provided by the caller. This latter action does not deliver the AST; it creates a description of it in a system-space buffer to be used later when delivery of the AST is requested.

The description of the output request that is prepared by the `xx_write` routine and placed on the internal queue for asynchronous execution is stored in a `buf` structure. Most of the fields needed to describe the request already exist in the `buf` definition. Some existing unused fields will be redefined to hold new items specific to this driver. Of course it would also be legitimate to simply define a new structure type, but for the example it is simpler to use the existing `buf` definition.

Since no system-space memory is needed for the output data, buffers are not allocated from the kernel pool. Instead, the driver will declare a group of private external `buf` structures as follows:

```
struct buf xx_buf[NBUF];
```

The value of NBUF will depend on how many controllers are to be supported and how many outstanding asynchronous requests are to be allowed. To support overlapped I/O of the type shown in the example user program above on a single controller, NBUF = 2 would be adequate. The driver must also include routines `xx_getbuf` and `xx_rlsbuf` to get and release `buf` structures from the pool. We will not show these routines; they would use the B_BUSY flag to mark buffers in use and use a `sleep` and `wakeup` channel to allow `xx_getbuf` to wait for a buffer to become available.

The driver will need to redefine two `buf` fields to hold nonstandard items:

```
#define  b_event   b_forw   /* AST queuehead */
#define  b_saddr   b_caddr  /* status block pointer */
```

The AST queuehead at `b_event` stores two pointer values, so it will overlay both `b_forw` and `b_back`.

Here is the `xx_write` routine:

```
xx_write(dev)
int dev;
{
    struct buf *bp;        /* pointer to output buf */
    struct async_rq asr;   /* user request */
    struct async_st ass;   /* user status */
    struct ast_spec asa;   /* user ast description */


    if (u.u_count != RQSIZE)      /* check for valid request */
    {
      u.u_error = EINVAL;
      return;
    }

    iomove(&asr,RQSIZE,B_WRITE);  /* get request structure */
    if (asr.ast_mark != RQMARK)   /* double check validity */
    {
      u.u_error = EINVAL;
      return;
    }
```

(continued)

```
/* can user access data buffer? */
if (!useracc(asr.baddr,asr.count,B_READ))
{
  u.u_error = EACCES;            /* and is address valid? */
  return;
}

bp = xx_getbuf();              /* get a buf structure */
bp->b_ioaddr = asr.baddr;      /* fill in I/O specs */
bp->b_bcount = asr.count;
bp->b_saddr  = (caddr_t) asr.saddr;
bp->b_proc   = u.u_procp;
bp->b_flags |= B_PHYS;

/* get the ast descriptor */
copyin(asr.ast_desc,&asa, sizeof(struct ast_spec));

/* declare the ast */
dclast(u.u_proc,asa.handler,asa.param1,
       asa.param2,asa.priority,0, &bp->b_event);

vslock(asr.baddr,asr.count);  /* lock in the data buffer */
vslock(asr.saddr,STSIZE);     /* and the status block */

/* clear all status fields */
ass.done = ass.error = ass.count = 0;

copyout(&ass,asr.saddr,STSIZE); /* in user space */

xx_qio(bp);                    /* queue the request */

return;
}
```

We have omitted some error checking from this routine, so the following comments are in order. dclast can return a failure status if no clist space is available; if this happens the driver should either wait and try again or return a failure to the caller.

It is also important that a driver not lock down too much memory. vslock must be executed while the caller is the current process; therefore, memory must be locked in advance for all queued asynchronous I/O requests. The kernel does not perform any kind of quota check on vslock calls; if one or more drivers attempt to lock too much memory, a system deadlock will occur. Therefore a driver should set an upper limit on the amount of memory that it will lock at one time and either sleep or return an error if the limit would be exceeded. For a system with one megabyte of physical memory, an upper limit of 256 kilobytes set within a driver would be reasonable. If more physical memory is available, the driver limit could be larger.

The xx_write routine calls xx_qio to place the output request on the driver queue. We will not show the code for that routine or for the xx_start routine which is also required. These routines will be similar to the ones with the same names presented in Example 3 in Chapter 6. Note that in xx_write the flag B_PHYS was set to inform iomaddr that the buffer to be mapped is in a user process address space.

The final routine required is the interrupt handler. In addition to its usual functions in this example, it must also update the user I/O status block, unlock the user memory buffers, and deliver the AST.

```
xx_intr(devno,csr,dp)

int devno;
int csr;
struct xx_device *dp;
{
   struct buf *bp;
   struct async_st ass;

   dp->xx_cr = CR_CA;              /* clear the interrupt */

   bp = xx_qhed;                   /* point to completed buf */
   xx_qhed = xx_qhed->av_forw;     /* remove it from the queue */
   if (xx_qhed != NULL)
      xx_start();                  /* start the next one */

   /* unlock the data buffer */
   vspunlock(bp->b_proc,bp->b_ioaddr,bp->b_bcount, B_WRITE);

   ass.done = 1;                   /* set up status values */
   ass.error = 0;
   ass.count = bp->b_bcount;

   /* write the status block */
   pcopyout(bp->b_proc,&ass,bp->b_saddr, STSIZE);

   /* and unlock it */
   vspunlock(bp->b_proc,bp->b_saddr,STSIZE, B_READ);

   delast(bp->b_event);            /* deliver the AST */

   xx_rlsbuf(bp);                  /* return buf to pool */
}
```

A

SUMMARY OF EXECUTIVE
HEADER FILES

Table A-1 summarizes the header files related to device drivers. Most of these files are found in `/usr/include/sys`. However, `fcntl.h` and `errno.h` are found in `/usr/include` and `ast.h` is found in both places.

TABLE A-1. Driver Header Files

ast.h	Defines the `ast_spec` structure used by a user program to pass an AST specification to a device driver. `/usr/include/ast.h` is intended for use by user programs. Device drivers should use `/usr/include/sys/ast.h`.
buf.h	Defines the `buf` structure used to pass I/O requests to the `strategy` routine of a block driver.
cblock.h	Defines the `cblock` structure used to hold `clist` data and declared ASTs. Not usually included by drivers, but could be used to alter one of the parameters of a declared AST.
conf.h	Included by the `conf.c` file; defines the `bdevsw`, `cdevsw`, and `linesw` structures.
elog.h	Used for error logging; defines the `iostat` data structure which can be used to count I/O operations. Defines required device major numbers for error logging.
erec.h	Used for error logging; defines `eblock` and other structures that hold error data.
errno.h	Defines the error codes that are returned to a user process by a driver. The codes EIO, ENXIO,

EACCES, EBUSY, ENODEV, and EINVAL are used by drivers.

fcntl.h	Defines I/O mode flags supplied by user programs to open and fcntl system calls.
file.h	Defines I/O mode flags passed to driver open, close, and ioctl routines.
io.h	Defines miscellaneous device information; a structure definition needed in conf.c can be placed here. See also peri.h.
iobuf.h	Defines the iobuf structure used by block drivers to hold controller and device state information.
ioctl.h	Defines commands for ioctl routines in various drivers.
mtio.h	Defines commands and structures for magtape operations.
param.h	Defines a large number of constants and macros used throughout the RTU executive.
peri.h	Defines miscellaneous device information; a structure definition needed in conf.c can be placed here. See also io.h.
proc.h	Defines the proc structure which defines a user process; not usually included by drivers.
space.h	Defines major executive data areas; should not be included by drivers.
sysinfo.h	Defines structures that hold global executive state information.
sysmacros.h	(System V.3 only) Defines macros for manipulating system variables and data types.
systm.h	Defines global executive variables.
tty.h	Defines parameters and structures associated with interactive terminals. Defines the clist structure and can be included by any driver that uses that structure.
types.h	Defines the special data types used by the executive.
user.h	Defines the user structure which describes a user process and passes information about I/O requests to drivers.

Table A-2 lists special data types used by the executive. These data types are defined in types.h.

TABLE A-2. System Data Types

`caddr_t`	Main memory virtual address
`daddr_t`	Block device address
`dev_t`	Device major and minor numbers
`ino_t`	Inode index
`label_t`	Vector for `setjmp`/`longjmp`
`off_t`	File offset
`paddr_t`	Main memory physical address
`time_t`	System time
`ushort`	`unsigned short`

Table A-3 lists the I/O status flags in the `buf` field `b_flags` that are used by drivers. This table does not list the flags in the `iobuf` field `b_flags`. The only flag in the `iobuf` field `b_flags` that is used by drivers is `B_TAPE` to determine whether a device is a magnetic tape.

TABLE A-3. I/O Status Flags in buf

B_READ   Set if the operation is a read, cleared for a write. There is a pseudoflag `B_WRITE` with the value zero, which can be used as function argument.

B_DONE   Cleared when a request is passed to `strategy`; must be set by the driver (usually by calling `iodone`) when the operation has been completed or aborted.

B_ERROR   Used by the device driver to indicate an error.

B_BUSY   Indicates that the buffer is in use. Drivers must not alter this flag for buffers from the executive block buffering cache; they can read and write it to coordinate access to private `buf` structures.

B_PHYS   Indicates that the associated data is in user address space. Must be set for raw I/O before `iomaddr` is called.

B_WANTED   If set, a `wakeup` should be issued on the `buf` address. This operation is handled in `brelse` for executive buffers; for a private `buf` the driver should test the flag and call `wakeup` if necessary. `B_BUSY` should be cleared at the same time. It is not necessary to call `wakeup` for block I/O because the `iodone` routine does it for you.

The following flag bits are specific to RTU and may not be used in other UNIX-like systems:

B_CMD   Set if this `buf` is a mode setting command rather than a data transfer request. It should be processed immediately.

B_URGON   Set by the data acquisition driver in a command buffer to order a disk driver to enter "urgent" mode. While that mode is in effect only buffers with the `B_URGNT` flag set are to be processed.

B_URGNT   See `B_URGON`. The routine `disksort` queues all buffers with this flag set ahead of those for which it is not set.

B_URGOF   Set to terminate urgent mode. When urgent mode terminates, all queued I/O requests with the `B_URGNT` flag not set can be processed.

KERNEL I/O
SUPPORT ROUTINES

This appendix describes kernel I/O support routines that are used by device drivers. Table B-1 lists the routines with a brief description. The reference sections that follow describe each routine in detail.

TABLE B-1. Kernel I/O Support Routines

brelse	Release a buffer
canast	Cancel an AST
cantimeout	Cancel a timeout request
clist	Storage management for small FIFO queue
cmn_err	Print system errors
copyin	Copy data from user space to system space
copyout	Copy data from system space to user space
cpass	Get character from user-space buffer
dclast	Declare an AST
delast	Deliver an AST
delay	Sleep for a specified number of clock ticks
disksort	Sort I/O requests into a queue
fmtberr	Format an error record for a block device
fubyte,fushort,fuword	Fetch datum from user space
getc	Get character from driver internal queue
getcb,getcf	Get cblock from clist queue or free list
geteblk	Get a free block buffer
gsignal	Send signal to process group
hibyte	Retrieves the high-order byte from a short word
hiword	Retrieves the high-order word from an integer
iodone	Release buffer and issue wakeup
iomaddr	Set up the I/O map for an I/O transfer to a buffer
iomalloc	Allocate I/O map registers
iomapvaddr	Set up the I/O map for an I/O transfer to a process
iomove	Move block of characters to or from user-space buffer

`iowait`	Wait for I/O completion
`lobyte`	Retrieves the low-order byte of a short word
`loword`	Retrieves the low-order word of an integer
`major`	Retrieve the major device number
`makedev`	Generate a complete device number
`memall`	Allocate memory
`memfree`	Free pages of physical memory
`minor`	Retrieve minor device number
`minphys`	Limit DMA to 252 kbytes
`panic`	Crash the system
`passc`	Put character to user-space buffer
`pcopyin`	Copy data from space of arbitrary process
`pcopyout`	Copy data to space of arbitrary process
`physck`	Check validity of raw DMA request
`physio`	Perform I/O to or from user-space buffer
`printf`	Print message on the system console
`psignal`	Send signal to a process
`putc`	Put character on driver internal queue
`putcb,putcf`	Put cblock on clist queue or free list
`signal`	Send signal to process
`sleep`	Suspend process until event occurs
`spl0, spl1, ..., spl7,` `splv, splx`	Set processor priority level
`subyte,sushort,suword`	Write datum in user space
`suser`	Determine if current user is superuser
`swab, swabl`	Reverse byte ordering
`timeout`	Declare a timeout interval and handler
`uprintf`	Display message on user terminal
`useracc`	Check user access to memory
`v_page_lock`	Lock user buffer in physical memory
`v_page_unlock`	Unlock user buffer from physical memory
`vmemall`	Allocate memory, always succeeding
`vmemfree`	Free virtual memory
`vslock`	Lock user buffer in physical memory
`vspunlock`	Unlock buffer from physical memory for arbitrary process
`vsunlock`	Unlock user buffer from physical memory
`wakeup`	Wake processes sleeping on event
`wmemall`	Allocate nonpaged memory in the kernel
`wmemfree`	Free nonpaged memory in the kernel

BRELSE   (RTU and System V.3)

NAME

brelse – release a buffer, with no I/O implied

SYNOPSIS

```
brelse(bp)
struct buf *bp;
```

DESCRIPTION

brelse returns the buffer described by the header structure pointed to by bp list of free buffers. The B_WANTED, B_BUSY, B_ASYNC, and B_AGE bits in bp->b_flags are cleared after the buffer is put on the appropriate free list.

RTU

RTU actually maintains several free lists that are searched separately when allocating buffers. The heads of these lists are kept in the array bfreelist. bfreelist[BQ_LOCKED] contains buffers that have been "locked" into the buffer cache. For example, file system super-blocks for mounted file systems and the current bitmap free-list block are locked into the buffer cache, and these buffers cannot be reallocated by subsequent calls to getblk, geteblk, bread, or breada. Locked buffers are identified by a nonzero bp->b_locked field.

bfreelist[BQ_AGE] is a list of buffers that contain no valid data or contain data that is not expected to be reused soon. brelse puts buffers containing no valid data (bp->b_valid equal to zero) at the front of this list. Buffers that contain data that is not expected to be reused soon (B_AGE set in bp->b_flags) are placed at the end of this list.

All other buffers are placed on bfreelist[BQ_LRU], a list of buffers containing valid data that may be referenced again soon. This list is kept in "least recently used" order: brelse adds buffers to the end of this list, and getblk searches this list from the beginning when looking for a block to reuse.

If brelse is not being called from interrupt level and runrun is set, brelese will call qswtch to allow higher priority processes to run. brelse uses the B_ASYNC bit in bp->b_flags to determine whether it was called from interrupt level.

System V.3

brelse performs basically the same operation in System V.3 as in RTU. However, the management of the buffer free list is substantially simpler. If an error has occurred (indicated by the B_ERROR bit being set in bp->b_flags), B_STALE and B_AGE are set in bp->b_flags. Any buffer with B_AGE set in bp->b_flags is placed at the front of the buffer free list. All other buffers are placed at the end of the list. This is essentially the bfreelist[BQ_LRU] list managed by RTU.

RETURNS

No return value.

SEE ALSO

getblk, geteblk, bread, breada, bwrite, bawrite, and bdwrite.

DIAGNOSTICS

None.

CANAST   (RTU)

NAME

canast – cancel an AST

SYNOPSIS

```
canast(event)
struct cblock *event;
```

DESCRIPTION

The canast routine is called to cancel a previously-declared AST. This routine is called by the exit routine for processes, so that AST's are not delivered to a non-existent process. The AST is removed from both the pending (delivered) queue, and from the active (declared) queue for a particular process.

This routine may also be called by device a driver, for instance, in a close routine, or in response to an ioctl.

RETURNS

None.

SEE ALSO

dclast and delast.

CANTIMEOUT   (RTU)

NAME

cantimeout – cancel a timeout call

SYNOPSIS

```
cantimeout(id)
int id;
```

DESCRIPTION

cantimeout cancels a previously scheduled function call timeout.   id
should be the identifier returned by a previous call to timeout.

RETURNS

cantimeout returns the number of ticks remaining until the function
would be called, or –1 if the timeout had already expired (that is, if the
specified timeout was not found on the pending list of timeouts).

Note that untimeout, the System V.3 equivalent of cantimeout does
not return a value.

SEE ALSO

timeout and untimeout.

NAME

clist – storage management for small FIFO queues

SYNPOSIS

```
#include <sys/types.h>
#ifdef RTU
#include <sys/cblock.h>
#endif
#include <sys/tty.h>
```

This declares:

```
#ifdef RTU
#define CLSTSIZE 24
#endif

#ifdef SYSV3
#define CLSTSIZE 64
#endif

struct cblock {
      struct      cblock *c_next;
      char  c_first;
      char  c_last;
      char  c_data[CLSTSIZE];
};
```

and

```
struct clist {
#ifdef RTU
      lock_t      c_lk; /* lock for this queue */
      short c_cc;        /* character count */
#endif
#ifdef RTU
      int c_cc;          /* character count */
#endif
      struct cblock *c_cf;/* pointer to first */
      struct cblock *c_cl;/* pointer to last */
};
```

DESCRIPTION

A clist is conceptually a FIFO queue. Characters entered onto a clist using `putc` can be retrieved by calling `getc`. The number of characters that can be stored on a clist is not fixed. Instead, the queue is stored as a linked list of cblocks, each of which can store up to `CLSTSIZE` characters. This requires less total storage assuming only a few clists actually have a large number of characters queued. The total number of cblocks available on the system is specified at system configuration time.

Groups of characters can be moved efficiently to and from a clist using the calls `putcb` and `getcb`, which transfer whole cblocks to and from the clist. The number of characters stored in the cblock `cb` is `cb.c_last-cb.c_first`. These characters are stored in `cb.c_data[cb.c_first]` through `cb.c_data[cb.c_last-1]`.

Using these calls, a cblock is allocated using `getcf`. After data is stored in the cblock, the cblock is put on a clist by calling `putcb`. The cblock will be removed from the clist by a call to `getcb`, and the cblock is returned to the free list after the data is copied by calling `putcf`.

In RTU the actual declaration of the cblock structure is more complicated than the one shown here, although cblocks can be used in clists as if they were declared as shown here. RTU also uses cblocks for dynamic allocation of other small data structures. In particular, active and pending ASTs are stored in cblocks, as are the DACP buffer queues. cblocks can be allocated for any similar purpose using `getcf` and released using `putcf`.

Because cblocks are a limited resource, device drivers should avoid attempting to put an unbounded number of characters on a clist. For example, terminal drivers discard all input if the number of pending characters exceeds 256 and wait for the device if the length of the output queue exceeds some terminal dependent limit.

SEE ALSO

`getc`, `putc`, `getcb`, `putcb`, `getcf`, and `putcf`.

CMN_ERR (System V.3)

NAME

cmn_err – print system errors

SYNOPSIS

```
#include <cmn_err.h>

cmn_err(severity, format, var1,...)
int severity;
char *format;
unsigned var1,...;
```

DESCRIPTION

cmn_err is essentially a scaled-down version of the C library routine printf with an additional argument to indicate the severity of an error. severity is one of CE_CONT, CE_NOTE, CE_WARN, and CE_PANIC. An error message is printed using format and the rest of the arguments as arguments to printf. Only %s, %u, %d (==%u), %o, %x, %c, and %D are recognized. If the first character of format is a vertical bar (|), the message is only stored in an internal buffer, putbuf. If the first character of format is a caret (^), the message is only printed on the system console. Otherwise the message is sent to both destinations.

The message is preceded by NOTE, WARNING, or PANIC for severity levels C_NOTE, CE_WARN, or CE_PANIC. If the severity level is CE_PANIC, the system enters an infinite loop after printing the error message.

Note that cmn_err often works by disabling all interrupts while printing messages, so aside from debugging, cmn_err should be used sparingly.

SEE ALSO

printf, panic, and printf(3).

COPYIN   (RTU and System V.3)

NAME

copyin – copy bytes from user address space to kernel address space

SYNOPSIS

```
copyin(from, to, cnt)
caddr_t from;
caddr_t to;
unsigned int cnt;
```

DESCRIPTION

copyin copies cnt bytes from the user virtual address from to the kernel virtual address to.

If some portion of the user virtual address space from from to from + cnt is not readable by the user, copyin returns –1 (without altering u.u_error). Some portion of the data may have been copied.

copyin optimizes the copy operation using larger data types where possible.

RETURNS

Zero if successful, –1 otherwise.

SEE ALSO

copyout, pcopyin, pcopyout, and iomove.

DIAGNOSTICS

An attempt to copy from a user virtual address that is mapped to a non-sensical physical page cause a panic ("copyin").

COPYOUT _____ (RTU and System V.3)

NAME

copyout – copy bytes from kernel address space to user address space

SYNOPSIS

```
copyout(from, to, cnt)
caddr_t from;
caddr_t to;
unsigned int cnt;
```

DESCRIPTION

copyout copies cnt bytes from the kernel virtual address from to the user virtual address to.

If some portion of the user virtual address space from to to to + cnt is not writable by the user, copyout returns –1 (without altering u.u_error). Some portion of the data may have been copied.

copyout optimizes the copy operation by using larger data types where possible.

RETURNS

Zero if successful, –1 otherwise.

SEE ALSO

copyin, pcopyout, pcopyout, and iomove.

DIAGNOSTICS

An attempt to copy from a user virtual address that is mapped to a non-sensical physical page cause a panic ("copyout").

CPASS

NAME

cpass – get a character from user virtual space

SYNOPSIS

    int cpass()

DESCRIPTION

The cpass routine returns an integer that is the character at the user virtual address specified by u.u_base. It decrements u.u_count and increments u.u_offset and u.u_base.

RETURNS

If u.u_count is zero when cpass is called, it returns a –1. Otherwise, it returns the character fetched from user space. The returned value is an integer.

In System V.3, cpass will set u.u_error to EFAULT if u.u_base refers to an invalid user virtual address.

SEE ALSO

passc and fubyte. A discussion of the efficiency of this routine is included under fubyte.

DCLAST   (RTU)
_____

NAME

   dclast – declare an AST

SYNOPSIS

```
dclast(proc, handler, p1, p2, pri, flag, event)
struct proc *proc;
caddr_t handler;
int p1;
int p2;
int pri;
int flag;
struct cblock **event;
```


DESCRIPTION

   A user process calls dclast to declare that it wants to receive an AST
   when a certain event occurs. ASTs are stored in cblock structures as a
   doubly-linked list.   dclast builds an AST cblock structure and adds it
   to the queue named in event.

   proc is a pointer to the entry in the process table for the process to
   which the AST should be sent.

   handler is the address of a low-level handler that provides the interface
   to either C or Fortran code.

   p1 is typically the address of a high level routine. This routine will be
   passed control when the AST is delivered. This routine will usually be
   called with a calling argument, p2. The actual interpretation of p1 and
   p2 is a function of the language-dependent low-level handler.

   p2 is the argument to be passed to the high level routine when the AST
   is delivered.

   pri is the priority of the AST. This is an AST delivery priority and is not
   related to hardware interrupts or to signal priorities.

   flag specifies whether or not the AST should be automatically redeclared every time it is delivered. The only flag value currently defined is
   AST_AUTO. MASSCOMP reserves the right to expand the values of this
   argument in the future.

`event` is the address of a link word to be used to insert the AST into the active queue. Multiple ASTs can be declared for a given event. An event list should be declared as:

```
struct cblock *event[2];
```

and used

```
dclast (proc, handler, p1, p2, pri, flag, event);
```

`dclast` adds the cblock holding the AST description to the active queue. `delast` causes the AST to be removed from the active queue and delivered to the user process. Delivery to the user process entails placing the AST on a pending queue. ASTs are received from the pending queue of the process in order by AST delivery priority. `sanast` removes the AST from both the active queue and the pending queue.

RETURNS

The `dclast` routine returns zero if there are no clists available. It returns one if the routine is successful.

SEE ALSO

`delast, canast, ast(2), asthandler(2),` and `setpri(2).`

DELAST   (RTU)

NAME

delast – deliver an AST

SYNOPSIS

```
delast(event)
struct cblock *event;
```

DESCRIPTION

The delast routine delivers the first AST on the AST queue that was
declared on event with a call to dclast. The delast routine places
the AST on a pending queue in the user area.

Actual delivery of the AST will be postponed if either the process is
sleeping on a priority less than or equal to PZERO or if the AST delivery
priority is currently higher than the priority of the specified AST. In
both of these cases, delivery will be triggered when the various system
priorities once again allow it.

Multiple ASTs can be pending delivery on a process at a given time.
They will be received by the process in AST delivery-priority order.

After an AST has been delivered, it is removed from the declared-ASTs
queue. However, if AST_AUTO was set in the flag argument to the
dclast routine, it will be automatically redeclared.

To deliver just one AST on an event queue use:

```
        if (event[0])
                delast(event[0]);
or
        while(event[0)
                delast(event[0]);
```

where event is a the address of a clist structure declared in the
user's code.

To deliver just one AST on an event queue use:

```
        if (event[0])
                delast(event[0]);
```

For ASTs that are delivered to represent a particular event (such as pushing a button), it is generally required to deliver only one AST. If the event is more general (for example, failure of some auxiliary processor), all ASTs should be delivered.

`delast` does not return any value. It is an error to call `delast` if no AST has been declared.

SEE ALSO

`dclast` and `canast`.

DELAY   (RTU and System V.3)

NAME

delay – sleep for a specified number of clock ticks

SYNOPSIS

delay (*ticks*)

DESCRIPTION

delay causes the calling process to sleep for the number of clock ticks
specified by ticks and wakes it up when that number of ticks has
passed.

NOTES

Do not call delay at device initialization time. Do not call delay in
any context in which it is not appropriate to call sleep.

SEE ALSO

sleep, wakeup, and timeout.

DISKSORT   (RTU)
_____

NAME

　　disksort – sort I/O requests onto a queue

SYNOPSIS

```
#define  b_cylin  b_resid
disksort(devptr, bufptr)
struct iobuf *devptr;
struct buf *bufptr;
```

DESCRIPTION

　　The disksort routine sorts the I/O requests for a disk onto a queue
　　based on the seek location of the requests. The purpose of this routine is
　　to optimize seeks to the disk.

　　The argument devptr contains a pointer to the I/O request queue for
　　the device. The bufptr argument contains a pointer to the buffer for
　　this I/O request. This routine depends on the driver having placed the
　　cylinder number in the field b_resid.

　　The algorithm used by this routine is a one-directional elevator algo-
　　rithm.　 disksort assumes that the heads are at the cylinder specified
　　by the first request in the queue. The first request is followed by I/O
　　requests for cylinders, in order from low to high, which have not been
　　passed on this sweep of the disk. Requests for cylinders that have
　　already been passed on this sweep are placed in order from low to high
　　following the first list and will be processed on the next sweep.

　　For example, the queue might contain requests for cylinders:

　　　　　start　　100
　　　　　　　　　150
　　　　　　　　　151
　　　　　　　　　200
　　　　　　　　　 2
　　　　　　　　　 3
　　　　　　　　　 10

　　All I/O requests with B_URGNT set are placed in FIFO order before all
　　other buffers. Buffers with B_CMD set are placed in FIFO order after
　　B_URGNT requests but before all other I/O requests. Therefore, driver
　　commands that do not require I/O and have B_CMD set are acted upon
　　quickly.

RETURNS

None.

WARNINGS

MASSCOMP reserves the right to use alternative algorithms in the `disksort` routine. Notice also that not all versions of UNIX use this algorithm.

FMTBERR (RTU)

NAME

fmtberr – format an error record for a block device

SYNOPSIS

```
fmtberr(dp, cyl)
struct iobuf *dp;
int cyl;
```

DESCRIPTION

fmtberr manipulates various structures prior to logging the error with logberr.

If dp->io_erec is not zero when fmtberr is called, the e_rtry field is incremented and fmtberr returns.

Fmtberr uses the following:

```
dp->io_stp
dp->io_stp->io_ops
dp->io_stp->io_misc
dp->io_stp->io_unlog
dp->i_addr
dp->i_nreg
dp->b_dev
dp->b_actf
```

and the buffer header pointed to by dp->b_actf to construct an error logging record whose address is saved in dp->io_erec. dp->b_actf is assumed to point to the buffer header describing the transfer causing the error. However, the error logger uses dp->b_dev as the device number for the device causing the error rather than dp->b_actf->bp->b_dev. The device numbers stored in dp->b_dev are declared in /usr/include/sys/elog.h.

FUBYTE   (RTU)

NAME

fubyte, fushort, fuword – fetch a byte, short, or word from user
virtual space

SYNOPSIS

```
char fubyte(addr)
caddr_t addr;
short fushort(addr)
caddr_t addr;
fuword(addr)
caddr_t addr;
```


DESCRIPTION

fubyte, fushort, and fuword are used to get a single byte, short, or
word from user virtual address space. The byte, short, or word is the
return value from the routine. A word is defined to be an integer, which
is four bytes on the MASSCOMP machines.

These routines do not access or modify the u.u_base or u.u_count
fields while cpass and iomove do.

These routines are commonly used in standard UNIX but not on the
MASSCOMP system, because the MC68000 is not good at accessing single bytes and words in user virtual address space while executing in system mode. If more than a few bytes are to be moved, a single call to
iomove or copyin will be more efficient.

RETURNS

If the specificied user address is invalid, these routines will all return –1.
Note fuword does not distinguish between this error and fetching a
valid value of –1 from user space.

SEE ALSO

cpass, passc, subyte, copyin, copyout, and iomove.

GETC   (RTU and System V.3)

NAME

getc – get a character from the front of a clist

SYNOPSIS

```
getc(p)
struct clist *p;
```

DESCRIPTION

getc removes the character from the front of the clist pointed to by p
and returns that character. If that character is the last character in the
cblock at the front of the clist, the cblock is returned to the free cblock
list.

RETURNS

getc returns −1 if there are no characters currently on the specified clist.

SEE ALSO

clist, putc, getcf, getcb, putcf, and putcb.

GETCB   (RTU and System V.3)

___

NAME

getcb – get a cblock from a clist

SYNOPSIS

```
struct cblock *getcb(p)
struct clist *p;
```


DESCRIPTION

getcb removes the cblock from the front of the clist specified by p and returns a pointer to that cblock.

getcb is used by the system to flush clists quickly (remove all characters regardless of the contents).   getcb is also used by ttread, the common terminal read system call routine, when the requested number of characters is greater than or equal to CLSTSIZE.

The number of characters stored in the cblock cb is cb.c_last-cb.c_first.   These   characters   are   stored   in cb.c_data[cb.c_first] through cb.c_data[cb.c_last-1]. After the data is copied out of the cblock, it should be returned to the free cblock list by calling putcf.

RETURNS

A pointer to the cblock removed from the front of the clist.

SEE ALSO

clist, getc, getcf, putc, putcf, and putcb.

GETCF   **(RTU and System V.3)**

NAME

getcf – allocate a cblock (get a cblock from the free list)

SYNOPSIS

```
struct cblock *getcf()
```

DESCRIPTION

getcf allocates a cblock from the system list of free cblocks
(cfreelist).

RETURNS

The address of the allocated cblock, or zero if no cblocks are available.

SEE ALSO

getc, getcb, putc, putcb, and putcf.

GETEBLK   (RTU and System V.3)

NAME

geteblk – get an empty block buffer

SYNOPSIS

```
struct buf *geteblk()
```

DESCRIPTION

geteblk allocates a buffer from the pool of disk buffers and returns a pointer to a buffer header structure describing the buffer. The buffer will not be associated with any disk driver or block number and can be used for arbitrary purposes by device drivers or other system routines. The buffer is released to the pool using brelse.

Note that geteblk returns a pointer to a buffer header. If this pointer is stored in a variable bp, the data buffer itself is accessed as bp->b_un.b_addr.

RETURNS

A pointer to a buffer header describing the data buffer.

SEE ALSO

brelse, wmemall, and wmemfree.

DIAGNOSTICS

None.

WARNINGS

Sleeps at high priority (PRIBIO + 1) if no buffers are available. geteblk will call bwrite (with B_ASYNC set in b_flags) for all dirty buffers on the free list geteblk finds while searching for a clean buffer to return.

GSIGNAL   (RTU)

NAME

gsignal – send a signal to members of a process group

SYNOPSIS

```
gsignal(pgroup, signal)
int pgroup;
int signal;
```

DESCRIPTION

The gsignal routine is used to send a specified signal, signal, to all
of the processes in a given process group, pgroup. This is used by terminal drivers to send signals such as SIGHUP and SIGINT.

The processes in a process group are normally all those processes that
were forked by a particular instance of a login shell. The setgrp system call can be used to change the process group. Note that the C shell
uses a different process group for every job.

The signal, signal, can be any of those listed in
/usr/include/signal.h. This routine calls the psignal routine to
send the signals to each process.

NOTE

The equivalent routine in System V.3 is called signal.

RETURNS

None.

SEE ALSO

psignal and signal.

HIBYTE   (RTU and System V.3)
_____

NAME

hibyte – retrieves the high order (most signifcant) byte

SYNOPSIS

```
hibyte(word)
ushort word;
```

DESCRIPTION

The hibyte macro retrieves the high order byte from a short word. It is defined in /usr/include/sys/param.h.

SEE ALSO

hiword, lobyte, and loword.

HIWORD   (RTU and System V.3)

NAME

hiword – retreives the high order word

SYNOPSIS

```
hiword(longword)
int longword;
```

DESCRIPTION

The `hiword` macro retrieves the high order (most significant) word (16 bits) from an integer. It is defined in `/usr/include/sys/param.h`.

This routine reflects PDP-11 naming conventions where integer data types are `bytes`, `words`, and `longwords`. The other common naming convention refers to these as `bytes`, `halfwords`, and `words`.

SEE ALSO

`hibyte`, `lobyte`, and `loword`.

IODONE   (RTU and System V.3)

NAME

iodone – mark I/O complete on a buffer

SYNOPSIS

```
int iodone(bp)
struct buf *bp;
```

DESCRIPTION

The basic function of iodone is to indicate that an I/O operation has completed on a specified buffer and either wakeup processes waiting for that I/O to complete or to release the buffer following an asynchronous I/O operation.

Under System V.3, the action of iodone is simple. iodone first sets B_DONE in bp->b_flags. If the I/O operation is asynchronous (B_ASYNC is set in bp->b_flags), then iodone releases the buffer by calling brelse. iodone also decrements the variable basyncnt and wakes up any processes sleeping on &basyncnt if basyncnt is now zero (this allows the sync system call to wait for all writebehinds to complete before returning).

If the I/O operation is not asynchronous, iodone checks B_WANTED in bp->b_flags to determine if any process is waiting for the I/O to complete. If B_WANTED was set, iodone clears B_WANTED and calls wakeup(bp).

Under RTU the operation of iodone is more complex in order to deal with paging I/O operations and clustered block I/O.

iodone performs several functions. First, it marks the buffer, *bp as being complete by setting B_DONE in bp->b_flags. Second, if the I/O is asynchronous, iodone releases the buffer.

iodone will call the completion routine whose address is in bp->b_completion if it is not equal to NULL.

If none of B_CMD, B_PHYS, or B_UAREA is set in bp->b_flags, iodone assumes the buffer header was set up for block clustering and modifies bp->bio, bp->b_resid[], bp->b_error[], bp->b_eflag, and bp->b_error, based on the values of bp->b_resid, bp->b_bcount, and bp->b_mask. If B_CMD or B_PHYS is set, iodone does not modify any of these fields. It simply sets the done bit and does the wakeup call.

If B_DIRTY is set in bp->b_flags, iodone calls pageclean and returns before calling a completion routine or releasing the buffer. It is assumed that pageclean will do this.

Finally, iodone performs a wakeup call on anyone who is sleeping on the buffer *bp.

If B_ASYNC is set, iodone clears B_BUSY and releases the buffer. It does not modify any of the fields described above and does not call pageclean or wakeup.

Except when B_ASYNC is set, iodone does not clear B_BUSY. B_BUSY is cleared by brelse when the buffer is released.

DIAGNOSTICS

The iodone routine panics if the buffer *bp is already marked as complete (i.e., panic ("dup iodone")).

SEE ALSO

iowait.

IOMADDR   (RTU)

NAME

iomaddr – set up the I/O map for an I/O transfer to a buffer

SYNOPSIS

```
paddr_t iomaddr(bp, addr, count, base)
struct buf *bp;
paddr_t addr;
unsigned int count;
int base;
```

DESCRIPTION

iomaddr is designed to be called from a device driver implementing the
block device interface. bp is a pointer to an I/O buffer. addr designates the starting memory address of the I/O transfer and may be an
address in the buffer cache, a user process virtual address space, a system per process data area, or the user page tables. count specifies the
size of the transfer in bytes. base is the base address in the I/O map to
be used for the transfer, i.e., the return value of a previous call to
iomalloc.

Bits in the b_flags word control the action of iomaddr.

B_CMD   Causes iomaddr to ignore this buffer and return.

B_DIRTY   Indicates that this I/O transaction is writing out a
             dirty memory page for the I/O system. The I/O map
             is set up from the page table of process two (the page
             daemon) rather than from the process specified by
             b_proc.

B_UAREA   Indicates that addr is to be interpreted relative to the
             start of the per process user data area, u. The I/O
             map registers are initialized from bp->b_proc->
             p_addr[i].

B_PHYS   Indicates a raw I/O transfer (i.e., bypassing the disk
             block cache). addr is to be interpreted as a virtual
             address in the process specified by bp->b_proc.

B_PAGET   Indicates that addr is to be interpreted as an offset
             within the page tables for the process specified by
             bp->b_proc.

If none of these bits are set, `addr` is treated as a system virtual address. This includes system buffers. Device drivers generally do not need to be aware of these bits. These bits are set up (if needed) by system routines to perform paging or swapping.

RETURNS

The MULTIBUS address to be used by the transfer, i.e., the data address that should be passed to the I/O controller.

SEE ALSO

`iomalloc, iomfree, iomapvaddr,` and `iomload.`

DIAGNOSTICS

If the I/O map was loaded incorrectly (i.e., the page number read back from the map differs from the page number written), `iomaddr` prints the I/O map register address, the physical memory page number being loaded, the erroneous contents of I/O map register, and the current contents of the I/O map register (all in hexadecimal radix), and then calls `panic("iomaddr")`.

Attempts to direct I/O to physical memory page zero will result in a `panic("iomaddr: zero entry")`.

WARNINGS

Note that `addr` and `count` are passed explicitly as arguments rather than being picked up from `bp->b_ioaddr` and `bp->b_bcount`. This allows device drivers to break large transfers into smaller ones if this was not already done by `physio` or `swap`.

IOMALLOC   (RTU)

NAME

iomalloc – allocate I/O map registers

SYNOPSIS

```
iomalloc (size, flag)
unsigned size;
int flag;
```

DESCRIPTION

Allocates enough registers in the MULTIBUS I/O map for transferring
size bytes.   iomalloc assumes that the data transfer is not page
aligned. If flag is zero, iomalloc will allocate I/O map registers for
addresses totally contained in the low megabyte of the Multibus address
space (i.e., 20-bit addresses). If flag is nonzero, the allocated I/O map
addresses will require more than 20 bits.

RETURNS

The base index of the I/O map registers allocated.

SEE ALSO

iomfree, iomload, iomaddr, and iomapvaddr.

DIAGNOSTICS

None.

WARNINGS

If sufficient space in the I/O map is not available, iomalloc calls
sleep at priority PSWP+1 waiting for space to be freed.

BUGS

It should be possible to allocate space in the low 64K bytes of the I/O
map (i.e., 16-bit addresses).

There should be a flag to cause `iomalloc` to return an error value rather than waiting for available space. This will probably be implemented by treating `flag` as a bit vector of flags. Therefore, programs should use only the values zero or one.

IOMAPVADDR   (RTU)

NAME

iomapvaddr – set up the I/O map for an I/O transfer to a process

SYNOPSIS

```
paddr_t iomapvaddr(base, addr, count)
int base;
paddr_t addr;
unsigned int count;
```

DESCRIPTION

iomapvaddr is designed to be called from device drivers implementing a raw device (i.e., DMA directly to a process address space) but not using the buffer device interface. addr designates the starting address (in the virtual address space of the current process) of the I/O transfer. count specifies the size of the transfer in bytes. base is the base address in the I/O map to be used for the transfer, i.e., the return value of a previous call to iomalloc.

RETURNS

The MULTIBUS address to be used by the transfer, i.e., the data address that should be passed to the I/O controller.

SEE ALSO

iomalloc, iomfree, iomvaddr, and iomload.

DIAGNOSTICS

If the I/O map was loaded incorrectly (i.e., the page number read back from the map differs from the page number written), iomapvaddr prints the I/O map register address, the physical memory page number being loaded, the erroneous contents of I/O map register, and the current contents of the I/O map register (all in hexadecimal radix), and then calls panic("iomapvaddr").

Attempts to direct I/O to physical memory page zero will result in a panic("iomapvaddr: zero entry").

IOMOVE   (RTU and System V.3)

NAME

`iomove` – move data between user and system virtual space

SYNOPSIS

```
int iomove(addr, count, direction)
caddr_t addr;
unsigned count;
int direction;
```

DESCRIPTION

`iomove` is used to move data in the direction, `direction`, which is either `B_READ` or `B_WRITE`. `B_READ` is used to write data to the user process (the user has issued a `read`), and `B_WRITE` is used to get data from the user area (the user has issued a `write`). The `count` is the number of bytes to be transferred.

The `addr` argument is the address of a buffer in virtual address space. If `u_segflag` is equal to one, `addr` is interpreted as an address in the current processes virtual address space. If `u_segflag` is equal to zero, `addr` is interpreted as a system virtual address. If `u_segflag` is two `addr` is interpreted as a reference to instruction space in the current process. On MASSCOMP systems, user instruction space is the same as user data space, but would be different on machines implementing separate instruction and data spaces, such as some PDP-11s.

The other address is taken from `u_base`.

The fields `u.u_base`, `u.u_count`, and `u.u_offset` are updated by the number of bytes moved.

RETURNS

If `count` is zero, `iomove` just returns. If `copyin` or `copyout` return error codes, `iomove` sets `u.u_error` to `EFAULT` and returns.

SEE ALSO

`copyin` and `copyout`.

IOWAIT   (RTU and System V.3)

_____

NAME

iowait – wait for I/O completion on a buffer

SYNOPSIS

```
iowait(bp);
struct buf *bp;
```


DESCRIPTION

This routine sleeps at the appropriate priority until the I/O for the buffer
*bp has been completed.   iowait causes sleeps at PRIBIO. Since
PRIBIO is less than PZERO, no signals can be received. It then calls the
geterror routine to log any errors that may have occurred.

RETURNS

None.

SEE ALSO

geterror and iodone.

LOBYTE   (RTU and System V.3)

NAME

lobyte – retreives the low order byte

SYNOPSIS

```
lobyte(word)
ushort word;
```

DESCRIPTION

The lobyte macro retrieves the low order byte from a short word. It is defined in /usr/include/sys/param.h.

SEE ALSO

hiword, hibyte, and loword.

LOWORD   (RTU and System V.3)

NAME

loword – retreives the low order word

SYNOPSIS

```
loword(longword)
int longword;
```

DESCRIPTION

The loword macro retrieves the low order word (short) from an integer. It is defined in /usr/include/sys/param.h.

SEE ALSO

hibyte, hiword, and lobyte.

MAJOR   (RTU and System V.3)

NAME

major – retreive the major device number

SYNOPSIS

```
major(device)
dev_t device;
```

DESCRIPTION

major is a macro that gets the major device number from a device number, device.

In RTU this macro is defined in /usr/include/sys/param.h.

In System V.3 this macro is defined in /usr/include/sys/sysmacros.h.

SEE ALSO

minor and makedev.

MAKEDEV   (RTU and System V.3)

NAME

    makedev – generates a complete device number

SYNOPSIS

```
makedev(major, minor)
ushort major;
ushort minor;
```

DESCRIPTION

    makedev is a macro that generates a device number of type dev_t from the major and minor numbers for the device.

    In RTU this macro is defined in /usr/include/sys/param.h.

    In System V.3 this macro is defined in /usr/include/sys/sysmacros.h.

SEE ALSO

    major and minor.

MEMALL   (RTU)

NAME

memall – allocate memory

SYNOPSIS

```
memall(pte, size, p, type)
struct pte *pte;
int size;
struct proc *p;
int type;
```

DESCRIPTION

memall allocates size pages of physical memory, filling in the page
map pointed to by pte. The allocated memory "belongs" to the process
specified by p. type is one of:

CTEXT   The allocated memory is part of a user shared text seg-
         ment.

CDATA   The allocated memory is part of a user data segment.

CSTACK   The allocated memory is part of a user stack segment.

CSYS   The allocated memory is part of system virtual address
         space.

The page table entries are filled in with the physical page numbers of the
allocated memory with all other fields in the page table entry zero.

RETURNS

Zero if there is not enough free memory to satisfy the request (in which
case no page table entries are modified) or one if the memory allocation
succeeds.

SEE ALSO

vmemall, wmemall, vmemfree, memfree, and wmemfree.

WARNING

Device drivers should generally use wmemall rather than calling
memall directly.

NAME

memfree – free pages of physical memory

SYNOPSIS

```
memfree(vpte, size, detach)
struct pte *vpte;
int size;
```

DESCRIPTION

Returns size pages of physical memory described by the page table entries pointed to by vpte to the free list. The page frames being returned are inserted to the head/tail of the free list depending on whether there is any possible future use of them.

If detach is nonzero then the page table entries are invalidated in memory and in the TB cache.

If the freemem count had been zero, the processes sleeping for memory are awakened.

RETURNS

No return value.

SEE ALSO

memall, vmemall, wmemall, vmemfree, and wmemfree.

DIAGNOSTICS

If size is not a multiple of CLSIZE then memfree calls panic("memfree").

If any page table entry points to a physical memory page less than firstfree or greater than maxfree and is not mapped to physical memory, then memall calls panic("bad mem free").

If any page is already on the free list, `memall` calls `panic("dup mem free")`.

WARNING

Device drivers should use `wmemfree` rather than calling `memfree` directly.

MINOR   (RTU and System V.3)

NAME

minor – retreive the minor device number

SYNOPSIS

```
minor(device)
dev_t device;
```

DESCRIPTION

minor is a macro that gets the minor device number from a device number, device.

In RTU this macro is defined in /usr/include/sys/param.h.

In System V.3 this macro is defined in /usr/include/sys/sysmacros.h.

SEE ALSO

major and makedev.

MINPHYS   (RTU)

NAME

minphys – break a transfer up into manageable chunks

SYNOPSIS

```
minphys(bp)
struct buf *bp;
```

DESCRIPTION

The minphys routine that is delivered with RTU looks at the b_bcount field of the bp structure. If this field is larger than one page less than one-quarter megabyte (252*1024 bytes), it is overwritten with the value (252*1024).

This value is used to facilitate DMA transfers that may not be page aligned. The allocation made of the iomap of one-quarter megabytes will be adequate if the system version of the minphys routine is called.

This is intended to be used with physio.

RETURNS

This routine returns nothing, but may overwrite the value of bp->b_bcount.

NOTE

In System V.3 DMA transfers are broken into small pieces by the routine dma_breakup, which is used in conjunction with a special strategy routine.

SEE ALSO

physio and dma_breakup.

PANIC   (RTU and System V.3)

NAME

`panic` – hang system after a fatal error

SYNOPSIS

```
panic(msg)
char *msg;
```

DESCRIPTION

If an RTU system is configured with the kernel debugger `kdb`, control passes to the command interpreter of `kdb`. This enables you to examine memory or processor register contents, take a stack backtrace, or perform other actions to determine the source of the problem. Attempting to continue from `panic` will resume its standard action which first synchronizes the disks with a call to the `update` routine. It then prints the message, `msg` on the system console. Finally, the `panic` routine places the system in an infinite loop.

Under System V.3, `panic` simply prints a message on the system console and then places the system in an infinite loop.

RETURNS

The `panic` routine never returns.

SEE ALSO

`cmn_err` and `printf`.

WARNINGS

This routine should only be used in the case of unrecoverable errors that threaten the integrity of the system as a whole, or when something indicates that integrity has already been lost.

PASSC   (RTU and System V.3)

NAME

passc – pass a character to user virtual space

SYNOPSIS

```
passc(c)
char c;
```

DESCRIPTION

The passc routine places the character c at the address specified by
u.u_base. It decrements u.u_count and increments u.u_offset
and u.u_base.

RETURNS

passc returns a –1 when u.u_count reaches zero. Until then, zero is
returned.

SEE ALSO

cpass and subyte.

PCOPYIN
(RTU)

NAME

pcopyin – copy bytes from another user address space to kernel address space

SYNOPSIS

```
pcopyin(procp, from, to, cnt)
struct proc *procp;
caddr_t from;
caddr_t to;
unsigned int cnt;
```

DESCRIPTION

pcopyin copies cnt bytes from virtual address from in the process specified by procp to the kernel virtual address to.

pcopyin assumes that memory from from to from+cnt is readable by the user in process procp, and that the physical memory for these addresses has been locked into memory using vslock or v_page_lock. Typically this will be done as part of the "top half" of some device driver, and pcopyin will be called at interrupt time.

pcopyin optimizes the copy operation by copying larger data types (ints) where possible.

RETURNS

No return value.

SEE ALSO

copyin, pcopyout, and iomove.

DIAGNOSTICS

If either from or to has any of the high-order eight bits set, pcopyin calls panic("pcopyin-- 'from'") or ("pcopyin-- 'to'").

Attempts to copy from a user virtual address that is mapped to a non-sensical physical page cause a panic("pcopyin").

PCOPYOUT   (RTU)

NAME

pcopyout – copy bytes from kernel address space to another user address space

SYNOPSIS

```
pcopyout(procp, from, to, cnt)
struct proc *procp;
caddr_t from;
caddr_t to;
unsigned int cnt;
```

DESCRIPTION

pcopyout copies cnt bytes from the kernel virtual address from to the virtual address to in the process specified by procp.

pcopyout assumes that memory from to to to+cnt is writeable by the user in process procp, and that the physical memory for these addresses has been locked into memory using vslock or v_page_lock. Typically this will be done as part of the "top half" of some device driver and pcopyout will be called at interrupt time.

pcopyout optimizes the copy operation by copying larger data types (ints) where possible.

RETURNS

No return value.

SEE ALSO

copyout, pcopyin, and iomove.

DIAGNOSTICS

If either from or to has any of the high-order eight bits set, pcopyout calls panic("pcopyout -- 'from'") or ("pcopyout -- 'to'").

If `pcopyout` finds a nonresident page it calls `panic("pcopyout: pagein")`.

Attempts to copy from a user virtual address that is mapped to a nonsensical physical page cause a `panic ("pcopyout")`.

PHYSCK   (RTU and System V.3)

NAME

physck – perform physical device access checks

SYNOPSIS

```
physck(nblocks, flag)
daddr_t nblocks;
int flag;
```

DESCRIPTION

The physck routine determines whether the user is attempting to access beyond the end of a logical disk unit. It uses u.u_offset and u.u_count to determine the blocks that the user is trying to access. physck relies on its calling arguments for the size of the device in blocks and the type of access. The type of access is specified with flag as either B_READ or B_WRITE.

If an attempt is made to write beyond the unit or if u.u_offset is beyond the end of the unit, physck returns an error code.

If u.u_offset is within the size of the unit and flag is B_READ, physck will alter u.u_count by the size of the read beyond the end of the unit.

RETURNS

A value of one is returned if physck recognizes an error condition (in System V.3 physck also sets u.u_error to ENXIO). Otherwise, zero is returned.

WARNINGS

The RTU version of physck assumes BSIZE bytes per block while the System V.3 version assumes 2**SCTRSHIFT bytes per block.

PHYSIO   (RTU)

NAME

    physio – perform the steps required for physical (raw) I/O

SYNOPSIS

```
physio(strat, bp, dev, flag, minphys)
int (*strat)();
register struct buf *bp;
short dev;
int flag;
unsigned (*minphys)();
```

DESCRIPTION

The physio routine performs most of the steps that are required for raw I/O. The dev argument is the minor device number for the device. (Only the minor device number is important here.) First, the useracc routine is called to determine if the request is valid with respect to the user's access rights to the address range in question. This function relies on the flag argument being set to B_READ if the user has issued a read request, and to B_WRITE if the user has issued a write request. If the addresses specified by u.u_base and u.u_count are invalid, u.u_error is set to EFAULT, and physio returns.

Next, the buf structure pointed to by bp is filled in. Part of this involves calling the minphys routine to adjust the requested count to be less than or equal to the largest allowable transfer for that device. It is called with the bp argument. This routine can either be the one supplied with the system or one that the user has supplied.

The physio routine calls vslock to lock the affected areas into physical memory, bp->b_bcount as modified by the minphys routine.

Next the strat routine is called with the bp argument. strat is a pointer to a strategy routine entry point for the device. This routine is one of the standard entry points for a block device. After calling the strat routine, the physio routine sleeps at priority PRIBIO until this I/O operation is complete. It then calls vsunlock to unlock the pages that were previously locked into physical memory with the vslock routine.

Finally, it updates the u.u_count, u.u_base, and u.u_offset fields for the transfer. This process is repeated until all the data is transferred or until an error occurs.

Note that `physio` will automatically wait (`sleep`) for a buffer marked
`B_BUSY` to become available, and in turn will issue a `wakeup` if
`B_WANTED` is set when the transfer is complete.

RETURNS

The `physio` routine does not return any value, but the `u.u_error`
field will be set if any error was recognized.

SEE ALSO

`minphys`, `vslock`, `vsunlock`, and `useracc`.

WARNINGS

A strategy routine called by `physio` must not call `sleep` at interruptible priorities (`<=ZERO`) or must catch signals using `PCATCH` or `setjmp`
(`u.u_gav`). Otherwise raw I/O lock errors will result.

PHYSIO   (System V.3)

NAME

> physio – perform the steps required for physical (raw) I/O

SYNOPSIS

```
physio(strat, bp, dev, flag)
int (*strat)();
register struct buf *bp;
short dev;
int flag;
unsigned (*minphys)();
```

DESCRIPTION

The physio routine performs most of the steps that are required for raw I/O. The dev argument is the minor device number for the device. (Only the minor device number is important here.) First, the userdma routine is called to determine if the request is valid with respect to the user's access rights to the address range in question and to lock that portion of the processes virtual memory into physical memory. This function relies on the flag argument being set to B_READ if the user has issued a read request, and to B_WRITE if the user has issued a write request. If the addresses specified by u.u_base and u.u_count are invalid, u.u_error is set to EFAULT and physio returns.

Next, the buf structure pointed to by bp is filled in. If bp is NULL, a buffer header will be allocated from a pool of buffer headers (separate from the block device buffers).

Next the strat routine is called with the bp argument. strat is a pointer to a strategy routine for the device. It is customary to use a special strategy routine for raw devices rather than the standard block device strategy routine. The raw device strategy routine is responsible for performing very large transfers as several smaller transfers to overcome limitations of DMA channels that may only be able to transfer limited amounts of data. This raw device strategy routine will usually invoke dma_breakup to make sure that no individual transfer is too large or crosses certain address boundaries. dma_breakup is passed the address of another strategy routine that is usually the standard block device strategy routine.

After calling the strat routine, the physio routine sleeps at priority PRIBIO until this I/O operation is complete. It then calls undma to unlock the pages that were previously locked into physical memory with the userdma routine.

Finally, it updates the `u.u_count, u.u_base,` and `u.u_offset` fields for the transfer. This process is repeated until all the data is transferred or until an error occurs. If a buffer header had been allocated by `physio`, it is returned to the pool of raw I/O buffer headers.

Note that `physio` will *not* wait (`sleep`) for a buffer marked `B_BUSY` to become available.

RETURNS

The `physio` routine does not return any value, but the `u.u_error` field will be set if any error was recognized.

SEE ALSO

`dma_breakup, userdma,` and `undma.`

PRINTF   **(RTU and System V.3)**

NAME

printf – printf on the system console device

SYNOPSIS

```
printf(format, var1,...)
char *format;
unsigned var1,...;
```

DESCRIPTION

This is a scaled-down version of the C library routine, printf, which
always goes to the system console. Only %s, %u, %d (==%u), %o, %x,
%c, and %D are recognized. In RTU, the %O and %X formats are
equivalent to their lowercase versions.

Note that printf often works by disabling all interrupts while printing
messages, so aside from debugging, printf should be used sparingly.

SEE ALSO

printf, cmn_err, and printf(3).

PSIGNAL   (RTU and System V.3)

NAME

psignal – send a signal to a process

SYNOPSIS

```
psignal(proc, signal)
struct proc *proc;
int signal;
```

DESCRIPTION

The psignal routine is used to send a signal to a process. The signal to be sent, signal, must appear in the file /usr/include/signal.h. The process to which the signal will be sent is specified as a pointer to the entry for the process in the process table.

If the process to which the signal is sent is sleeping at a priority less than or equal to PZERO, the signal will be held pending the waking of the process. Potentially, delivery could be postponed until the current system call for the process completes. Otherwise, the signal will be delivered immediately.

RETURNS

None.

SEE ALSO

sleep, gsignal, and wakeup.

NOTE

A previously sent signal that is still pending will be wiped out.

PUTC (RTU and System V.3)

NAME

putc – put a character at the end of a clist

SYNOPSIS

```
putc(c, p)
char c;
struct clist *p;
```

DESCRIPTION

putc puts the character c at the end of the clist pointed to by p. If the clist is currently empty, or the last cblock on the clist is already full, putc will allocate a new cblock from the free list and put it at the end of the clist.

RETURNS

The character c, if c was successfully put at the end of the clist. –1 if the clist was empty or the last cblock was full and the free list was empty.

SEE ALSO

clist, getc, getcb, getcf, putcb, and putcf.

WARNINGS

If putc returns –1, the standard terminal line discipline routines will simply drop characters on both input and output.

PUTCB   (RTU and System V.3)

NAME

putcb – get a cblock from a clist

SYNOPSIS

```
putcb(bp, p)
struct cblock *bp;
struct clist *p;
```

DESCRIPTION

putcb put the cblock pointed to by bp at the end of the clist p.

Data should be copied into the cblock prior to calling putcb. A cblock
can be allocated by calling getcf. The number of characters stored in
the cblock cb is cb.c_last-cb.c_first. These characters are
stored in cb.c_data[cb.c_first] through cb.c_data
[cb.c_last-1].

SEE ALSO

clist, getc, getcb, getcf, putc, and putcf.

PUTCF   (RTU and System V.3)

───

NAME

putcf – free a cblock (put a cblock on the free list)

SYNOPSIS

```
putcf(bp)
struct cblock *bp;
```

DESCRIPTION

putcf frees a cblock for future use by putting it on the system list of free cblocks (cfreelist).

SEE ALSO

getc, getcf, getcb, putc, and putcb.

SIGNAL   (System V.3)

NAME

signal – send a signal to members of a process group

SYNOPSIS

```
signal(pgroup, signal)
int pgroup;
int signal;
```

DESCRIPTION

The signal routine is used to send a specified signal, signal, to all of the processes in a given process group, pgroup. This is used by terminal drivers to send signals such as SIGHUP and SIGINT.

The processes in a process group are normally all those processes that were forked by a particular instance of a login shell. The setgrp system call can be used to change the process group. Note that the C shell uses a different process group for every job.

The signal, signal, can be any of those listed in /usr/include/ signal.h. This routine calls the psignal routine to send the signals to each process.

NOTE

The equivalent routine in RTU is called gsignal.

RETURNS

None.

SEE ALSO

psignal and gsignal.

SLEEP   **(RTU and System V.3)**

NAME

sleep - voluntarily suspend process execution

SYNOPSIS

```
sleep(channel, pri)
caddr_t channel;
int pri;
```

DESCRIPTION

The caller of sleep gives up the processor until a call to wakeup on the same channel is given. The argument, channel, is arbitrary, but is generally an address that is uniquely associated with the event for which you are sleeping. For example, with block I/O it is common to sleep on the address of the I/O buffer. channel is generally in system virtual address space but sleep does not reference any data through channel

When the process is awakened, it enters the scheduling queue at priority, pri. The most important effect of pri is that when pri<=PZERO, signals (and ASTs in RTU) cannot disturb the sleep; if pri>PZERO signals and ASTs will be processed as they are received.

Callers of sleep must be prepared for premature return, and check that the reason for sleeping has gone away.

The appropriate values for pri are given in the file /usr/include/sys/ param.h.

If the PCATCH bit is set in pri and the rest of pri is greater than PZERO, sleep returns zero if the sleep terminated normally, and a nonzero value if the sleep was terminated as the result of a signal or an AST.

SEE ALSO

wakeup and signal.

WARNINGS

The sleep system routine should never be accessed from interrupt level or by a strategy routine.

SPL   (RTU and System V.3)

NAME

spl*n* – set the hardware interrupt level *n*

SYNOPSIS

```
int spl0(), spl1(), spl2(), spl3(), spl4(), spl4(),
spl5(), spl6(), spl7()
```

DESCRIPTION

There are eight routines: spl0, spl1, spl2, spl3, spl4, spl5, spl6, and spl7. The spl*n* routines set the hardware interrupt level of the CPU to level *n*. This means that devices whose interrupt level is greater than *n* will be serviced immediately on an interrupt.

Not all machines will support all these interrupt levels, and the significance of any level depends not only on the machine type but also on the system configuration. However, spl0 is the lowest level and will enable all interrupts while spl7 is the highest level and will not allow any interrupts. On some processors (such as the MC68000) level seven interrupts cannot be disabled completely. Refer to the manufacturers documentation for more information about the way interrupts operate on your system.

RETURNS

The return value of the spl*n* routines is an integer that is suitable for use with the splx routine to reset the hardware interrupt level.

SEE ALSO

splv and splx.

SPLV   (RTU)
_____

NAME

splv – set the hardware interrupt priority to a specified level

SYNOPSIS

```
int splv(pri)
int pri;
```

DESCRIPTION

This routine sets the hardware interrupt priority to a variable level and returns the previous priority level, pri.

RETURNS   •

An integer that is suitable for use with splx or splv to restore the hardware interrupt priority level.

SEE ALSO

splx, spl0, spl1, ...

WARNINGS

The argument pri is currently copied directly into the processor status register. The caller must ensure that all appropriate bits are set. For the MC-500, the PS_SUP bit (defined in /usr/include/sys/psl.h) must be set. Since splv is considered a function call by the C compiler, it is permissable to destroy the other condition code bits. The bit patterns for interrupt levels one through seven are defined in /usr/include/sys/psl.h as IPL1 through IPL7.

SPLX   (RTU and System V.3)

NAME

splx – reinstate the hardware interrupt level

SYNOPSIS

```
splx(pri)
int pri;
```

DESCRIPTION

This routine returns the hardware priority interrupt level to the level
that it was prior to issuing the last spl*n* command. The pri argument
is the return value from the previous spl*n*.

This command affects which hardware interrupts will be serviced
immediately and which will be held pending the lowering of the
hardware interrupt priority level.

SEE ALSO

spl*n*.

RETURNS

None.

WARNING

It does not work to give as an argument some value other than that
which was returned by the previous call to spl*n*.

SUBYTE   **(RTU and System V.3)**

NAME

subyte, sushort, suword – set a byte, short, or word in user virtual space

SYNOPSIS

```
char subyte(addr, value)
caddr_t addr;
char value;

short sushort(addr,value)
caddr_t addr;
short value;

suword(addr, value)
caddr_t addr;
int value;
```

DESCRIPTION

subyte, sushort, and suword are used to set a single byte, short, or word in user virtual address space. addr will be set to the value value.

These routines are commonly used in standard UNIX but not on the MASSCOMP system, because the MC68000 is not good at accessing single bytes and words in user virtual address space while executing in system mode. If more than a few bytes are to be moved, a single call to iomove or copyout will be more efficient.

These routines do not access or modify the u.u_base or u.u_count fields while passc and iomove do.

SEE ALSO

cpass, passc, fubyte, copyin, copyout, and iomove.

SUSER   **(RTU and System V.3)**

NAME

suser – determine if current user is superuser

SYNOPSIS

suser ()

DESCRIPTION

suser allows you to determine whether the owner of the current process is superuser. This allows your driver to determine whether to override restrictions on some device operations.

RETURNS

suser returns zero if the current user is not superuser and one if the current user is superuser.

On System V.3 and 4.3BSD, suser sets u.u_error to EPERM if it returns zero and sets a flag bit indicating that the process has used superuser privileges if it returns one.

SWAB   **(RTU)**

NAME

swab – swap the bytes in a short word

SYNOPSIS

```
swab(value)
int value;
```

DESCRIPTION

The swab routine swaps the bytes in a short word.

RETURNS

swab returns the swapped value.

SWABL (RTU)

NAME

swabl – swap the bytes in a long word

SYNOPSIS

```
short  swabl(value)
short  value;
```

DESCRIPTION

The swabl routine reverses the order of 8-bit bytes in a 32-bit word.

RETURNS

swabl returns the swapped value.

TIMEOUT   (RTU and System V.3)

NAME

timeout – call a function after an elapsed time

SYNOPSIS

```
timeout(function, argument, time)
int (*function)();
caddr_t argument;
int time;
```

DESCRIPTION

timeout is called to arrange that function(argument) is called in time clock ticks unless cancelled first. There are HZ clock ticks per second. HZ is declared in /usr/include/sys/param.h.

RETURNS

The identifier of the entry in the timeout table for this instance of timeout. This identifier can used with cantimeout (RTU) or untimeout (System V.3) to cancel the timeout before it has expired.

SEE ALSO

cantimeout, untimeout, and sleep.

DIAGNOSTICS

timeout will panic if there is no room left in the timeout table (i.e., panic("timeout table overflow")).

UPRINTF   **(RTU)**

NAME

uprintf – printf on the terminal of the current process

SYNOPSIS

```
uprintf(format, var1, ...)
char *format;
unsigned var1,...;
```

DESCRIPTION

This is a scaled-down version of the C library routine, `printf`(3), which always goes to the terminal of the current user process. Only `%s`, `%u`, `%d` (`==%u`), `%o`, `%x`, `%c`, and `%D` are recognized. The `%O` and `%X` formats are equivalent to their lowercase versions.

`uprintf` should not be called from an interrupt handler since the current process at interrupt time is unpredictable. `uprintf` is intended for reporting device errors from top-half routines, such as device-not-ready in an open routine.

SEE ALSO

`printf`(SYS) and `printf`(3).

USERACC   **(RTU and System V.3)**

NAME

useracc – check a virtual address for user accessibility

SYNOPSIS

```
useracc(vaddr, count, access)
caddr_t vaddr;
unsigned count;
int access;
```

DESCRIPTION

useracc determines that the user has the right to access of type access through the range of vaddr through vaddr plus count. access must be either B_READ or B_WRITE. This routine is usually used when performing raw I/O.

Under System V.3, useracc will lock the addressed range of virtual memory into physical memory if B_PHYS is set in access. However, drivers should generally call userdma to get this behavior.

WARNINGS

Under RTU, useracc returns zero if the user is allowed access of type access at virtual address vaddr. If access is not allowed, one is returned.

The return value of useracc in System V.3 has the opposite sense: a return value of zero indicates the access was not allowed.

Note that if the user is performing a read, then he must have write permission on the buffer. Likewise, if the user is performing a write, he must have read permission on the buffer. A common snippet of code is:

```
useracc(vaddr, count, flag==B_READ ? B_WRITE : B_READ);
```

SEE ALSO

userdma.

V_PAGE_LOCK   (RTU)

NAME

v_page_lock – lock a segment of user address space into memory

SYNOPSIS

```
v_page_lock(base, count)
caddr_t base;
int count;
```

DESCRIPTION

Locks a segment of count bytes at virtual address base in the current process user space into physical memory. For each page, if the page is not valid it is faulted in, and the page is marked as locked into memory.

Unlike vslock, v_page_lock does not increment u.u_procp->p_lock.

The SDLYU bit is set in u.u_procp->p_flags to keep pagein from unlocking pages, so pages faulted in by v_page_lock will already be locked. It is cleared when v_page_lock returns.

RETURNS

No return value.

SEE ALSO

vslock, vsunlock, vspunlock, and v_page_unlock.

DIAGNOSTICS

If v_page_lock is unable to fetch a byte to fault a nonvalid page in, then v_page_lock calls panic("v_page_lock").

If a nonvalid page is not valid after v_page_lock faults that page in, then v_page_lock calls panic("v_page_lock: page not valid").

If a page faulted in by v_page_lock is not referenced (locked) after the page fault then v_page_lock calls panic("v_page_lock: page not referenced").

V_PAGE_UNLOCK   (RTU)

NAME

v_page_unlock – unlock a segment of user address space

SYNOPSIS

```
v_page_unlock(procp, base, count, rw)
struct proc *procp;
caddr_t base;
int count;
int rw;
```

DESCRIPTION

Unlocks a segment of count bytes at virtual address base in the current process user space. If rw is B_READ (a read from a device will write memory), the modified bit is set in all pages in the segment. Unlike vsunlock, v_page_unlock does not decrement u.u_procp->p_lock.

RETURNS

No return value.

SEE ALSO

vslock, vsunlock, v_page_lock, and v_page_unlock.

VMEMALL (RTU)

NAME

vmemall – allocate memory, always succeeding

SYNOPSIS

```
vmemall(pte, size, p, type)
struct pte *pte;
int size;
struct proc *p;
int type;
```

DESCRIPTION

vmemall allocates size pages of physical memory, filling in the page map pointed to by pte. The allocated memory "belongs" to the process specified by p. type is one of:

CTEXT The allocated memory is part of a user shared text segment.

CDATA The allocated memory is part of a user data segment.

CSTACK The allocated memory is part of a user stack segment.

CSYS The allocated memory is part of system virtual address space.

The page table entries are filled with the physical page numbers of the allocated memory; all other fields in the page table entry are set to zero.

RETURNS

One (i.e., it always succeeds).

SEE ALSO

memall, wmemall, vmemfree, memfree, and wmemfree.

WARNING

Device drivers should generally call wmemall rather than calling vmemall directly.

VMEMFREE (RTU)

NAME

vmemfree – free virtual memory

SYNOPSIS

```
vmemfree(vpte, count)
struct pte *vpte;
int count;
```

DESCRIPTION

Free valid and reclaimable page frames belonging to the count pages starting at vpte. If a page is valid or reclaimable and locked (but not a system page), then the page is marked as cm_gone and the pageout daemon will free the page when it is through with it. If a page is reclaimable and already in the free list, then the page is marked as cm_gone and is not freed here. These pages are invalidated in the TB for the owning process.

Pages mapped to physical memory (i.e., with pg_phys set) are ignored.

Determines the largest contiguous cluster of valid pages and frees them in one call to

RETURNS

The number of physical memory pages returned to the free list.

SEE ALSO

memall, wmemall, vmemall, memfree, and wmemfree.

DIAGNOSTICS

If count is not a multiple of CLSIZE then vmemfree calls panic("vmemfree").

If the page was fill on demand from the vread system call and the per-process reference count of vread pages becomes less than zero for that file or the system-wide reference count of vread pages for that inode becomes less than zero, then vmemfree calls panic("vmemfree `vrpages")` or `("vmemfree vfdcnt")`, respectively.

`vread` is not supported on MASSCOMP systems.

WARNING

Device drivers should generally call `wmemfree` rather than caling `vmemfree` directly.

VSLOCK   (RTU)

NAME

vslock, vsmlock – lock a segment of user address space into memory

SYNOPSIS

```
vslock(base, count)
caddr_t base;
int count;

vsmlock(base,count)
caddr_t base;
int count;
```

DESCRIPTION

Locks a segment of count bytes at virtual address base in the current process user space into physical memory. For each page if the page is not valid, it is faulted in and is marked as locked into memory. If it was valid but incompatible with the caller's memory preference (see mpad-vise(2)), vsmlock will relocate the page.

vslock and vsmlock also increment u.u_procp->p_lock to lock the page tables for the current process in memory (that is, it makes the current process unswappable).

vslock is called from physio to ensure that the pages participating in raw i/o are valid and locked. vsmlock is called from plockin to ensure memory preference adherence.

SDLYU is set in u.u_procp->p_flags to keep pagein from unlocking pages, so pages faulted in by vslock will already be locked. SDLYU is cleared when vslock returns.

RETURNS

No return value.

SEE ALSO

vsunlock, vspunlock, v_page_lock, and v_page_unlock.

DIAGNOSTICS

If `u.u_procp->p_lock` overflows, `vslock` calls `panic("vslock: p_lock overflow")`.

If `vslock` is unable to fetch a byte to fault a nonvalid page in, `vslock` calls `panic("vslock")`.

If a nonvalid page is not valid after `vslock` faults that page in, `vslock` calls `panic("vslock: page not valid")`.

If a page faulted in by `vslock` is not referenced (locked) after the page fault, `vslock` calls `panic("vslock: page not referenced")`.

VSUNLOCK   (RTU)

NAME

vsunlock – unlock a segment of user address space

SYNOPSIS

```
vsunlock(base, count, rw)
caddr_t base;
int count;
int rw;
```

DESCRIPTION

Unlocks a segment of count bytes at virtual address base in the current process user space. If rw is B_READ (a read from a device will write memory), the modified bit is set in all pages in the segment. Also for B_READ, when base and count completely span a page, the page is marked globally consistent in all caches.

vsunlock decrements u.u_procp->p_lock to unlock the process page tables.

RETURNS

No return value.

SEE ALSO

vslock, vspunlock, v_page_lock, and v_page_unlock.

DIAGNOSTICS

If u.u_procp->p_lock becomes negative, then vsunlock calls panic("vsunlock: p_lock underflow");

WAKEUP (RTU and System V.3)

NAME

wakeup - wakeup all processes sleeping on a channel

SYNOPSIS

```
wakeup(channel)
caddr_t channel;
```

DESCRIPTION

The wakeup routine wakes up all processes that are sleeping on the channel, channel. This should be the same value on which the process went to sleep. You may issue a wakeup on a channel for which no process is sleeping.

RETURNS

None.

WARNINGS

Note that all processes sleeping on the channel are awakened by a single call to wakeup. This makes it necessary for every process that sleeps to recheck the event on which it is sleeping when it is awakened.

SEE ALSO

sleep.

WMEMALL   (RTU)

NAME

wmemall, wmemallx – allocate nonpaged memory in the kernel

SYNOPSIS

```
caddr_t wmemall(pmemall, n)
int (*pmemall)();
int n;
caddr_t wmemallx(pmemall,n,attr)
int (*pmemall)();
int n;
int attr;
```

DESCRIPTION

Allocates n bytes of memory (in kernel virtual address space), allocates physical memory (using the memory allocator specified by pmemall which should be either memall or vmemall), sets the page table entries to allow read/write access, cache enabled, and invalidates any current translations for those virtual addresses.

If you do not want the cache enabled or want other than read/write access, use wmemallx specifying attr (e.g.,, PG_V|PG_CACHE|PG_RX).

RETURNS

The system virtual address of the memory allocated.

If virtual memory space is unavailable (kept in the resource map kernelmap) or physical memory is unavailable (if pmemall is memall), then wmemall returns zero and modifies neither the page table entries nor the translation buffer.

SEE ALSO

wmemfree.

WMEMFREE   (RTU)

NAME

wmemfree – free nonpaged memory in the kernel

SYNOPSIS

```
wmemfree(va, n)
caddr_t va;
int n;
```

DESCRIPTION

Releases n bytes of memory in kernel virtual address space.

RETURNS

No return value.

SEE ALSO

`memall`, `vmemall`, `wmemall`, `memfree`, and `vmemfree`.

TEMPLATE CHARACTER DRIVER

This appendix contains listings of the source code for the template character driver discussed in Chapter 8. The files shown are:

- chdriver.c
- ch.master
- ch.dfile
- ch.make
- ch.files
- ch.test
- chex.c

```
/**************************************************************************/
/*                                                                        */
/*   chdriver.c -- template character driver                              */
/*                                                                        */
/*   This template driver is delivered with the MASSCOMP "GUIDE TO        */
/*   WRITING A UNIX DEVICE DRIVER" as an example of a typical character    */
/*   driver.                                                              */
/*                                                                        */
/**************************************************************************/


/*

        This is a complete, working device driver that does not use any hard-
    ware; it can be added to any MASSCOMP system and executed as an example.  It
    provides working examples of many typical driver features and can also be
    used as a starting point for implementing other character drivers.

        The pseudodevices supported by this driver act somewhat like UNIX
    pipes; characters written to the device are passed to any process that reads
    it on a first-in-first-out basis.  Up to D_MAX characters will be buffered
    within the driver for each device.  If a writer tries to write more charac-
    ters than will fit, the 'start' routine sleeps until a reader removes some
    stored characters.  If a reader finds the device empty, the 'read' routine
    sleeps until more characters are written.

        A read or write sequence on a device is terminated by an EOF character
    (a Control-D) in the data stream.  Once this character has appeared further
    reads and writes are inhibited until all processes have closed the device.

        The 'init' routine demonstrates the use of fault trapping to determine
    whether the controllers are online.  Because this demonstration driver does
    not use hardware, arbitrary MULTIBUS address are used, and the controllers
    are always found to be offline.  The other routines ignore the offline
    status.  The driver also demonstrates the use of multidevice controllers
    and one form of "exclusive open" logic.  Each controller supports two
    devices.  If one of them has been opened, it owns the controller, and the
    other device cannot be opened.

        The driver also demonstrates the use of bits within the device minor
    number to set device modes.  The four low-order bits of the minor number
    select the device.  The fifth bit is a mode bit; if it is on, the device
    converts all alphabetic characters written to it to upper case.

        The 'write', 'start', and 'intr' routines include code that demon-
    strates the use of an output queue to link the top and bottom halves of a
    character driver.  The 'write' routine fills the queue up to a specified
    maximum size (O_MAX) and then sleeps until it has been reduced by 'intr' and
    method that restores top-half context only once per O_MAX-O_MIN bytes
    instead of for every byte.  Because the template driver has no hardware to
    generate interrupts, some of this code is never executed.

*/
```

```
/**********/
/*
/*   Standard include files needed in most drivers.  The symbol KERNEL must
/*   be defined -- it enables conditional declarations of executive data
/*   structures in 'user.h' and other include files.
/*
/**********/

#define KERNEL                          /* flag: need system variables */

#include <sys/param.h>                  /* system typedefs etc. */
#include <sys/systm.h>                  /* system global data structures */
#include <sys/dir.h>                    /* needed by user.h */
#include <sys/user.h>                   /* current process data */


/**********/
/*
/*   Other include files used in this driver
/*
/*   The 'ch' entry in the master configuration file causes a 'tty' structure
/*   to be defined for each 'ch' device.  They are used as control structures
/*   to hold device status information.
/*
/**********/

#include <sys/tty.h>                    /* used as control structures */


/**********/
/*
/*   Macros for trace print
/*
/*   Trace print is generated if the variable 'ch_trace' is TRUE.  Trace print
/*   is initially turned on by the 'init' routine and can be turned on and off
/*   by calls to 'ioctl'.  Two print functions are supplied:
/*
/*      TRACE_TXT -- print a string
/*      TRACE_VAL -- print a string and a value
/*
/*   The second function prints the value in octal, decimal, and hexadecimal.
/*   Each line of print includes the device minor number.
/*
/**********/

#define TRACE_TXT(text) \
    if (ch_trace)        \
       printf ("chdriver (minor %d): text\n", minor(dev))

#define TRACE_VAL(text,val)      \
    if (ch_trace)                 \
       printf ("chdriver (minor %d): text -- val = %o(O), %d(D), %x(X)\n", \
               minor(dev), val, val, val)
```

```
/**********/
/*
/*  General-purpose symbols
/*
/**********/

#define FALSE 0                            /* general false flag */
#define TRUE  1                            /* general true flag */


/**********/
/*
/*  Macros to convert the device number to other useful numbers.
/*
/*  On MASSCOMP systems device numbers of the type 'dev_t' passed to drivers
/*  contain the minor number only.  However, for the sake of consistency and
/*  portability we extract the minor number by using the standard macro
/*  'minor'.
/*
/*  This driver assumes that the low-order four bits of the minor number
/*  define the device unit number and that there are two devices per
/*  controller.  Unit numbers are consecutive integers beginning at zero.
/*
/**********/

#define   dev_to_unit(dev)    minor(dev)&0xf          /* unit number */
#define   dev_to_cont(dev)    (dev_to_unit(dev))>>1   /* controller number */
#define   dev_to_dsp(dev)     &ch__tty[dev_to_unit(dev)] /* dev status block */
#define   dev_to_csp(dev)     &ch_cs[dev_to_cont(dev)]   /* cnt status block */


/**********/
/*
/*  Macro to convert lower case ASCII to upper case.
/*
/**********/

#define upper(x) (( x>='a' && x<='z' ) ? x+('A'-'a') : x)
```

```
/**********/
/*
/*   Device and Controller Status Flags
/*
/*
/*   CM_UPR  is a mask used to locate the upper case flag bit in the device
/*           minor number.
/*
/*   CD_EOF  is set after an EOF is seen in the data stream; it prevents
/*           further I/O.
/*
/*   CC_BUSY indicates that a controller is busy; that is, one of its
/*           devices is open.
/*
/*   CC_ACTV indicates that a hardware operation has been initiated and an
/*           interrupt is expected.  It is included as an example and is never
/*           set in this template driver.
/*
/*   CC_WAKE set by the 'write' routine to indicate that it is sleeping until
/*           the output queue reaches its low water mark.  Never set by the
/*           template driver.
/*
/**********/

#define CM_UPR 0x10                     /* force upper case */

#define CD_RDY 0                        /* pseudo-flag: device ready */
#define CD_EOF 1                        /* device off after EOF */

#define CC_BUSY 1                       /* controller is busy */
#define CC_ACTV 2                       /* controller is active */
#define CC_WAKE 4                       /* writer wants wakeup */


/**********/
/*
/*   Special Function Commands
/*
/*   Used as the 'command' argument in 'ioctl' calls.
/*
/**********/

#define TRON  1                         /* trace print on */
#define TROFF 2                         /* trace print off */
#define NUMC  3                         /* return character count */
```

```
/**********/
/*
/*   Defined Parameters
/*
/*   C_MAX   is the maximum number of controllers that the driver can support.
/*
/*   EOF     When seen in the data stream, terminates further writing to a
/*           device until it is closed.
/*
/*   D_MAX   is the upper limit on the number of characters that will be held
/*           in the "device".  When that limit is reached, the 'write' routine
/*           will sleep until some characters are read.
/*
/*   O_MIN   set limits on the size of the output queue.  They appear in
/*   O_MAX   example logic and are never really used in the template driver.
/*
/**********/

#define C_MAX 3                         /* max # of controllers */
#define EOF 4                           /* end-of-file indicator */

#define D_MAX 50                        /* max # of buffered characters */

#define O_MIN  5                        /* limits on size of output queue */
#define O_MAX 24

/**********/
/*
/*   Controller hardware and software structures
/*
/*   The 'ch_device' structure represents the controller hardware registers.
/*   Since there is no real hardware for this driver, the definition is just
/*   an example.  MULTIBUS address passed to the driver are defined as
/*   pointers to a structure of this type.  The 'ch_cstat' structure type is
/*   used to store controller status information.
/*
/**********/

struct ch_device                        /* device CSR definition: */
{
   char status;                         /*    status register */
   char command;                        /*    command register */
   char rdbuf;                          /*    read buffer */
   char wrbuf;                          /*    write buffer */
};

struct ch_cstat                         /* controller status block: */
{
   int cc_flags;                        /*    binary flags */
   dev_t cc_owner;                      /*    device currently open */
} ch_cs[C_MAX];
```

```
/**********/
/*
/*   External variables and structures
/*
/*   The variables declared in the following 'extern' statements are defined
/*   in 'conf.c' based on the 'ch' data in the system configuration data files.
/*
/**********/

extern int ch__ccnt;                    /* count of controllers */
extern int ch__cnt;                     /* count of devices */

extern struct tty ch__tty[];            /* device status blocks */
extern struct ch_device *ch__addr[];    /* controller register addresses */


/**********/
/*
/*   The following variable is a flag that is set TRUE or FALSE to
/*   control the generation of trace print.
/*
/**********/

int ch_trace;                           /* flag for trace print */
```

```
/**************************************************************************/
/*                                                                        */
/*  Entry Point:  init                                                    */
/*  Purpose:      Driver Initialization                                   */
/*  Description:                                                          */
/*                                                                        */
/*  The 'init' routine checks all controllers to see whether they are     */
/*  online.  Since the template driver has no hardware, all controller    */
/*  will be declared offline, but the other routines ignore this          */
/*  status.                                                               */
/*                                                                        */
/*  The device and controller status blocks are also initialized.         */
/*                                                                        */
/**************************************************************************/

ch_init ()

{
    struct ch_device *dp;              /* ptr to controller CSR */
    struct tty *dsp;                   /* ptr to dev status block */
    struct ch_cstat *csp;              /* ptr to cnt status block */

    int i;
    char temp;
    dev_t dev = 0;                     /* dummy for trace print */


    ch_trace = TRUE;                   /* start with trace on */
    TRACE_VAL (ch_init, ch__cnt);


/**********/
/*
/*  Check whether the controllers are online
/*
/**********/

    for (i=0; i<ch__ccnt; i++)                   /* check all controllers */
      {
        dp = ch__addr[i];                        /* get the CSR address */
        printf("chdriver: controller at %x\n", dp);/* announce the device */
        if (setjmp(u.u_tsav) == 0)               /* save the fault vector */
          {
            u.u_nofault = TRUE;                  /* enable fault handling */
            temp = (ushort)dp->status;           /* touch the controller */
            u.u_nofault = FALSE;                 /* continue if it's there */
            /*******/
            /*
            /* for real devices, initialize the hardware here */
            /*
            /*******/
          }
        else                                     /* arrive here on fault */
          {
            ch__addr[i] = 0;                     /* mark it offline */
            printf("          device is not online\n");
          }
      }
```

```
/**********/
/*
/*  Mark each controller not busy, and mark each device ready for I/O with
/*   empty input and output queues.
/*
/**********/

    for (i=0; i<ch__ccnt; i++)                      /* for all controllers */
      {
        csp = &ch_cs[i];
        csp->cc_flags = 0;                          /* controller not busy */
      }

    for (i=0; i<ch__cnt; i++)                       /* for all devices */
      {
        dsp = dev_to_dsp(i);                        /* point to control block */
        dsp->t_cflag = CD_RDY;                      /* flag: ready for I/O */
        dsp->t_rawq.c_cc = 0;                       /* queues are empty */
        dsp->t_outq.c_cc = 0;
      }

}
```

```
/*****************************************************************************/
/*                                                                         */
/*  Entry Point:  open                                                     */
/*  Purpose:      Open Device                                              */
/*  Description:                                                           */
/*                                                                         */
/*  This routine checks to see whether the device and controller          */
/*  numbers are valid.  Because the template driver does not use real     */
/*  devices, it does not check to see whether the controller is           */
/*  offline.  The open fails if another device is already open on the     */
/*  same controller.                                                      */
/*                                                                         */
/*****************************************************************************/


ch_open (dev, flag)

dev_t dev;                                      /* device (minor) number */
int flag;                                       /* read/write flag */
{
   int unit;                                    /* device number */
   int cont;                                    /* controller number */
   struct tty *dsp;                             /* dev status block */
   struct ch_cstat *csp;                        /* cont status block */

   TRACE_VAL (open, flag);

/**********/
/*
/*  Check for legal controller and unit
/*
/**********/

   cont = dev_to_cont(dev);                     /* get the controller # */
   TRACE_VAL (open, cont);
   if (cont >= ch__ccnt || cont >= C_MAX)       /* if illegal controller */
    {
      u.u_error = ENXIO;                        /* return same error */
      return;
    }

   unit = dev_to_unit(dev);                     /* get device number */
   TRACE_VAL (open, unit);
   if (unit >= ch__cnt)                         /* if bad unit number */
    {
      u.u_error = ENXIO;                        /* return an error */
      return;
    }

/**********/
/*
/*  The following is commented out for the template driver -- its devices are
/*  always offline.  It should be included in a driver for a real device.
/*
/*   if (ch__addr[cont] == 0)                   /* check for offline */
/*    {
/*      u.u_error = ENODEV;                      /* error if so */
/*      return;
/*    }
/*
/**********/
```

```
/**********/
/*
/*   Check whether the controller is busy with the other unit.
/*
/**********/

    csp = &ch_cs[cont];                          /* get cont status pointer */
    TRACE_VAL(open, csp->cc_flags);
    TRACE_VAL(open, csp->cc_owner);

    if (csp->cc_flags&CC_BUSY && csp->cc_owner != dev)
      {
        u.u_error = EBUSY;                       /* can't open -- busy */
        return;
      }
    else
      {
        csp->cc_flags |= CC_BUSY;                /* set controller busy */
        csp->cc_owner = dev;                     /* show the owner */
      }
}                                                /* successful open */
```

```
/**************************************************************************/
/*                                                                        */
/*  Entry Point:  close                                                   */
/*  Purpose:      Close Device                                            */
/*  Description:                                                          */
/*                                                                        */
/*  The controller is marked not busy, and the device is marked ready     */
/*  for I/O.  If there are any characters stored in the device (in the    */
/*  't_rawq' list), they will stay there and can be read later.           */
/*                                                                        */
/**************************************************************************/


ch_close (dev, flag)

dev_t dev;                                  /* device (minor) number */
int flag;                                   /* read/write flag */
{
    struct tty *dsp;                        /* dev status block ptr */
    struct ch_cstat *csp;                   /* cnt status block ptr */
    int a_char;


    TRACE_VAL (close, flag);

    csp = dev_to_csp(dev);                  /* get cont status pointer */
    csp->cc_flags &= ~CC_BUSY;              /* clear the busy flag */

    dsp = dev_to_dsp(dev);                  /* get dev status pointer */
    dsp->t_cflag = CD_RDY;                  /* mark it ready for I/O */
}
```

```
/***********************************************************************/
/*                                                                     */
/*  Entry Point:  write                                                */
/*  Purpose:      Write Data                                           */
/*  Description:                                                       */
/*                                                                     */
/*  This routine is written as though there were an output device that */
/*  generates an interrupt after each byte is transmitted.  It places  */
/*  bytes in an output queue and if the hardware is idle, calls the    */
/*  'start' routine to activate it.  When the queue reaches a maximum  */
/*  size it sleeps until the queue falls to its minimum size.          */
/*                                                                     */
/*  Since the template driver does not use hardware, the 'start' routine*/
/*  completes the output synchronously.  Therefore the characters do   */
/*  not accumulate in the output queue, and the 'write' routine never  */
/*  calls 'sleep'.  (There is a second call to 'sleep' that may be ex- */
/*  ecuted very rarely if the system clist space is exhausted.)        */
/*                                                                     */
/*  Output continues until the user's request is satisfied or until an */
/*  EOF character appears in the data.  In the latter case the device  */
/*  is marked as being in the "off" state, and no further output is    */
/*  allowed until the device is closed and reopened.                   */
/*                                                                     */
/***********************************************************************/


ch_write (dev)

dev_t dev;                                  /* device (minor) number */
{
   struct tty *dsp;                         /* device status pointer */
   struct ch_cstat *csp;                    /* controller status ptr */
   int a_char;                              /* temp for holding data */
   int oldpri;                              /* old CPU priority */


   TRACE_VAL(write, u.u_count);

   dsp = dev_to_dsp(dev);                   /* get dev status pointer */
   csp = dev_to_csp(dev);                   /* and controller status */
   TRACE_VAL(write,dsp->t_rawq.c_cc);

   if (dsp->t_cflag&CD_EOF)                 /* do nothing if dev off */
      return;


/**********/
/*
/*  Transfer bytes from user process space to the output queue.  Start up
/*  the hardware whenever the device has become inactive.  Sleep for a
/*  while if the queue gets too big.
/*
/**********/

   while (u.u_count)                        /* while user has data */
     {
       a_char = cpass();                    /* get the next byte */
       if (dev&CM_UPR)                      /* if minor flag on */
          a_char = upper(a_char);           /* force to upper case */
```

```
        while (dsp->t_outq.c_cc >= O_MAX)           /* wait for output space */
         {
           csp->cc_flags |= CC_WAKE;                /* ask for a wakeup call */
           sleep(&dsp->t_outq, PSLEP);              /* and wait for it */
         }

        while (putc(a_char, &dsp->t_outq))          /* put it on the queue */
         {
           TRACE_TXT (write: no clist space -- waiting one second);
           sleep (&lbolt, PWAIT);                   /* wait for system space */
         }

        oldpri = spl6();                            /* raise priority */
        if (!(csp->cc_flags&CC_ACTV))               /* if the hardware is idle */
           ch_start(dev);                           /* start it up */
        splx(oldpri);                               /* restore priority */

        if (a_char == EOF)                          /* if end of file */
         {
           dsp->t_cflag |= CD_EOF;                  /* mark end of I/O */
           break;                                   /* and return */
         }
     }


/**********/
/*
/*  The following belongs only in the template driver -- it wakes up any
/*  reader that may be waiting for input characters.
/*
/**********/

   TRACE_VAL(write, dsp->t_rawq.c_cc);
   TRACE_TXT(write: done -- waking the reader);

   wakeup(&dsp->t_rawq);                            /* in case reader waiting */
}
```

```
/**************************************************************************/
/*                                                                        */
/* Entry Point:  read                                                     */
/* Purpose:      Read Data                                                 */
/* Description:                                                            */
/*                                                                        */
/* Move characters from the input queue into user process space.  If      */
/* the queue becomes empty before the request is satisfied and there      */
/* has not been an EOF, send a 'wakeup' to the writer and sleep until      */
/* he sends one back.                                                      */
/*                                                                        */
/**************************************************************************/


ch_read (dev)

dev_t dev;
{
    struct tty *dsp;                            /* control block pointer */
    int a_char;


    TRACE_VAL (read, u.u_count);

    dsp = dev_to_dsp(dev);                      /* Get dev status pointer */
    TRACE_VAL (read, dsp->t_rawq.c_cc);
    TRACE_VAL (read, dsp->t_cflag);

    while (u.u_count)                           /* while user wants chars */
      {
        if ((a_char=getc(&dsp->t_rawq)) >= 0)   /* ask for the next one */
          {
            passc(a_char);                      /* put it in user space */
            if (a_char == EOF)                  /* and check for EOF */
                dsp->t_cflag |= CD_EOF;
          }
        else                                    /* else the device is empty */
          {
            if (dsp->t_cflag&CD_EOF)
                break;                          /* device off -- give up */
            TRACE_TXT (read: queue is empty -- waking the writer);
            wakeup (&dsp->t_outq);              /* wake up the writer  */
            sleep (&dsp->t_rawq, PSLEP);        /* and wait for him */
          }
      }
}
```

```
/**********************************************************************/
/*                                                                    */
/* Entry Point:  ioctl                                                */
/* Purpose:      Special Functions                                    */
/* Description:                                                        */
/*                                                                    */
/* Three special function commands are implemented:                   */
/*                                                                    */
/*     TRON -- turn trace print on                                    */
/*     TROFF -- turn trace print off                                  */
/*     NUMC -- return number of characters stored in device           */
/*                                                                    */
/* The argument 'argp' is not used with the first two commands.  For  */
/* the NUMC command it is a pointer to an integer where the character */
/* count will be stored.                                              */
/*                                                                    */
/**********************************************************************/


ch_ioctl (dev, cmd, argp)

dev_t dev;                                  /* device (minor) number */
int cmd;                                    /* The command */
int *argp;                                  /* The argument or pointer */
{
   struct tty *dsp;                         /* dev status pointer */
   int temp;                                /* temporary for NUMC */

   TRACE_VAL (ioctl, cmd);

   switch (cmd)                             /* handle command cases: */
    {
     case TRON:                             /* turn trace print on */
      ch_trace = TRUE;
      break;

     case TROFF:                            /* turn trace print off */
      ch_trace = FALSE;
      break;

     case NUMC:                             /* return character count */
      dsp = dev_to_dsp(dev);
      temp = dsp->t_rawq.c_cc;              /*c_cc is a short */
      copyout(&dsp->t_rawq.c_cc, argp, sizeof(int));
      break;

     default:
      u.u_error = EINVAL;                   /* else return an error */
    }
}
```

```
/**********************************************************************/
/*                                                                    */
/*  Entry Point:  intr                                                */
/*  Purpose:      Handle Interrupts                                   */
/*  Description:                                                      */
/*                                                                    */
/*  For the template driver there is no device to issue interrupts, but */
/*  this routine may be called as part of a poll.  Therefore, it always */
/*  returns a zero to indicate that the poll should continue.         */
/*                                                                    */
/*  The routine also contains the code that would be needed to handle */
/*  a device interrupt; in the template driver this code will never be */
/*  executed.  The routine clears the CC_ACTV flag and, if there is   */
/*  another byte in the output queue, calls 'ch_start'.  If the size of */
/*  the queue drops to O_MIN and a 'write' routine is waiting to write */
/*  more characters (CC_WAKE is set) it issues a 'wakeup' call.       */
/*                                                                    */
/**********************************************************************/


ch_intr(devno, dp)

int devno;                              /* device index */
struct ch_device *dp;                   /* pointer to CSR */
{
   dev_t dev;                           /* device (minor) number */
   struct ch_cstat *csp;                /* controller status ptr */
   struct tty *dsp;                     /* device status pointer */


/**********/
/*
/*  Code goes here to determine whether the interrupt came from this
/*  device and if so, clear it in the hardware.
/*
/**********/

   if (TRUE) return(0);                 /* assume it is not ours */

/**********/
/*
/*  The following code will not be executed by the template driver.
/*
/**********/

   csp = &ch_cs[devno];                 /* get controller status ptr */
   csp->cc_flags &= ~CC_ACTV;           /* clear device active flag */
   dev = csp->cc_owner;                 /* get device number */
   dsp = dev_to_dsp(dev);               /* pointer to device status */

   if (dsp->t_outq.c_cc)                /* any more characters? */
      ch_start(dev);                    /* if so, start device */

   if (dsp->t_outq.c_cc <= O_MIN &&     /* if at low point */
      csp->cc_flags&CC_WAKE)            /* and someone is sleeping */
   {
      wakeup(&dsp->t_outq);             /* wake the writer */
      csp->cc_flags &= ~CC_WAKE;
   }
```

```
/***********************************************************************/
/*                                                                     */
/*  Local Routine: start                                               */
/*  Purpose:        Write (and read) a Character                       */
/*  Description:                                                        */
/*                                                                     */
/*  In a driver that controlled a real device, this routine would      */
/*  initiate a hardware output operation and set the CC_ACTV flag.  In */
/*  the template driver it merely moves the character from the output  */
/*  queue to the input queue.                                          */
/*                                                                     */
/***********************************************************************/

ch_start(dev)

dev_t dev;
{
    struct tty *dsp;                         /* device status pointer */
    struct ch_cstat *csp;                    /* controller status ptr */
    int a_char;                              /* temporary byte store */
    struct ch_device *dp;                    /* pointer to device CSR */


    dsp = dev_to_dsp(dev);                   /* get status block ptrs */
    csp = dev_to_csp(dev);
    dp = ch__addr[dev_to_cont(dev)];         /* get hardware CSR pointer */

    if (csp->cc_flags&CC_ACTV)               /* dev can't be active */
       panic("ch_start: device is active");
    if ((a_char=getc(&dsp->t_outq)) == -1)   /* has to be a byte */
       panic("ch_start: no character");


/*********/
/*
/*  Writes to hardware registers would go here.  The following code is for
/*  the template only.
/*
/*********/

    while (dsp->t_rawq.c_cc >= D_MAX)        /* if device is full */
      {
        TRACE_TXT (start: device is full -- waking the reader);
        wakeup(&dsp->t_rawq);                /* wake up the reader */
        sleep(&dsp->t_outq);                 /* and wait for him */
      }

    while (putc(a_char, &dsp->t_rawq))       /* transfer the byte */
      {
        TRACE_TXT (start: no clist space -- waiting one second);
        sleep (&lbolt, PWAIT);               /* wait for system space */
      }
}

/*  End of chdriver.c   */
```

```
##########################################################################
#                                                                        #
#  ch.master -- Template Character Driver entry in master configuration  #
#                  file                                                  #
#                                                                        #
#  The following line of data is in the file 'ch.master'.  These         #
#  comments are not in the file.                                         #
#                                                                        #
##########################################################################

ch    137    4    ch_    4    0    0    0    24    2    2    tty

# end of ch.master




##########################################################################
#                                                                        #
#  ch.dfile -- Template Character Driver entry in device description      #
#                  file                                                   #
#                                                                        #
#  The following lines of data are in the file 'ch.dfile'.  These        #
#  comments are not in the file.                                         #
#                                                                        #
##########################################################################

ch        ffa000        2        2
ch        ffb000        2        1

#end of ch.dfile




##########################################################################
#                                                                        #
#  ch.make -- makefile for template character driver                     #
#                                                                        #
#  This is a makefile for the template character driver 'chdriver'       #
#  supplied with the MASSCOMP "GUIDE TO WRITING A DEVICE DRIVER".  It     #
#  compiles the driver source code and places a copy of 'chdriver.o'     #
#  in the directory '/usr/drivers/uts'.                                  #
#                                                                        #
##########################################################################


chdriver.o:    chdriver.c
               cc -O -c chdriver.c
               cp chdriver.o /usr/drivers/uts

# End of ch.make
```

```
##############################################################################
#                                                                          #
#   ch.files -- create device special files for chdriver                   #
#                                                                          #
#   This csh script is executed by the 'Install' procedure in order to     #
#   create three device special files for the template character driver.   #
#   The value of MAJOR must be changed here and in 'ch.master' if the       #
#   value used below has been used by another driver.  Note that device     #
#   'ch1' has the "upper case" bit set.                                     #
#                                                                          #
##############################################################################

set MAJOR = 24

mknod /dev/ch0 c $MAJOR 0
mknod /dev/ch1 c $MAJOR 17
mknod /dev/ch2 c $MAJOR 2

chmod a+rw /dev/ch0
chmod a+rw /dev/ch1
chmod a+rw /dev/ch2

#   End of ch.files


##############################################################################
#                                                                          #
#   ch.test -- test the template character driver                          #
#                                                                          #
#   This csh script starts a copy of the device '/dev/ch0' to the file      #
#   'temp' in the background and then copies itself to that device.  In     #
#   order to make the copies terminate the last character in this file      #
#   is a 'Control-D'.  After this script has been executed a complete       #
#   copy of 'ch.test' should be found in 'temp'.                            #
#                                                                          #
##############################################################################


if (-e ch.temp) rm temp

echo ""
echo " Starting a reader..."
set verbose

cp /dev/ch0 temp &
unset verbose

echo ""
echo " Copying this script to the device..."
set verbose

cp ch.test /dev/ch0
unset verbose

echo ""
echo " There should now be a copy of this file in 'temp'."

#   End of ch.test (except for terminating ^D)
```

```
/**************************************************************************/
/*                                                                        */
/*   chex.c -- exercise chdriver                                          */
/*                                                                        */
/*   This program performs several operations that demonstrate the oper- */
/*   ations of the template character driver 'chdriver'.  It              */
/*                                                                        */
/*      - Opens 'ch' devices but fails to open two devices on the same    */
/*        controller.                                                     */
/*      - Writes and reads both normal and upper case devices.           */
/*      - Uses the three 'ioctl' commands.                               */
/*                                                                        */
/**************************************************************************/


#include <fcntl.h>

#define TRON  1
#define TROFF 2
#define NUMC  3

main()
{
   int fd1,fd2;                              /* file descriptors */
   char stuff[50], fluff[50];                /* string storage */
   int count;                                /* returned count */

   if ((fd1=open("/dev/ch0", O_RDWR)) == -1)  /* this open will succeed */
      perror("chex: could not open ch0");

   if ((fd2=open("/dev/ch1", O_RDWR)) == -1)  /* this one will fail */
      perror("chex: could not open ch1");

   if ((fd2=open("/dev/ch2", O_WRONLY)) == -1) /* this one will succeed */
      perror("chex: could not open ch2");


   strcpy(stuff, "This is a test");          /* create a test string */
   write(fd1, stuff, strlen(stuff));         /* write to normal device */
   ioctl(fd1, NUMC, &count);                 /* check the stored count */
   printf("ch0 holding %d characters\n", count);

   read(fd1, fluff, count);                  /* read it back */
   printf("got from ch0: <%s>\n", fluff);

   close(fd1);                               /* close that device */
   ioctl(fd2, TROFF, 0);                     /* trace off for a while */

   fd1 = open("/dev/ch1", O_RDWR);           /* open upper case device */
   write(fd1, stuff, strlen(stuff));         /* write same string to it */
   close(fd1);                               /* close it */
   fd1 = open("/dev/ch1", O_RDONLY);         /* and open again */

   fluff[0] = 0;                             /* clear the result */
   read(fd1, fluff, strlen(stuff));          /* should still have bytes */
   printf("got from ch1: <%s>\n", fluff);

   ioctl(fd1, TRON, 0);                      /* restore the trace */
                                             /* closes are automatic */
}
/*  End of chex.c  */
```

D

TEMPLATE BLOCK DRIVER

This appendix contains listings of the source code for the template block driver discussed in Chapter 8. The files shown are:

- bkdriver.c
- bk.master
- bk.dfile
- bk.make
- bk.files
- bk.test
- bkex.c

```
/***************************************************************************/
/*                                                                       */
/*  bkdriver.c -- template block driver                                  */
/*                                                                       */
/*  This template driver is delivered with the MASSCOMP "GUIDE TO        */
/*  WRITING A UNIX DEVICE DRIVER" as an example of a typical block       */
/*  Driver.                                                              */
/*                                                                       */
/***************************************************************************/


/*

     This is a complete, working driver that does not use any hardware.
It can be added to a MASSCOMP RTU executive and executed as an example.
It can also be used as a starting point for implementing other block
drivers.

     The pseudodevices supported by this driver act just like real disks.
They can be used as unstructured storage devices, or you can use mkfs to
build a UNIX file system on them and mount them.

     The driver also supports raw (character) devices and raw I/O to the
block devices by the executive.  These raw read and write routines
demonstrate the use of the executive routines physio and physck.  They
also demonstrate the use of a driver routine to limit the size of a data
transfer. A special routine bk_trim is included for this purpose.

*/

/**********/
/*
/*  Standard include files needed in most drivers.  The symbol KERNEL must
/*  be defined -- it enables conditional declarations of executive data
/*  structures in 'user.h' and other include files.
/*
/**********/

#define KERNEL                          /* flag: need system variables */

#include <sys/param.h>                  /* system typedefs etc. */
#include <sys/systm.h>                  /* system global data structures */
#include <sys/dir.h>                    /* needed by user.h */
#include <sys/user.h>                   /* current process data */


/**********/
/*
/*  Other include files used in this driver
/*
/*  All block drivers refer to symbols defined in the 'buf.h' and
/*  'iobuf.h' files.
/*
/**********/

#include <sys/buf.h>
#include <sys/iobuf.h>
```

```
/**********/
/*
/*  Macros for trace print
/*
/*  Trace print is generated if the variable 'bk_trace' is TRUE.  Trace print
/*  is initially turned on by the 'init' routine and can be turned on and off
/*  by calls to 'ioctl'.  Two print functions are supplied:
/*
/*      TRACE_TXT -- print a string
/*      TRACE_VAL -- print a string and a value
/*
/*  The second function prints the value in octal, decimal, and hexadecimal.
/*  Each line of print includes the device minor number.
/*
/**********/

#define TRACE_TXT(text)          \
    if (bk_trace)                \
       printf ("bkdriver (minor %d): text\n", minor(dev))

#define TRACE_VAL(text,val)      \
    if (bk_trace)                \
       printf ("bkdriver (minor %d): text -- val = %o(O), %d(D), %x(X)\n", \
               minor(dev), val, val, val)

/**********/
/*
/*  General-purpose symbols
/**********/

#define FALSE 0                          /* general false flag */
#define TRUE  1                          /* general true flag */


/**********
*
* Macros to convert the device number to other useful numbers.
*
**********/

#define  dev_to_unit(dev)   minor(dev)

/**********/
/*
/*  Defined Parameters
/*
/*  These are arbitrary values that define the characteristics of the
/*  driver and pseudodevices.
/*
/**********/

#define  U_MAX    2                      /* number of units supported */

#define  U_CLST   2                      /* device size in clusters */
#define  U_BLKS   U_CLST*CLUSTER         /* device size in blocks */

#define  U_MAXXFR 10*BSIZE               /* maximum DMA transfer */
```

```
/**********/
/*
/*   External Variables and Structures
/*
/*
/*   The variables declared in the 'extern' statements are defined in 'conf.c'
/*   based on the 'bk' data in the system configuration data files.
/*
/*   The 'bk_tab' structure contains device status information and queue heads
/*   used by the executive and by the driver.
/*
/*   The 'bk_store' arrays form the memory areas for the pseudodevices.
/*
/*   The 'bk_rbuf' structures are used by the 'read' and 'write' routines to
/*   perform raw I/O.
/*
/*   'bk_trace' is a boolean flag that determines whether synchronous trace
/*   print will appear on the console.
/*
/**********/

extern int bk__ccnt;                    /* count of controllers */
extern int bk__cnt;                     /* count of units */
struct iobuf bk_tab = tabinit(8,0);     /* device control block */

char bk_store[U_MAX][U_BLKS*BSIZE];     /* block device memory */
struct buf bk_rbuf[U_MAX];              /* buf's for raw I/O */

int bk_trace;                           /* trace print flag */
```

```
/**************************************************************************/
/*                                                                      */
/*  Entry Point:  init                                                  */
/*  Purpose:      Driver Initialization                                 */
/*  Description:                                                         */
/*                                                                      */
/*  In this template driver the only useful function performed by the   */
/*  'init' routine is to turn on synchronous trace print.  In a driver  */
/*  for a real device it would verify that all configured controllers   */
/*  are online and would initialize all hardware.                       */
/*                                                                      */
/*  As an example this routine allocates a small group of I/O Map reg-  */
/*  isters and saves their base index in the driver 'iobuf' structure.  */
/*                                                                      */
/**************************************************************************/


bk_init()

{
   dev_t dev = 0;                       /* dummy for trace print */


   bk_trace = TRUE;                     /* begin with trace on */
   TRACE_VAL(bk_init, bk__cnt);


/**********/
/*
/*  At this point a driver for real devices should probe the hardware and
/*  mark it offline if it does not respond.  See 'chdriver' for an example
/*  of the required code.
/*
/**********/


/**********/
/*
/*  The following line allocates registers in the I/O Map.  These registers
/*  are allocated and later loaded with mapping values as examples -- the
/*  template driver does not actually use them.
/*
/**********/

   bk_tab.io_mapbase = iomalloc(U_MAXXFR, 0); /* allocate I/O map space */

}
```

```
/**************************************************************************/
/*                                                                        */
/*  Entry Point:   open                                                   */
/*  Purpose:       Open Device                                            */
/*  Description:                                                           */
/*                                                                        */
/*  This routine checks to see whether the unit number (which is equal    */
/*  to the device minor number) is in the legal range.                    */
/*                                                                        */
/**************************************************************************/


bk_open(dev, flag)

dev_t dev;                              /* device (minor) number */
int flag;                               /* read/write flag */


{
    int unit;                           /* device unit number */


    TRACE_VAL (bk_open, flag);

    unit = dev_to_unit(dev);            /* get the unit number */
    if (unit>=bk__cnt || unit>=U_MAX)   /* check for invalid */
       u.u_error = ENXIO;               /* return an error */


/**********/
/*
/*  The following test should appear in a driver for a hardware device.
/*
/*    if (bk__addr[dev_to_cont(dev)] == 0)
/*        u.u_error = ENODEV;
/*
/**********/

}
/**************************************************************************/
/*                                                                        */
/*  Entry Point:   close                                                  */
/*  Purpose:       Close Device                                           */
/*  Description:                                                           */
/*                                                                        */
/*  In most cases the 'close' routine for a block driver does not need    */
/*  to do anything.                                                       */
/*                                                                        */
/**************************************************************************/


bk_close(dev,flag)

dev_t dev;                              /* device (minor) number */
int flag;                               /* read/write flag */


{

    TRACE_VAL (close, flag);
}
```

```
/************************************************************************/
/*                                                                    */
/*  Entry Point: strategy                                             */
/*  Purpose:        Queue Read and Write Requests                     */
/*  Description:                                                      */
/*                                                                    */
/*  This routine checks the 'buf' passed to it to verify that the unit */
/*  and device address are legal.  If they are it places the 'buf' at */
/*  the end of the device active request queue and, if the device hard-*/
/*  ware is idle, calls 'bk_start' to activate it.  If the hardware is */
/*  active the interrupt handler will call 'bk_start' when the current */
/*  action is completed.                                              */
/*                                                                    */
/*  This template driver does not have any hardware, so the device is  */
/*  never active.  The 'bk_start' routine always completes the I/O     */
/*  synchronously, so the 'buf' structures never accumulate on the     */
/*  queue.                                                            */
/*                                                                    */
/************************************************************************/


bk_strategy (bp)

struct buf *bp;                         /* pointer to I/O request */
{
    int unit,blk;                       /* unit and block numbers */
    int oldpri;                         /* old CPU priority */
    struct iobuf *ip;                   /* pointer to device info */
    dev_t dev;                          /* needed for trace print */


    dev = bp->b_dev;                    /* Set the device number */
    TRACE_VAL (strategy, bp->b_flags);
    TRACE_VAL (strategy, bp->b_bcount);
    TRACE_VAL (strategy, bp->b_ioblkno);

    unit = dev_to_unit(dev);            /* get device unit number */
    blk = bp->b_ioblkno;                /* and device address */

    if (unit<0 || unit>=U_MAX || unit>=bk__cnt) /* check for legal unit */
      {
        bp->b_flags |= B_ERROR;
        bp->b_error = ENXIO;
        TRACE_TXT (strategy -- bad unit);
        iodone(bp);
      }
    else if (blk<0 || blk>=U_BLKS)        /* check for legal address */
      {
        if (bp->b_flags&B_READ && blk==U_BLKS)  /* if reading off end */
          {
            bp->b_resid = bp->b_bcount;     /* just read nothing */
            bp->b_error = 0;
            TRACE_TXT (strategy -- read off end);
          }
        else                            /* else its an error */
          {
            bp->b_flags |= B_ERROR;
            bp->b_error = EINVAL;
            TRACE_TXT (strategy -- bad address);
          }
```

```
            iodone(bp);
        }

    else                                    /* queue the request */
      {
        ip = &bk_tab;                       /* get ptr to device struct */
        bp->av_forw = NULL;                 /* buf goes at end of queue */
        oldpri = spl6();                    /* block interrupt handler */
        if (ip->b_actf == NULL)             /* if queue is empty */
           ip->b_actf = bp;                 /* new one will be first */
        else
           ip->b_actl->av_forw = bp;        /* else link to last one */
        ip->b_actl = bp;                    /* new one definitely last */

        if (!ip->b_active)                  /* if hardware idle */
           bk_start();                      /* fire it up */
        splx(oldpri);
      }
}

/**************************************************************************/
/*                                                                        */
/*  Local Routine: trim                                                   */
/*  Purpose:       Limit DMA Transfers                                    */
/*  Description:                                                          */
/*                                                                        */
/*  When 'physio' is called from 'read' and 'write' to perform raw        */
/*  transfers it calls this routine to allow the byte count to be         */
/*  reduced if necessary.  The value U_MAXXFR is an arbitrary example     */
/*  that has no special meaning.                                          */
/*                                                                        */
/**************************************************************************/


bk_trim(bp)

struct buf *bp;
{
    dev_t dev;


    dev = bp->b_dev;
    TRACE_VAL (trim, bp->b_bcount);

    if (bp->b_bcount > U_MAXXFR)            /* if count is too large */
        bp->b_bcount = U_MAXXFR;            /* reduce it */
}
```

```
/**********************************************************************/
/*                                                                    */
/*  Entry Point:  read                                                */
/*  Purpose:      Read Raw Data                                       */
/*  Description:                                                      */
/*                                                                    */
/*  This routine is called when a 'read' system service call is made  */
/*  to a character device (raw device) associated with this driver. It */
/*  may also be called by the executive file system to perform raw    */
/*  reads on the block device.                                        */
/*                                                                    */
/**********************************************************************/


bk_read (dev)

dev_t dev;                              /* device (minor) number */
{


    TRACE_VAL (read,u.u_offset);
    TRACE_VAL (read,u.u_count);

    if (physck(U_BLKS, B_READ))         /* reject or truncate I/O? */
        physio (bk_strategy, &bk_rbuf[dev_to_unit(dev)], dev, B_READ, bk_trim);
}
```

```
/*****************************************************************************/
/*                                                                         */
/*  Entry Point:  write                                                    */
/*  Purpose:      Write Raw Data                                           */
/*  Description:                                                           */
/*                                                                         */
/*  This routine is called when a 'write' system service call is made      */
/*  to a character device (raw device) associated with this driver.  It    */
/*  may also be called by the executive file system to perform raw         */
/*  writes on the block device.                                            */
/*                                                                         */
/*****************************************************************************/


bk_write (dev)

dev_t dev;                              /* device (minor) number */
{

   TRACE_VAL (write, u.u_offset);
   TRACE_VAL (write, u.u_count);

   if (physck (U_BLKS, B_WRITE))        /* reject or truncate I/O? */
      physio (bk_strategy, &bk_rbuf[dev_to_unit(dev)], dev, B_WRITE, bk_trim);
}



/*****************************************************************************/
/*                                                                         */
/*  Entry Point:  ioctl                                                    */
/*  Purpose:      Special Functions                                        */
/*  Description:                                                           */
/*                                                                         */
/*  No special function commands are implemented -- this routine always    */
/*  returns an error.                                                      */
/*                                                                         */
/*****************************************************************************/


bk_ioctl (dev, cmd, argp)

dev_t dev;                              /* device (minor) number */
int cmd;                                /* The command */
int *argp;                              /* The argument or pointer */
{
   struct tty *dsp;                     /* dev status pointer */


   TRACE_VAL (ioctl, cmd);

   switch (cmd)                         /* handle command cases: */
    {

     default:
      u.u_error = EINVAL;               /* else return an error */
    }
}
```

```
/*************************************************************************/
/*                                                                     */
/*  Entry Point:  intr                                                 */
/*  Purpose:      Handle Interrupts                                    */
/*  Description:                                                       */
/*                                                                     */
/*  The pseudodevices supported by this template driver do not issue   */
/*  interrupts; therefore this routine does nothing (and could in fact */
/*  be omitted).  For a real device this routine must                  */
/*                                                                     */
/*      - determine whether the interrupt is to be handled by this     */
/*        driver                                                       */
/*      - clear the interrupt in the hardware and indicate in the iobuf*/
/*        that the device is not active                                */
/*      - remove the completed buf from the queue and call 'iodone' to */
/*        release it                                                   */
/*      - if there is another buf queued, call the 'start' routine     */
/*                                                                     */
/*************************************************************************/


bk_intr(devno, dp)

int devno;                              /* device index */
struct bk_device *dp;                   /* pointer to CSR */
{


    if (TRUE)
        return(0);                      /* assume it is not ours */
}
```

```
/*************************************************************************/
/*                                                                     */
/*  Local Routine: start                                               */
/*  Purpose:        Initiate Device Activity                           */
/*  Description:                                                        */
/*                                                                     */
/*  In a driver for a real device this routine issues commands to the  */
/*  hardware to initiate I/O and perform other control operations.  In */
/*  in this template driver the routine actually performs the read and */
/*  write operations to the pseudodevice.                              */
/*                                                                     */
/*  If the flag B_PHYS is on the data buffer is in user space and the  */
/*  'copyin' and 'copyout' routines must be used.  Otherwise the buffer */
/*  is in system space and the data can be moved with a simple assign- */
/*  ment loop.  Note that this is a limited implementation that does   */
/*  not check the B_UAREA and B_PAGET flags -- this driver does not    */
/*  support a swap file.                                               */
/*                                                                     */
/*  As an example the template driver loads the allocated I/O Map reg- */
/*  isters and obtains the DMA MULTIBUS address.  In a driver for a    */
/*  real device the value returned by 'iomaddr' would be loaded into   */
/*  the controller address register.  In the template driver the I/O   */
/*  Map is not actually used.                                          */
/*                                                                     */
/*************************************************************************/


bk_start()

{
    struct iobuf *ip;               /* device structure pointer */
    struct buf *bp;                 /* request to process */
    char *from, *to;                /* source and dest pointers */
    dev_t dev;                      /* device number */
    int locnt;                      /* local byte count */
    paddr_t mbaddr;                 /* device DMA address */


/*** >>>>>>  NOTE: THIS ROUTINE EXECUTES AT ELEVATED PRIORITY  <<<<<< ***/


    ip = &bk_tab;                   /* locate the device queue */
    bp = ip->b_actf;                /* find the first request */
    dev = bp->b_dev;                /* get the unit number */


/**********/
/*                                                                     */
/*  Load the I/O Map.                                                  */
/*                                                                     */
/**********/

    mbaddr = iomaddr(bp,paddr(bp),bp->b_bcount,ip->io_mapbase);


/**********/
/*                                                                     */
/*  Determine the source and destination addresses.                    */
/*                                                                     */
/**********/
```

```
                                          /* assume this is a read */
    from = &bk_store[dev_to_unit(dev)] [bp->b_ioblkno*BSIZE];
    if (bp->b_flags&B_READ)               /* if it is... */
      to = bp->b_ioaddr;                  /* write to memory */
    else                                  /* else reverse it */
      {
      to = from;                          /* to the device */
      from = bp->b_ioaddr;                /* from memory */
      }


/**********/
/*
/*  Copy the data, either between user and system space or entirely
/*  within system space.
/*
/**********/

    if (bp->b_flags&B_PHYS)               /* if buffer in user space */
      {
      if (bp->b_flags&B_READ)             /* move in right direction */
          copyout(from, to, bp->b_bcount);
      else
          copyin(from, to, bp->b_bcount);
      }
    else                                  /* else copy in system space */
      {
      locnt = bp->b_bcount;
      while (locnt--)
          *to++ = *from++;
      }


/**********/
/*
/*  Dequeue and release the request buf.
/*
/**********/

    bp->b_resid = 0;                      /* clear error indicators */
    bp->b_error = 0;

    ip->b_actf = bp->av_forw;             /* take buf off the queue */
    TRACE_VAL (start, bp->b_flags);
    iodone(bp);                           /* and return it */
}




/* End of bkdriver.c */
```

```
#  bk.master -- Template Block Driver entry in master configuration file
#
#  The following line of data is in the file 'bk.master'.  These comments
#  are not in the file.
#

bk     737    54    bk_    0    0    0    8    23    2    0

# End of bk.master



#  bk.dfile -- Template Block entry in Device Description File
#
#  The following line of data is in the file 'bk.dfile'.  These comments
#  are not in the file.
#


bk        0        0        0
# End of bk.file




############################################################################
#                                                                          #
#  bk.make -- makefile for template block driver                           #
#                                                                          #
#  This is a makefile for the template block driver 'bkdriver'             #
#  supplied with the MASSCOMP "GUIDE TO WRITING A DEVICE DRIVER".  It       #
#  compiles the driver source code and places a copy of 'bkdriver.o'        #
#  in the directory '/usr/drivers/uts'.                                    #
#                                                                          #
############################################################################


bkdriver.o:     bkdriver.c
                cc -O -c bkdriver.c
                cp bkdriver.o /usr/drivers/uts

# End of bk.make
```

```
##########################################################################
#                                                                        #
#  bk.files -- create device special files for bkdriver                  #
#                                                                        #
#  This csh script is executed by the 'Install' procedure in order to    #
#  create four device special files for the template block driver.       #
#  The values of BMAJOR and CMAJOR must be changed here and in           #
#  'bk.master' if the current values have been used by another driver.   #
#  See Chapter 6 for a complete discussion.                              #
#                                                                        #
##########################################################################


set BMAJOR = 8
set CMAJOR = 23

mknod /dev/bk0 b 8 0
mknod /dev/bk1 b 8 1
mknod /dev/rbk0 c 23 0
mknod /dev/rbk1 c 23 1

chmod a+rw /dev/bk0
chmod a+rw /dev/bk1
chmod a+rw /dev/rbk0
chmod a+rw /dev/rbk1

#  End of bk.files
```

```
#######################################################################
#                                                                     #
#   bk.test -- demonstrate operation of template block driver         #
#                                                                     #
#   This demonstration C shell procedure creates a file system on the #
#   block device '/dev/bk0', mounts the device, and copies a group of #
#   files to it.                                                       #
#                                                                     #
#######################################################################


echo ""
echo " Test of bkdriver -- must be run by the superuser"
echo ""
echo ""

echo " Creating file system on the device..."
echo ""
set echo
mkfs /dev/bk0 16
unset echo

echo ""
echo " Creating a mount directory and mounting the device..."
echo ""
set echo
mkdir mntbk
mount /dev/bk0 $cwd/mntbk
unset echo

echo ""
echo " Copying files to the mounted device..."
echo ""
set echo
cp bk.* mntbk
unset echo

echo ""
echo "Device contents and free space:"
echo ""
ls -ls mntbk
df

umount /dev/bk0
rmdir mntbk


echo ""
echo " The device has been unmounted.  If you mount it again its contents"
echo " will still be intact."
echo ""


# End of bk.test
```

```
/**************************************************************************/
/*                                                                        */
/*  bkex -- exercise bkdriver                                             */
/*                                                                        */
/*  This program exercises the template driver 'bkdriver' by performing  */
/*  simple operations on the raw device '/dev/rbk1' and on the block     */
/*  device '/dev/bk1'.                                                    */
/*                                                                        */
/*  First it writes five individual blocks to the raw device.  Then it   */
/*  reads 16 blocks in one operation -- the driver routine 'bk_trim',    */
/*  which limits device transfers to 10 blocks, causes this read to be   */
/*  performed in two parts.  Finally the program reads five individual   */
/*  blocks form the block device.  These reads are mediated by the       */
/*  executive block buffering system and are seen by the driver as       */
/*  eight-block cluster reads.                                           */
/*                                                                        */
/**************************************************************************/


#include <fcntl.h>

extern errno;


main()
{
    int i;
    char dbuf[8192];
    int fd;
    int temp;


/**********/
/*
/*  Open the raw device.
/*
/**********/

    if ((fd=open("/dev/rbk1", O_RDWR)) < 0)
      {
        perror("bkex: can't open rbk1");
        exit(0);
      }


/**********/
/*
/*  Write the first two and last three blocks on the device.
/*
/**********/

    for (i=0; i<16; i++)
      {
        if (i==2) i = 13;
        printf("\nwrite raw block %d: ", lseek(fd, i<<9, 0) >> 9);
        scanf("%c",&temp);
        dbuf[0] = i;
        if (write(fd, dbuf, 512) != 512)
            perror("bkex: could not write raw device");
      }
```

```
/**********/
/*
/*  Read the entire device with one call.
/*
/**********/

    lseek(fd, 0, 0);
    printf("\nread 16 raw blocks: ");
    scanf("%c", &temp);
    if (read(fd, dbuf, 512*16) < 512*16)
        perror("bkex: could not do large read");


/**********/
/*
/*  Close the raw device and open the corresponding block device.
/*
/**********/

    close(fd);
    if ((fd=open("/dev/bk1", O_RDWR)) < 0)
     {
        perror("bkex: can't open bk1");
        exit(0);
     }


/**********/
/*
/*  Read the five blocks that were written earlier.
/*
/**********/

    for (i=0; i<16; i++)
     {
        if (i==2) i = 13;
        printf("\nread block %d: ", lseek(fd, i<<9, 0) >> 9);
        scanf("%c",&temp);
        if (read(fd, dbuf, 512) != 512)
            perror("bkex: could not write block device");
        if (dbuf[0] != i)
            perror("bkex: inconsistent value on bk1");
     }
}

/* End of bkex.c */
```

E

XENIX

The XENIX interface to device drivers differs in some details from the interface described in the rest of this book. This appendix describes those differences. This appendix is not a complete treatment of the internals of XENIX. Specific details provided here are for the implementation of XENIX on the Intel iAPX 286 microprocessor.

The areas of difference that are important to people writing device drivers are:

- Memory management
- System configuration
- Additional kernel support routines
- Interrupt vector usage

· Memory Management ·

As discussed in Chapter 3, the mapping of physical address space to logical address space differs based on hardware architecture and on the implementation of the particular UNIX variant on the hardware. The iAPX 286 can operate in either of two modes: Real Mode and Protected Mode. This section describes XENIX memory management on the iAPX 286 in Protected Mode.

Logical Address Space

The address space of the machine is divided into global and local address spaces. The global address space maps the kernel's working memory. The local address space contains task-specific information. The 32-bit pointer used to specify a logical address contains fields to allow you to select which address space to reference, as well as the index into the selected address space.

The logical address pointer is two 16-bit fields that make up a 32-bit pointer. The two fields are:

- effective offset—the offset in bytes from location zero of the segment
- segment selector—a value that uniquely identifies the segment

The segment selector is made up of the following bit fields:

Bits	Use
zero and one	Request Privilege Level (RPL)
two	Table Indicator (TI)
three	INDEX

The Request Privilege Level is part of the system protection mechanism.

The Table Indicator bit specifies whether the selector references global or local address space. If the TI bit is set (one), the reference is to local address space, and the segment descriptor will be found in the Local Descriptor Table. If the TI bit is not set (zero), the reference is to global address space, and the segment descriptor will be found in the Global Descriptor Table.

The remaining bits in the segment selector act as an index to the descriptor table, which records the mapping scheme that relates the logical address space to the physical address space. This offset is used to locate a unique descriptor entry in the table indicated by the TI bit (GDT or LDT). The iAPX 286 processor then sums the offset field of the descriptor—with the physical address field contained in the descriptor—to produce the physical address for the memory reference.

Descriptor Tables.   The Local Descriptor Table and Global Descriptor Table are both made up of individual entries that map the logical address to the physical address. Each descriptor table entry is 8 bytes long. Each descriptor table may contain from one to 8,192 entries.

There is only one Global Descriptor Table. It contains as many entries as needed to completely describe the system's global address space. There may be many Local Descriptor Tables since the LDT describes a particular task's own private local address space. Therefore, there must be as many LDTs as there are tasks. Each LDT in turn contains as many entries as needed to completely describe the task's local address space.

• Configuration •

The distributed XENIX system contains provisions for some common types of device drivers. These drivers are preconfigured into the master configuration file. Their names are compiled into c.o, and null routines in the kernel libraries provide name references for the linker when the drivers are not present. You can determine what devices have been preconfigured by looking at master. If your device is preconfigured, you can skip the next section.

For nonpreconfigured devices, the process of incorporating your device driver into the XENIX kernel is very similar to that described in Chapter 4. The kernel-to-driver interface file output by `config` on the XENIX system is `/usr/sys/conf/c.c` rather than `conf.c`, but it contains the same information. The hardware interface file output by `config` on the XENIX system is named `space.c`

Master Configuration File

The files described above are generated from the master configuration file, as described in Chapter 4. The fields in part 1 of `master` differ from those as follows:

Field	XENIX	System V	RTU
2	number of interrupt vectors	number of interrupt vectors	device mask
3	device mask	device mask	device type indicator
4	device type indicator	device type indicator	handler prefix
5	handler prefix	handler prefix	device address size
6	always zero	device address size	CSR offset
7	major device number for block devices	major device number for block devices	IRQ bit mask for CSR
8	major device number for character devices	major device number for character devices	major device number for block devices
9	maximum number of devices per controller	maximum number of devices per controller	major device number for character devices
10	interrupt level	interrupt level	maximum number of devices per controller
11 to 14	vectors on which this device can interrupt	optional configuration table structure declarations	11 is the interrupt level and 12 through 14 are the optional configuration table structure declarations

The same information is contained in `master` on each of the systems described above, but it is not always in the same field. Please check the manual pages for the `master` file in the reference manual that comes with your system to verify the fields.

System Configuration File

The system configuration file on XENIX systems is called `xenixconf` and corresponds to `/usr/uts/SYSNAME` as described in Chapter 4, or `dfile` as described in the `config` entry in the *UNIX Programmer's Manual*.

Vector Numbers

Whether your device driver is preconfigured or nonpreconfigured, you will need to determine your device's vector number before you can configure your driver into the kernel. The vector number is needed to inform the kernel that your device driver should be called when there is an interrupt pending for the device associated with that vector number.

Computing the Vector Number.   On unmapped XENIX systems, the XENIX vector number is the same as the bus request number on which your device interrupts.

On mapped XENIX systems, the XENIX vector number does not correspond directly to the bus request number. Rather, the vector number is mapped to logical vector numbers in order to allow for slave interrupt controllers connected to the master interrupt controller. Thus, for the master controller the vector number is the bus request number, but for the slave controllers you must compute it using the following algorithm:

1. Multiply the request line that the slave controller uses in the master controller (on the 80286 this should be two) by eight (the number of vectors per controller).

2. Add eight (the number of vectors on the master controller).

3. Add the number of the request line you are using on the slave controller.

Vector Numbers for Preconfigured Devices.   For preconfigured drivers all the driver entry points as described in Chapter 9 are already provided except for the interrupt handler. There are, however, extra entry points with the suffix `-init` included for each preconfigured driver that might require an interrupt vector. Therefore, you must have a driver init routine that replaces the appropriate vector in `vectintsw` (defined in `/usr/sys/h/conf.h`) with a pointer to the device interrupt handler. The init routine should also set the interrupt priority level of the driver by patching `vecintlev` (also defined in `conf.h`).

Compiling Device Drivers

When you compile your device driver for the XENIX system, you must use the following options to the XENIX C compiler:

`-K`	Disable stack probes
`-DM_KERNEL`	Required for conditional code in standard header files
`-NT io_text`	Use `IO_TEXT` as the name of the text segment for driver code
`-M2em`	Enables 80286 instructions. You cannot use this option if you specify `-M0em`
`-M0em`	Uses only 8086 instructions. You cannot use this option if you specify `-M2em`

▪ Interrupt Vector Usage ▪

In addition to the general information about hardware interrupt handlers in Chapter 4, there are some specific concerns for drivers written for XENIX systems running on the IBM PC XT, AT, and compatibles.

XENIX systems implemented for the Intel 8086 microprocessor use a single programmable interrupt controller. The controller has eight vectors (as disucssed above) of which all but one are currently used. That is bus lead IRQ2. Therefore, the only vector availabe for use by your driver is number two. Drivers written using interrupt priority level five (see `spl5`) may use this vector safely.

XENIX systems implemented for the Intel 80286 microprocessor use two programmable interrupt controllers. On these systems, vectors nine through 12 and vector 15 are available for your drivers to use. Drivers written using interrupt priority level five can use these vectors safely.

There may be cases when you must use one of the other vectors. The safest way to do that is to simply replace the driver already using that vector with your driver. This is the recommended alternative.

You may consider sharing a vector between two drivers by writing a special interrupt handler to deal with the shared vector. This approach may result in lost interrupts. However, devices that can time out while waiting for a response to a request (for example, disks or tapes) and check for completion when the timeout occurs can share a vector without losing interrupts. Both devices sharing a vector must be written using the `timeout` routine. If only one of the two drivers sharing the vector uses `timeout`, there is still the possibility of lost interrupts.

The discussion in Chapter 4 of handlers for nonvectored interrupts on the MULTIBUS may provide some hints on how to set up an interrupt routine to deal with multiple devices on a single vector.

▪ Kernel Support Routines ▪

The following kernel I/O support routines described in Appendix B are also available on XENIX systems (see Appendix B for the full description):

- delay
- spl5, spl6, spl7, and splx
- sleep
- wakeup
- timeout
- copyin and copyout
- printf
- panic
- signal
- suser

In addition to the above, there are several kernel support routines that are specific to XENIX. These are:

in, out, inb, outb, ioinb, iooutb	interface to device registers
dscralloc, dscrfree, dscraddr, mmudescr	memory mapping
copyio	copy bytes between a logical address and a physical address
putchar	print one character on the console

Each of these routines is described on the following pages:

COPYIO (XENIX)

NAME

copyio – copy bytes between a physical address and a logical address

SYNOPSIS

```
copyio (addr, faddr, cnt, mapping)
```

DESCRIPTION

copyio allows you to copy bytes between physical and logical addresses. It is most commonly used for copying between kernel data and user space.

addr is the physical address to or from which the data is to be copied. Its data type is paddr_t. It is a 32-bit quantity.

faddr is the logical address to or from which the data is to be copied. Its data type is faddr_t.

cnt is an integer specifying the number of bytes to be copied.

mapping is an integer specifying the copy direction (to or from which type of address space). The values for mapping are defined in /usr/sys/h/user.h.

RETURNS

copyio returns –1 if the copy fails.

SEE ALSO

copyin and copyout.

DSCRADDR   (XENIX)

NAME

dscraddr – return the physical address of the memory addressed by the selector

SYNOPSIS

```
dscraddr (sel)
```

DESCRIPTION

dscraddr returns the physical address of the memory addressed by sel. sel is an unsigned short that specifies the selector number for which you want the physical address.

RETURNS

dscraddr returns the 32-bit physical address of the memory addressed by the selector.

SEE ALSO

dscralloc, dscrfree, and mmudescr.

DSCRALLOC   (XENIX)

NAME

dscralloc – allocate a descriptor from the Global Descriptor Table

SYNOPSIS

dscralloc ()

DESCRIPTION

dscralloc allocates a descriptor from the GDT pool.

RETURNS

dscralloc returns an unsigned short value specifying the selector number of the allocated descriptor. It returns zero if there are no more descriptors available.

SEE ALSO

dscrfree, dscraddr, and mmudescr.

DSCRFREE   (XENIX)

NAME

dscrfree – return a descriptor to Global Descriptor Table pool

SYNOPSIS

dscrfree (sel)

DESCRIPTION

dscrfree returns the specified descriptor to the GDT pool. sel is an unsigned short specifying the selector number of the descriptor to be freed. The selector number was obtained from a call to dscralloc.

SEE ALSO

dscralloc, dscraddr, and mmudescr.

IN (XENIX)

NAME

in – return the value of the word at the specified port

SYNOPSIS

in (port)

DESCRIPTION

in returns the value of the word specified by port.

port is an integer value that specifies the register address of the desired word.

RETURNS

in returns the value on the port.

SEE ALSO

inb and ioinb.

INB   **(XENIX)**

NAME

    inb – return the value of the byte at the specified port

SYNOPSIS

    `inb (port)`

DESCRIPTION

    inb returns the value of the byte specified by `port`.

    `port` is an integer value that specifies the register address of the desired byte.

RETURNS

    inb returns the value on the port.

SEE ALSO

    in and ioinb.

IOINB   **(XENIX)**

NAME

  ioinb – near version of inb

SYNOPSIS

```
ioinb (port)
extern int near ioinb();
```

DESCRIPTION

  ioinb returns the value of the byte specified by port. It provides faster execution than inb. You must declare ioinb as a near routine for
  all modules that use it, and you must compile them with the -NT
  io_text option to the XENIX C compiler to ensure that the text segment of the calling routine is the same as the ioinb text segment.

  port is an integer value that specifies the register address of the desired
  byte.

RETURNS

  ioinb returns the value on the port.

SEE ALSO

  in and inb.

IOOUTB (XENIX)

NAME

iooutb – set the byte at the specified address to the specified value

SYNOPSIS

iooutb (port,value)

DESCRIPTION

iooutb sets the byte located at the address specified by port to the value specified by value. This near version of outb provides faster execution.

You must declare iooutb as a near routine for all the modules that use it, and you must compile those modules with the -NT io_text option to the XENIX C compiler to ensure that the text segment of the calling routine is the same as the iooutb text segment.

SEE ALSO

out and outb.

NAME

mmudescr – initialize a descriptor to map an area of memory

SYNOPSIS

mmudescr (sel, addr, limit, access)

DESCRIPTION

mmudescr initializes a descriptor to map an area of memory.

sel is an unsigned short that specifies the selector number of a descriptor that was allocated using dscralloc.

addr is the physical address of the memory addressed by the selector.

limit is an unsigned short that specifies the limit of the memory area in bytes.

access is a byte that specifies the type of memory access to be permitted. The possible values for access are:

RW	read/write
RO	read/execute only
DSA_DATA	defined in /usr/sys/h/relsym.h

SEE ALSO

dscralloc, dscrfree, and dscraddr.

OUT   (XENIX)

NAME

out – set the word at the specified address to the specified value

SYNOPSIS

```
out (port,value)
```

DESCRIPTION

out sets the word located at the address specified by port to the value specified by value.

SEE ALSO

outb and iooutb.

OUTB   (XENIX)

NAME

outb – set the byte at the specified address to the specified value

SYNOPSIS

```
outb (port,value)
```

DESCRIPTION

outb sets the byte located at the address specified by port to the value specified by value.

SEE ALSO

out and iooutb.

APPENDIX

F

BERKELEY UNIX COMPATIBILITY

This appendix describes special aspects of writing device drivers for UNIX systems based on the 4.3 Berkeley Software Distribution (also called 4.3BSD, or just 4BSD). This version of UNIX is widely used on VAX computers and is also the basis for many commercial versions of UNIX (RTU is based in part on previous versions of BSD).

· VAX-11/780 I/O Architecture ·

Although 4BSD versions of UNIX have been implemented on many systems with very different I/O architectures, the basic structure of device drivers were originally designed to accommodate the VAX-11/780. Prior to the availability of the VAX, UNIX had been ported to systems that supported only a single I/O bus. The VAX was capable of supporting several I/O buses as shown in Figure F-1. The main system bus connects the central processor, memory, and the I/O bus adaptors. This bus is called the SBI for Synchronous Bus Interconnect. The SBI provides a 32-bit wide path for transferring data between elements attached to the bus.

In addition to a central processor and main memory, one or more I/O bus adaptors can be connected to the SBI. These I/O adaptors can be either UNIBUS adaptors or MASSBUS adaptors. The UNIBUS was originally developed by Digital Equipment Corporation for its PDP-11 family of processors and supports 8- and 16-bit data transfers using up to 18 bits of addressing. A wide variety of I/O devices including disk, tape, serial interfaces, printers, and plotters can be interfaced using the UNIBUS. The MASSBUS is a higher performance I/O bus supporting 32-bit data transfers. Generally only high speed disk and tape devices are interfaced using the MASSBUS.

The bus adaptors are more than simple bus protocol converters: each bus adaptor incorporates its own I/O map similar to the I/O maps described in Chapter 3. In addition, the UNIBUS adaptor on the VAX-11/780 includes several *buffered data paths*, which allow more efficient data transfers between the 16-bit wide UNIBUS and the 32-bit wide SBI. Rather than performing an SBI cycle for each UNIBUS cycle, a buffered data path temporarily stores data for sequential data transfers so it only needs to perform one SBI cycle for every other 16-bit UNIBUS cycle.

Other VAX systems have a similar architecture although a different bus may be used as the main system bus to which processor, memory, and I/O adaptors are connected. For example, the VAX-11/750 uses a CMI and is able to support one MASSBUS adaptor and one UNIBUS adaptor. It is perfectly feasible to have a VAX system with only one I/O bus adaptor so the architectural model can also be applied to simple systems. Although not all UNIBUS adaptor VAX systems include buffered data paths, the low level support for this feature is contained in standard system support routines that adapt to the particular processor.

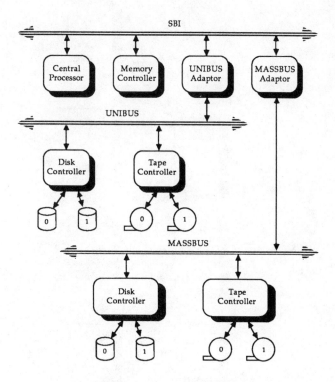

Fig. F-1. Device and Controller Connections on VAX-11/780

▪ Autoconfiguration Under 4BSD ▪

One of the challenges involved in supporting UNIX on the VAX-11/780 was dealing with the wide variety of I/O configurations that might be possible. For example, large VAX systems would often have separate MASSBUS adaptors for several disk drives in order to provide more aggregate bandwidth between I/O devices and memory. Smaller systems would connect all devices using a single UNIBUS adaptor in order to reduce the cost of the system. Intermediate systems would have several disk drives connected to a single MASSBUS adaptor.

The system support routines for device drivers accommodate the range of configuration options by using a set of internal data structures that mimic the connection of hardware components. This is shown graphically in Figure F-2. A system configuration contains one or more bus adaptors. I/O controllers are attached to these bus adaptors. Individual I/O devices such as a disk or tape drive are in turn attached to these controllers. 4BSD uses specific data structures for each bus adaptor, controller, and device in the system.

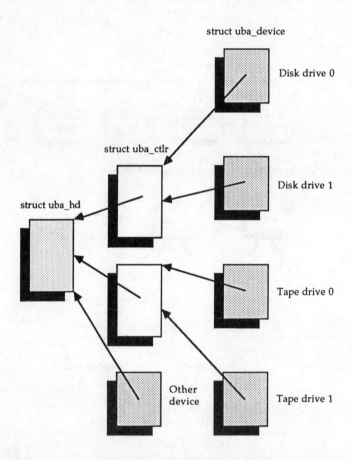

Fig. F-2. Device Configuration Data Structures for 4.3BSD

This is represented by a `mba_hd` structure for each MASSBUS adaptor on the system and a `uba_hd` structure for each UNIBUS adaptor. Each controller has a corresponding `mba_ctlr` or `uba_ctlr` structure depending on whether it is attached to the MASSBUS or UNIBUS. Finally, there is a `mba_device` or `uba_device` structure for each individual I/O device. Many controllers will not need separate device structures. The device structure is used primarily to manage the I/O maps and other resources associated with the bus adaptor. In particular, UNIBUS devices that do not need a buffered data path do not need a device structure. Notice that the configuration shown in Figure F-2 is not quite the same as the configuration of Figure F-1: only structures for UNIBUS devices are shown. In addition, Figure F-2 shows an "other" device directly connected to the UNIBUS.

Finally, there is a single data structure containing all the configuration information for a particular device driver. This includes the addresses of driver entry points used only during configuration or used by device drivers for a particular type of I/O bus (this data structure is not illustrated in Figure F-2).

These configuration data structures are linked together in various ways. For example, `uba_device` structures contain pointers to the `uba_ctlr` structure corresponding to the controller the device is attached to as well a pointer to the UNIBUS adaptor the controller is connected to. Other configuration information is also kept in these data structures instead of being stored in independent arrays. For example, the system virtual address to use when accessing a UNIBUS device is kept in the `uba_device` structure instead of being stored in a `xx_addr` array.

The configuration device structures are built by a `config` program that is very different from the `config` program supplied with AT&T System III or System V, and somewhat different from the one described in Chapter 4. The configuration file contains one line of information for each device or controller structure. For example, this portion of the configuration file:

```
controller    uba0    at nexus ?
controller    sc0     at uba? csr 0176700      vector upintr
disk          up0     at sc0 drive 0
disk          up1     at sc0 drive1
```

builds a `uba_hd` structure for the UNIBUS adaptor `uba0`. Attached to this is a `uba_ctlr` structure for a disk controller, `sc0`. The UNIBUS address of the controller is 0176700, and the interrupt handler for the driver is `upintr`. In addition, two `uba_device` structures are built (one for each disk attached to `sc0`) and linked to the `uba_ctlr` structure. The `config` program will also construct a `uba_driver` structure for `sc` controllers and `up` devices.

There are several special driver entry points that are used only during auto-configuration. These are:

- A probe routine to determine whether a controller is physically present in the system.

- A slave routine to determine whether devices attached to controllers (disk or tape drives) are present.

- An attach routine to finish initializing data structures for slave devices.

Probe Routines

For UNIBUS devices the probe routine will be called with a system virtual address where the controller status registers might be. The probe routine needs to determine whether a controller is present, what its interrupt priority is, and what interrupt vector it uses. This is normally done by attempting to issue a controller operation which will result in an interrupt. During configuration all interrupt vectors are diverted to standard handlers, which simply record the actual interrupt level and vector. On the VAX these are passed back to the configuration routine through register variables. This is accomplished by altering the entry point for probe routines so that they do not save all their register variables. Note that in order to work properly:

- Parameters to the probe routine must not be declared as register parameters.

- Two local variables, br and cvec, must be the first variables declared in the probe routine.

After the standard interrupt handler returns, br contains the interrupt level, and cvec contains the interrupt vector. It is possible to simply assign values to these parameters instead of causing an interrupt if it turns out to be difficult to generate an interrupt from the controller.

Probe routines are passed one or two additional parameters depending on whether the controller was described as a controller or a device in the configuration file. Controllers are passed the controller index and a pointer to the uba_ctlr structure built by config. Devices are passed a pointer to the uba_device structure built by config. It is usually not necessary to use any of these additional parameters.

The probe routine should return zero if the device is not present, or some nonzero value if the device was found. By convention, the probe routine returns the number of bytes of UNIBUS address space the controller responds to, although the actual value is immaterial as long as it is not zero. The probe routine does not need to explicitly check whether accessing the specified UNIBUS address results in a bus timeout or other error. The configuration routines will have already read from the base controller address before calling the probe routine. In addition, the configuration routine will print a warning message and ignore the value returned by the probe routine if the probe routine did not appear to generate an interrupt (this is determined by making sure the value of br changed as a result of calling the probe routine).

Slave Routines

Slave routines are only called for devices that are attached to controllers after the corresponding probe routine has been called and returned a nonzero value. The slave routine is passed a pointer to a uba_device structure and the system virtual address for the controller, which was previously passed to the probe routine. The slave routine should determine whether the device is present and return a nonzero value if the device is found. Device drivers are usually limited in their ability to determine whether a slave device is present. For example, it is usually not possible to distinguish a disk drive that is not spinning from a disk drive that isn't there. Similarly, a controller cannot usually distinguish a nonexistent tape drive from a drive that currently has no tape loaded or is offline. This ambiguity is usually resolved by returning zero for disk devices, unless the drive is currently online, and returning one for tape devices.

Attach Routines

If the slave routine indicates that a device is present, the attach routine is called with a pointer to the uba_device structure. The configuration routines will fill in most of the fields of the uba_device structure before calling the attach routine, but the attach routine needs to initialize any additional status variables used by the device driver. For example, the attach routine may record how many drives were found on each controller or may save the pointer to the uba_device structure in some table where it is easy to locate when the normal device interrupt handler is called.

· System Call Differences ·

The majority of system calls are identical in UNIX systems based on AT&T System V and 4.3BSD. These core system calls characterize any UNIX-based system. Although 4.3BSD implements many system calls not part of System V, the additional system calls have no effect on device drivers, with a few exceptions.

Scatter/Gather I/O

The readv and writev are similar to read and write in that they transfer data to or from files (which may, in fact, be devices). However, readv and writev implement *scatter-gather* I/O: when reading data from a file into memory, readv can scatter the data to many different data buffers rather than putting all the data into a single data buffer. Similarly writev can gather data from several data buffers and write it to consecutive bytes in a file in one system call.

At first glance, readv and writev appear superfluous since it is possible to transfer the same data using a sequence of ordinary read or write system calls. While this is true, using a single system call can eliminate much of the overhead of entering the operating system, fetching the arguments to a system call, determining which system call handler to invoke, and so forth.

More importantly, readv and writev are *atomic* operations for most types of files: if more than one process attempts to call readv or writev on the same file at essentially the same time, each process executes these system calls entirely without interference from other processes. This is typically used by *client* processes to communicate with a *server* process through a socket (for the purposes of this discussion a pair of sockets behave like a pipe, in that data written to the first socket by one process can be read from the second socket). The data written to the socket consists of a sequence of *messages* which may be variable length records and may contain data that a program would most conveniently store in several different variables or data structures. If a process wrote such a message using several write system calls, there would be a danger of two messages from separate processes getting jumbled together, but writev would guarantee that the messages did not get mixed up.

If writev were not available the programs would have to use some other mechanism to synchronize access to the socket, or the program could copy the data from several variables into a single data buffer and use an ordinary write system call (although System V.3 does not support sockets *per se*, writes to pipes or named pipes are also atomic provided each message is small enough to fit entirely within the temporary data storage for the pipe).

In order to efficiently support readv and writev, data is transferred to and from user virtual address space quite differently under 4.3BSD. Instead of using simple variables u.u_base and u.u_count to specify a data buffer,

4.3BSD uses a `uio` structure. The single base and count are replaced by an arbitrary number of base and count pairs. In addition, some other variables from the user structure are kept with the `uio` structure. The declaration for `uio` looks like:

```
struct iovec {        /* each iovec describes a piece */
  caddr_t iov_base;   /* of the scattered data buffer */
  int     iov_len;
};
struct uio {
  struct iovec *uio_iov; /* a pointer to all the iovecs for */
                         /* this system call */
  int    uio_iovcnt;  /* the number of pieces in the buffer */
  off_t  uio_offset;  /* the file offset (instead of u.u_offset) */
  int    uio_segflg;  /* segment the data resides in */
                         /* (instead of u.u_segflg) */
  int    uio_resid;   /* number of bytes not transferred */
};
```

Pointers to `uio` structures are passed explicitly to various routines inside the system as opposed to being passed implicitly through global variables within the user structure. In particular, the read and write entry points of device drivers are passed pointers to `uio` structures as their second argument. In addition, support routines that reference `u.u_base`, `u.u_count`, and `u.u_offset` are replaced by different routines that reference a `uio` structure.

Instead of calling `iomove`, device drivers for 4.3BSD systems will need to call `uiomove`. Similarly, calls to `passc` and `cpass` must be replaced with calls to `uread` and `uwrite` respectively.

Since `readv` and `writev` can be invoked for any device file, drivers for raw devices must be prepared to do scatter/gather I/O as well. This is usually done by the `physio` support routine, which must also be passed a pointer to a `uio` structure. The `physio` routine invokes the device strategy routine for each piece of the data buffer.

Arguments to `ioctls`

Instead of forcing each device driver to transfer data for extended arguments to `ioctls`, 4.3BSD establishes a convention where high order bits of the command specify whether the third argument to the `ioctl` system call is a pointer to additional data. Moreover, these bits specify how many bytes of data are referenced by this pointer, and whether the `ioctl` reads this data, writes it, or both. As a result, device driver routines for `ioctl` do not need to include explicit calls to `copyin` or `copyout`.

Network Connections

4.3BSD supports communication with other computer systems through various forms of network connections. Programs do not perform read and write calls directly to the network interface, but instead perform read and write

calls to sockets which may transmit data over a network interface. Consequently, device drivers for network interfaces are highly stylized and must
conform to a completely different set of conventions that are not described in this
book. You will need to consult the documentation that came with your system
for information about how to connect different network interfaces to your system.

· Other Internal Differences ·

In addition to changes required by different system calls or system call conventions, 4.3BSD uses very different underlying support routines for clists, buffered
I/O, I/O maps, and signals.

Clist Support Routines

While the actual format of clists and cblocks under 4.3BSD are different from
RTU, device drivers almost never need to access these data structures directly.
The basic support routines `putc` and `getc` are identical in 4.3BSD and RTU.
However, 4.3BSD has very different routines for moving large amounts of data
efficiently between user memory and clists. Instead of using `getcb` and `putcb`
to move an entire block of data onto a clist, 4.3BSD uses the routines `q_to_b`
and `b_to_q` to copy data from a clist into a buffer or from a buffer into a clist.

4.3BSD Block I/O system

The block I/O system in 4.3BSD serves the same function as a cache for data read
from block devices, particularly devices containing active file systems. However,
4.3BSD uses a different technique for transferring data between this cache and
the device in large block sizes and therefore achieves high file system
throughput. The data buffers managed by the 4.3BSD buffer system are
inherently variable sized. Typical file systems will contain large blocks of data
and several fragments at the end of files. The blocks are usually 4096 or 8192
bytes long while fragments are usually 512 or 1024 bytes. In addition, there can
be no more than 8 fragments per block.

   The routines implementing the block I/O system are basically unchanged,
although routines that allocate buffers such as `geteblk` must specify the size of
the data buffer to be allocated. Under 4.3BSD, this size must be less than the constant `MAXBSIZE`, which is defined in `param.h`.

   The fields inside a buffer header are also somewhat different. The fields
`b_ioaddr` and `b_ioblkno` are called `b_addr` and `b_blkno`. (Buffer headers
in RTU have fields with these names, but they are reserved for use by RTU and
should not be referenced or altered by device drivers.) A pointer to a completion
routine is stored in `b_iodone` instead of `b_completion`. In addition, the
B_CALL bit must be set in the `b_flags` field in order for the completion routine
to be called. 4.3BSD has no notion of urgent I/O, although the other flag bits
described in Chapter 5 are defined and have similar meanings.

I/O Mapping for DMA Transfers

A major complication of the VAX architecture is the presence of multiple I/O busses, each with its own address translation map. Since the entire address space of the UNIBUS is only 256K bytes, it is not feasible for device drivers simply to allocate large, static portions of the I/O map for dedicated use by that device. Therefore, I/O map entries have to be dynamically allocated for each transfer. Since this allocation may occur within interrupt handlers it is not always possible to use `sleep` and `wakeup` to wait until enough I/O map entries become available. In addition, many UNIBUS device drivers need to allocate buffered data paths to provide efficient data transfers.

The I/O mapping support routines in 4.3BSD can handle all these complications. The mapping routines are intimately related to the configuration data structures described earlier. For UNIBUS devices, the `uba_ctlr` and `ui_device` structures contain pointers to the `uba_hd` structure for the UNIBUS adaptor the controller or device is connected to. These fields are used by the support routines `ubago`, `ubadone`, `uballoc`, and `ubarelse`.

You can use the routines `uballoc` and `ubarelse` in much the same way you would use `iomapvaddr` and `iomfree`. You must indicate which UNIBUS adaptor to allocate resources as the first argument. The number of the UNIBUS adaptor is stored in both the `ui_ubanum` and `um_ubanum` fields of the device and controller structures. Flag bits indicate whether a buffered data path is needed, a buffered data path has already been allocated, the call is being made from interrupt level and therefore `uballoc` should not call `sleep`, or the controller can only transfer to the lower 64K bytes of UNIBUS address space. `uballoc` returns an integer that indicates all the UNIBUS resources that were allocated. The information is stored in the integer as shown in Figure F-3. If no resources were allocated, `uballoc` will return zero. The lower 18 bits of this value contain the UNIBUS address that the controller should use for DMA transfers. The high four bits contain the buffered data path, if any, that has been allocated for this transfer.

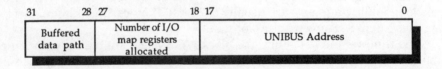

31 28 27	18 17	0
Buffered data path	Number of I/O map registers allocated	UNIBUS Address

Fig. F-3. Format of UNIBUS resource word

These resources are released by calling `ubarelse` with a pointer to a value previously returned by `uballoc`. Notice that if you have previously allocated a buffered data path but do not clear the high-order bits before calling `ubarelse`, the buffered data path will be released. Also, there is no separate routine for allocating buffered data paths. You must call `uballoc` to allocate a buffered data path, although you can use `ubarelse` to release the I/O map registers.

You should use buffered data paths for devices that transfer large quantities of data from sequential memory locations. For example, disk devices operate more efficiently using a buffered data path. However, for lower speed devices such as terminal multiplexors or line printers, the system overhead saved by using a buffered data path is insignificant. In almost all circumstances you should let uballoc allocate the buffered data path for you and release it when you are done.

Drivers that only need a small amount of memory for data buffers should allocate I/O map resources once when the device is opened and release them when the device is closed. An example of this would be a line printer driver that used a small, 132-character buffer to hold each line of output. However, if your driver will perform large, raw transfers on behalf of user programs it should allocate UNIBUS resources for each transfer.

If your driver needs to allocate UNIBUS resources at interrupt level, it should use ubago and ubadone instead of uballoc and ubarelse. The ubago routine uses fields of the uba_device structure to keep a queue of controllers that are waiting for UNIBUS resources to become available. This makes use of the ud_dgo entry point to the driver. This entry point is kept in the uba_driver structure, as opposed to the block device or character device switch.

The uba_go routine also requires that uba_ctlr structure for the device contains a queue of I/O buffer headers. uba_go will try to allocate UNIBUS resources for the first buffer header in this queue (it assumes umtab.b_actf->b_actf points to this buffer header). If resources are available, uba_go saves the value of UNIBUS resource in the um_ubinfo field of the uba_ctlr structure, calls the driver ud_dgo routine, and returns the value one. If the resources are not currently available, uba_go adds the current uba_device to a queue of devices on that UNIBUS adaptor waiting for resources and returns zero. This queue is examined whenever UNIBUS resources are released. If the UNIBUS resources needed by the device at the front of the queue are now available, the resources will be allocated and the ud_dgo will be called.

The ubago routine is also able to deal with controllers that have such severe latency requirements that no other devices should be allowed to use the UNIBUS at the same time. This is indicated by setting the ud_xclu field of the uba_driver structure to a nonzero value. Actually, ubago only guarantees that no other driver using ubago is active at the same time. Drivers that allocate UNIBUS resources using uballoc could potentially be using the bus at the same time. However, these are presumably lower speed devices that should not interfere with higher speed data transfers.

Drivers that use ubago to allocate UNIBUS resources should release these resources using ubadone instead of ubarelse.

You may notice that instead of having a single device start routine as used in the sample drivers in Chapter 8, device drivers for 4.3BSD will often have separate start and go routines. The start routine sets up most controller parameters but does not actually initiate the data transfer. Instead, the start routine calls ubago, and the device go routine is called after the UNIBUS resources have actually been allocated.

· Executive Header Files ·

One major difference in 4.3BSD is that while copies of header files are kept in
/usr/include/sys, system header files used for building systems are kept in a
special subdirectory of the file system containing the source files for the operating system. This directory is automatically searched before /usr/include/
sys so device drivers should normally contain statements such as

```
#include "buf.h"
```

instead of

```
#include <sys/buf.h>
```

In addition, several of the header files described earlier in this book do not
exist in 4.3BSD. These include:

```
ast.h
elog.h
erec.h
io.h
iobuf.h
peri.h
space.h
sysinfo.h
```

Instead, most device drivers must include one or more of the following header
files:

ubareg.h	Defines addresses of control registers and data structures used to allocate and use UNIBUS resources.
ubavar.h	Defines the kernel data structures used by device drivers for UNIBUS devices. These include the uba_hd, uba_ctlr, uba_device, and uba_driver structures.

· Kernel I/O Support Routines ·

Many of the support routines described in Appendix B are available with similar
or identical interfaces under 4.3BSD. These are summarized here. Routines that
are not available are also identified. Finally, we describe new routines that are
only available under UNIX systems derived from 4.3BSD.

brelse	Behaves very much like RTU, except 4.3BSD does not check runrun or call qswtch.
canast	Not available under 4.3BSD.
clist	The actual data structure used for clists under 4.3BSD is different, but clists are still suitable for relatively small, moderate speed FIFO queues.

Not all the clist routines from RTU or System V are available. For example, 4.3BSD uses different routines for moving blocks of data to or from a clist.

cmn_err
: Not available under 4.3BSD.

copyin, copyout
: Under 4.3BSD, these routines return zero if successful, an error code suitable for storing in u.u_error otherwise.

cpass
: Not available under 4.3BSD. Use the function uwritec instead.

dclast, delast
: Not available under 4.3BSD.

delay
: This works as described in Appendix B.

disksort
: 4.3BSD provides a disksort routine. The first argument is declared as struct buf * instead of struct iobuf *. However, it should be a pointer to a special header buffer. Also, the 4.3BSD version of disksort does not implement urgent I/O.

fmtberr
: Not available under 4.3BSD. (4.3BSD provides a mechanism for recording all messages printed by the system in a file, so device drivers log errors by simply printing an error message.)

fubyte, fushort, fuword
: These work as described in Appendix B.

getc
: This works as described in Appendix B.

getcb, getcf
: Not implemented in 4.3BSD. Use q_to_b to transfer large blocks of data from a clist to a data buffer efficiently.

geteblk
: Under 4.3BSD, geteblk takes one argument, which is used as the size of the block buffer to allocate. This must be less than or equal to MAXBSIZE, which is declared in param.h.

gsignal
: This works as described in Appendix B.

hibyte, hiword
: Not available under 4.3BSD.

iodone
: Under 4.3BSD, iodone is defined as a macro to invoke biodone, which performs essentially the same function. However, iodone does not appear in system symbol tables. Under 4.3BSD, the completion routine is stored in bp-> b_iodone and is called only if the B_CALL bit is set in bp->b_flags and does not implement block clustering.

`iomaddr`	Not available under 4.3BSD. There is no directly analogous routine, although the functions `uballoc` and `ubasetup` are similar.
`iomalloc`	Not available under 4.3BSD. The function `uballoc` is nearly identical, although it takes the number of a UNIBUS adaptor as its first argument and implements somewhat different flags.
`iomapvaddr`	Not available under 4.3BSD. There is no directly analogous routine, although the functions `uballoc` and `ubasetup` are similar.
`iomfree`	Not available under 4.3BSD. There is no directly analogous routine, although the function `ubarelse` is similar.
`iomload`	Not available under 4.3BSD.
`iomove`	Not available under 4.3BSD. Use the function `uiomove` instead.
`iowait`	Under 4.3BSD, `iowait` is defined as a macro to invoke `biowait`, which performs the same function. However, `iowait` does not appear in system symbol tables.
`lobyte, loword`	Not available under 4.3BSD.
`major, minor, makedev`	These macros are defined in `types.h` under 4.3BSD, but implement the same functions.
`memall, memfree`	Work as documented in 4.3BSD.
`minphys`	Under 4.3BSD, the system-supplied `minphys` routine enforces a maximum transfer size of 63K (63 * 1024) bytes.
`panic`	Works as documented in 4.3BSD.
`passc`	Not available under 4.3BSD. Use the function `ureadc` instead.
`pcopyin, pcopyout`	Not available under 4.3BSD.
`physck`	Not available under 4.3BSD.
`physio`	The 4.3BSD version of `physio` takes an additional argument that is a pointer to a `uio` structure. `physio` uses this structure to locate data buffers in user virtual address space instead of `u.u_base` and `u.u_count`. `physio` will call the strategy routine once for each `iovec` in the `uio` structure.
`psignal`	Works as documented in 4.3BSD.

putc	Works as documented in 4.3BSD.
putcb, putcf	Not available under 4.3BSD. Use `b_to_q` to efficiently transfer large blocks of data from a buffer to a clist.
sleep	The 4.3BSD version of `sleep` does not implement PCATCH and does not deal with ASTs.
spl0, ..., spl7, splv, splx	4.3BSD implements all of these except for `splv`. Many device drivers use abstract priority levels such as `splbio`. These are defined in `param.h`.
subyte, suword, sulong	These work as documented in 4.3BSD.
suser	This works as described in Appendix B.
swab, swabl	Not available under 4.3BSD.
timeout	The 4.3BSD version of `timeout` does not return a value. A timeout may be cancelled by calling `untimeout` with the same `function` and `argument` which will cancel *all* pending timeouts.
uprintf	The 4.3BSD version implements additional print formats described under `printf`.
useracc	The 4.3BSD version of `useracc` works like the RTU version: a return value of zero indicates the access was allowed, and a nonzero return indicates the access was not allowed.
v_page_lock, v_page_unlock	Not available under 4.3BSD.
vmemall, vmemfree	Works as documented in 4.3BSD.
vslock	The caller must set the S_PHYSIO bit in `u.u_procp->p_flag` (`u.u_procp->p_lock` does not exist under 4.3BSD).
vsmlock, vspunlock	Does not exist under 4.3BSD.
vsunlock	The caller should clear the S_PHYSIO bit in `u.u_procp->p_flag` (`u.u_procp->p_lock` does not exist under 4.3BSD).
wakeup	Works as documented in 4.3BSD.
wmemall, wmemallx, wmemfree	`wmemall` and `wmemfree` work as documented under 4.3BSD, but `wmemallx` is not available.

The pages that follow describe the kernel support routines that are unique to 4.3BSD systems, or that differ significantly from the same routines as implemented on RTU or System V systems.

B_TO_Q (4.3BSD)

NAME

b_to_q – copy a buffer to a clist

SYNOPSIS

```
b_to_q (cp, cc, q)
char *cp;
int cc;
struct clist *q;
```

DESCRIPTION

b_to_q copies cc characters from the data buffer addressed by cp to the clist pointed to by q.

b_to_q is substantially more efficient for copying a large number of characters to a clist than repeatedly calling putc but somewhat less efficient for moving only one or two characters.

RETURNS

b_to_q returns the number of characters that were not transferred. This will normally be zero unless b_to_q was unable to allocate additional cblocks when needed.

SEE ALSO

getc, putc, and q_to_b.

PHYSIO (4.3BSD)

NAME

physio – perform the steps required for physical (raw) I/O

SYNOPSIS

```
physio (strat, bp, dev, flag, minphys, uio)
int (*strat)();
register struct buf *bp;
short dev;
int flag;
unsigned (*minphys)();
struct uio *uio;
```

DESCRIPTION

The physio routine performs most of the steps that are required for raw I/O. The dev argument is the minor device number for the device. (Only the minor device number is important here.)

physio implements scatter/gather I/O by repeatedly calling the specified strategy routine for each element of the uio structure. For each iovec, the useracc routine is called to determine if the request is valid with respect to the user's access rights to the address range in question. This function relies on the flag argument being set to B_READ if the user has issued a read request and to B_WRITE if the user has issued a write request. If the addresses specified by the current iovec are invalid, u.u_error is set to EFAULT and physio returns.

Next, the buf structure pointed to by bp is filled in. Part of this involves calling the minphys routine to adjust the requested count to be less than or equal to the largest allowable transfer for that device. It is called with the bp argument. This routine can either be the one supplied with the system or one that the user has supplied.

The physio routine calls vslock to lock the affected areas into physical memory, bp->b_bcount as modified by the minphys routine.

Next the strat routine is called with the bp argument. strat is a pointer to a strategy routine entry point for the device. This routine is one of the standard entry points for a block device. After calling the strat routine, the physio routine sleeps at priority PRIBIO until this I/O operation is complete. It then calls vsunlock to unlock the pages that were previously locked into physical memory with the vslock routine.

Finally, the `uio` structure is updated to reflect the transfer.

This process is repeated until all the data is transferred or until an error occurs.

Note that `physio` will automatically wait (`sleep`) for a buffer marked `B_BUSY` to become available and in turn will issue a `wakeup` if `B_WANTED` is set when the transfer is complete.

RETURNS

The `physio` routine does not return any value, but the `u.u_error` field will be set if any error was recognized.

SEE ALSO

`minphys`, `vslock`, `vsunlock,` and `useracc`.

WARNINGS

A strategy routine called by `physio` must not call `sleep` at interruptible priorities (`<=ZERO`), or it must catch signals using `PCATCH` or `setjmp (u.u_gav)`. Otherwise, raw I/O locks errors will result.

Q_TO_B (4.3BSD)

NAME

q_to_b – copy characters from a clist to a data buffer

SYNOPSIS

```
q_to_b(q, cp, cc)
struct clist *q;
char *cp;
int cc;
```

DESCRIPTION

q_to_b copies up to cc characters from the clist pointed to by q to the data buffer pointed to by cp.

q_to_b is substantially more efficient than getc for copying large amounts of data from a clist but may be slightly less efficient when copying only one or two characters.

RETURNS

q_to_b returns the number of data bytes actually copied. This will be equal to cc unless the clist has less than cc characters on the list when q_to_b is called.

SEE ALSO

b_to_q, getc, and putc.

UBADONE   (4.3BSD)

NAME

ubadone – release UNIBUS adaptor resources for a controller

SYNOPSIS

```
ubadone(um)
struct uba_ctlr *um;
```

DESCRIPTION

ubadone releases the UNIBUS adaptor resources used by the current data transfer for the UNIBUS controller specified by um. The mapping registers and buffered data path to release are stored in um->ubinfo. ubadone also decreases the count of active devices for the UNIBUS adaptor the controller is connected to. This will eventually allow drivers waiting for exclusive access to the UNIBUS to proceed.

RETURNS

None.

SEE ALSO

ubago, uballoc, ubarelse, and ubasetup.

UBAGO   (4.3BSD)

NAME

ubago – start a UNIBUS transfer on a device

SYNOPSIS

```
ubago(ui)
struct uba_device *ui;
```

DESCRIPTION

ubago starts a transfer on the controller and UNIBUS adaptor that the device specified by ui is connected to. The controller the device is connected should must have a queue of buffer structures for pending data transfers at ui->ui_mi->um_tab.b_actf (the first buffer in this queue is ui->ui_mi->um_tab.b_actf->b_actf), although this queue may have just one buffer.

ubago always allocates a buffered data path for the transfer. In addition, ubago will wait until no other controller is using the UNIBUS adaptor if ui->ui_mi->um_driver->ud_xclu is nonzero.

If UNIBUS adaptor resources for this transfer are available, the resources are allocated, and ubago will call the device driver go routine ui->ui_mi->um_driver->ud_dgo), which should call ubadone when the transfer completes.

If UNIBUS adaptor resources for this transfer are not available, and this UNIBUS device is not at the front of the queue of devices waiting for resources on its corresponding UNIBUS adaptor, the device is added to the end of the queue of waiting devices.

RETURNS

ubago returns a nonzero value if UNIBUS adaptor resources were allocated. Otherwise, ubago returns zero.

SEE ALSO

uballoc, ubadone, ubarelse, and ubasetup.

UBALLOC   (4.3BSD)

NAME

uballoc – allocate UNIBUS adaptor resources

SYNOPSIS

```
#include "ubareg.h"
#include "ubavar.h"

uballoc(ubanum, addr, count, flags)
int ubanum;
caddr_t addr;
int count;
int flags;
```

DESCRIPTION

uballoc allocates resources on UNIBUS adaptor ubanum. These resources include sufficient I/O map registers for a data transfer of count bytes. These I/O map registers are initialized to access system virtual address space beginning at address addr and extending to addr+count. addr should not refer to the user portion of the processes virtual address space.

If UBA_NEEDBDP is set in flags, uballoc will allocate a buffered data path.

If UBA_NEED16 is set in flags, uballoc will allocate mapping registers corresponding to 16-bit UNIBUS addresses (bits 17 and 18 of the address will be zero).

If UBA_HAVEBDP is set in flags, uballoc will use the buffered data path specified in the high-order bits of flags.

If the requested resources are not currently available, uballoc will call sleep to wait for resources unless UBA_CANTWAIT is set in flags.

UNIBUS adaptor resources allocated by uballoc should be released by a subsequent call to ubarelse.

RETURNS

uballoc returns an integer describing the UNIBUS resources that were allocated. The low 18 bits of this value contain the UNIBUS address that should be used by a controller to access the data at system virtual addresses addr through addr+count.

The next ten bits contain the number of 512-byte pages of UNIBUS address space that were used to set up this mapping (since the UNIBUS address space is only 18 bits wide, at most nine bits of this field can be nonzero).

The high-order four bits contain the number of the buffered data path, if any, that has been allocated for this transfer.

The return value will be zero if no UNIBUS adaptor resources were allocated. This will happen only if `UBA_CANTWAIT` or `UBA_NEED16` is set in `flags` and the requested resources are not immediately available.

SEE ALSO

`ubadone, ubago, ubarelse,` and `ubasetup.`

UBARELSE   **(4.3BSD)**

NAME

ubarelse – release UNIBUS adaptor resources

SYNOPSIS

```
ubarelse(ubanum, resourcep)
int ubanum;
int *resourcep;
```

DESCRIPTION

ubarelse releases UNIBUS adaptor resources previously allocated by uballoc or ubasetup. resourcep should be a pointer to an integer containing the value of a previous call to one of these routines.

ubarelse will call ubago for controllers waiting for UNIBUS adaptor resources.

RETURNS

None.

SEE ALSO

ubadone, ubago, uballoc, and ubasetup.

UBASETUP   **(4.3BSD)**

NAME

ubasetup – allocate and setup UNIBUS adaptor resources for a buffer header

SYNOPSIS

```
#include "ubareg.h"
#include "ubavar.h"

ubasetup(ubanum, bp flags)
int ubanum;
struct buf *bp;
int flags;
```

DESCRIPTION

ubasetup allocates resources on UNIBUS adaptor ubanum. These resources include sufficient I/O map registers for a data transfer of bp->b_bcount bytes. These I/O map registers are initialized to access system virtual address space beginning at address addr and extending to addr+count. The address space that addr refers to is specified by flag bits in bp->b_flags. If the B_PHYS bit is set, addr is interpreted as an address in the user portion of the virtual address space. The caller should have previously locked the data into memory using vslock. If the B_UAREA bit is set, addr is interpreted as an offset into process user structure, u. If the B_PAGET bit is set, addr is interpreted as an offset into the process' page tables. Otherwise, addr is interpreted as a system virtual address.

If UBA_NEEDBDP is set in flags, ubasetup will allocate a buffered data path.

If UBA_NEED16 is set in flags, ubasetup will allocate mapping registers corresponding to 16-bit UNIBUS addresses (bits 17 and 18 of the address will be zero).

If UBA_HAVEBDP is set in flags, ubasetup will use the buffered data path specified in the high-order bits of flags.

If the requested resources are not currently available, ubasetup will call sleep to wait for resources unless UBA_CANTWAIT is set in flags.

UNIBUS adaptor resources allocated by ubasetup should be released by a subsequent call to ubarelse.

Device drivers will not usually call `ubasetup` directly. Instead, they will generally use `ubago`. Note that the `physio` routine will lock data buffers into memory and correctly set up flag bits in `bp->b_flags` for a subsequent call to `ubasetup` or `ubago`.

RETURNS

`ubasetup` returns an integer describing the UNIBUS resources that were allocated. The low 18 bits of this value contain the UNIBUS address that should be used by a controller to access the data at system virtual addresses `addr` through `addr+count`.

The next ten bits contain the number of 512-byte pages of UNIBUS address space that were used to set up this mapping (since the UNIBUS address space is only 18 bits wide, at most nine bits of this field can be nonzero).

The high-order four bits contain the number of the buffered data path, if any, which has been allocated for this transfer.

The return value will be zero if no UNIBUS adaptor resources were allocated. This will happen only if `UBA_CANTWAIT` or `UBA_NEED16` is set in `flags`, and the requested resources are not immediately available.

SEE ALSO

`physio`, `ubadone`, `ubago`, `uballoc`, `ubarelse`, and `vslock`.

UIOMOVE   (4.3BSD)

NAME

uiomove – move data between user and system virtual space

SYNOPSIS

```
int uiomove(addr, count, direction, struct uio *uio)
caddr_t addr;
unsigned count;
enum uio_rw directio;
```

DESCRIPTION

uiomove is used to move data in the direction direction, which is
UIO_READ or UIO_WRITE.   UIO_READ is used to write data to the user
process, (the user has issued a read), and UIO_WRITE is used to get
data from the user area (the user has issued a write).   count is the
number of bytes to be transferred.

The uio structure describes the buffer and virtual address space that
data should be transferred to.   uiomove implements scatter/gather
I/O by iterating over the iovec structures in uio.

uio->uio_segflg indicates the virtual address space the data is in. If
uio->uio_segflag is equal to UIO_USERSPACE, the iovecs are
interpreted as addresses in the current processes virtual address space.
If uio->uio_segflag is equal to UIO_SYSSPACE, the iovecs are
interpreted as system virtual addresses. If uio->uio_segflag is
UIO_USERISPACE, the iovecs are interpreted as references to instruction space in the current process. On VAX systems, user instruction
space is the same as user data space but would be different on machines
implementing separate instruction and data spaces.

The other address is taken from addr.

The structure pointed to by uio is updated to reflect the number of
bytes moved.

RETURNS

uiomove returns an error code suitable for storing in u.u_error. A
return value of zero indicates a successful transfer.

UREADC   (RTU and System V.3)

NAME

ureadc – return a character for a read system call

SYNOPSIS

```
ureadc(c, uio)
char c;
struct uio *uio;
```

DESCRIPTION

The ureadc routine places the character c at the address specified by
the uio structure pointed to by uio. ureadc updates the base and
length of the current iovec, the offset, and the residual count in the
uio structure.

RETURNS

ureadc returns EFAULT if an error occurs transferring the character to
the data buffer and zero if no such error occurs.

ureadc will call panic if the uio structure describes an empty data
buffer (uio->uio_iovcnt is zero).

SEE ALSO

uwritec and subyte.

UWRITEC   **(4.3BSD)**

NAME

uwritec – get a character for a write system call

SYNOPSIS

```
int uwritec(uio)
struct uio *uio;
```

DESCRIPTION

uwritec returns an integer that is the first character in the virtual I/O buffer addressed by uio. uwritec will update the base and length fields of the current iovec in uio and will also update the file offset and residual counts in uio.

RETURNS

uwritec returns –1 if uio->uio_resid is less than or equal to zero or if an error occurs while fetching the addressed character.

uwritec will call panic if there is no iovec (if uio->uio_iovcnt is less than or equal to zero).

SEE ALSO

ureadc and fubyte.

BIBLIOGRAPHY

Bach, M., *The Design of the UNIX Operating System*, Prentice-Hall, 1986.

Comer, D., *Operating System Design: The Xinu Approach*, Prentice-Hall, 1984.

Earhart, S., editor, *UNIX Programmer's Manual*, Holt, Rinehart and Winston, 1986.

Kernighan, B. and R. Pike, *The UNIX Programming Environment*, Prentice-Hall,1984.

Thomas, R., L.Rogers and J.L. Yates, *Advanced Programmer's Guide to UNIX System V*, Osborne McGraw-Hill, 1986.

Thomas, R. and J.L. Yates, *A User Guide to the UNIX System*, Osborne McGraw-Hill, 1985.

INDEX